DRIVING SCHOOL IMPROVEMENT
SECOND EDITION

PRACTICAL STRATEGIES AND TOOLS

PAMELA MACKLIN AND VIC ZBAR

amba press

Published in 2025 by Amba Press, Melbourne, Australia
www.ambapress.com.au

First published in 2020 by ACER Press, an imprint of
Australian Council *for* Educational Research Ltd

© 2025 Pamela Macklin and Vic Zbar

This book is copyright. All rights reserved. Except under the conditions described in the *Copyright Act 1968* of Australia and subsequent amendments, and any exceptions permitted under the current statutory licence scheme administered by Copyright Agency (www.copyright.com.au), no part of this publication may be reproduced, stored in a retrieval system, transmitted, broadcast or communicated in any form or by any means, optical, digital, electronic, mechanical, photocopying, recording or otherwise, without the written permission of the publisher.

Copying of the pro forma pages
The purchasing educational institution and its staff are permitted to make copies of the pages marked as blackline master pages, beyond their rights under the Act, provided that:

1. The number of copies does not exceed the number reasonably required by the educational institution to satisfy its teaching purposes.
2. Copies are made only by reprographic means (photocopying), not by electronic, digital means, and not stored or transmitted.
3. Copies are not sold or lent.
4. Every copy made clearly shows the footnotes ('© Pamela Macklin and Vic Zbar, *Driving School Improvement*, Australian Council for Education Research, 2017', '© Pamela Macklin and Vic Zbar, *Driving School Improvement 2nd Edition*, Australian Council for Education Research, 2020' or © Pamela Macklin and Vic Zbar, *Driving School Improvement 2nd Edition*, Amba Press, 2025').

For those pages not marked as pro forma pages the normal copying limits in the Act, as described above, apply.

Edited by Holly Proctor
Cover design by Nada Backovic
Text design and typesetting by ACER Creative Services
Cover image © Rawpixel.com; SpeedKingz; used under license from Shutterstock.com

ISBN: 9781923569027 (pbk)
ISBN: 9781923569034 (ebk)

A catalogue record for this book is available from the National Library of Australia.

FOREWORD BY MICHAEL FULLAN

I was just beginning my career in 1968 when the very first studies of educational innovation began to appear: John Goodlad's (1970) *Behind the classroom door* and Seymour Sarason's (1972) *The culture of the school and the problem of change*. Both brought an abrupt realisation that 'innovations' that were presumed to be operating in particular schools were simply not in evidence. It became quickly embarrassing when it turned out that researchers and practitioners had the language of *innovation*, but had not contemplated the language of *implementation*. The latter term was not used. It took almost a decade before implementation developed into usage. Initially, it referred more or less to the beliefs and practices that represented the new concept or idea in practice. Then came the implementation process—factors associated with the planning required for practice to change. Last to emerge were implementation outcomes.

During the 1970s and 1980s, research was focused on understanding implementation (and its lack of impact), not necessarily on the matter of how to improve the process, and to assess impact. I wrote the first complete book on the issue in 1982—*The meaning of educational change* (now in its 5th edition).

From then on, a very active field developed, cycling back and forth between the concepts of 'school improvement' (practitioners), and 'school effectiveness' (researchers). Thousands of books were written about 'change and innovation' to the point that Viviane Robinson in 2018 wrote a book to underscore that we should be about 'improvement'—not just change per se.

There you have 50 years expressed in a little more than 250 words!

There were, first under the radar, and then openly, a group of mainly practitioners, who worked systematically to improve the science of improvement. That is what we have before us in Macklin and Zbar's *Driving school improvement: Practical strategies and tools*. To 'drive' something, and to get anywhere, one needs a fair amount of conceptual savvy, as well as high quality tools. Quality tools in the hands of someone who doesn't know what they are doing are, well, dangerous: a fool with a tool is still a fool. By the same token, a person with ideas, but no tools, progresses very slowly.

Now we can get to the heart of Macklin and Zbar's contribution. Simply put, the book is about the close relationship between powerful ideas and tools that results in integrated quality change, and its impact on practice and related outcomes. The conceptual framework is superb—comprehensive, clear, and practical.

In chapter 1, the improvement challenge is put forth in terms of what difference a school can make. Second, the improvement challenge is modest but powerful: diagnose, focus on a manageable amount, and carry people with you. In the middle of this analysis, the authors focus on why and how leadership is crucial in terms of building capacity, and a culture for all. Then three critical conditions for success are laid out:

i preconditions (leadership, high expectations, a safe and orderly environment, and a solid program)
ii building teacher capacity (especially around an instructional model and effective professional learning)
iii improving classroom practice across the school (through good learning goals, success criteria and a system of feedback).

The authors underscore the preconditions by showing how classroom observation and quality feedback are crucial, especially feedback from students. We get a clear sense from these chapters how the day-to-day culture works. The clincher in terms of what the reader can take away are the vignettes and 'tools' for analysis and action. There are 47 figures dispersed throughout the book that provide data, comparison of schools, roles and responsibilities, explicit lesson procedures, instructional models, use of data and so on.

Parallel to the figures, chapter by chapter, are 49 tables, such as: diagnosing leadership behavior, processing self-assessment, getting a fix on the team, assessing your effectiveness, evaluating the effectiveness of the team, developing and assessing learning goals, and more.

In the end we have a systematic set of ideas and tools to assess and improve the schools we work in. The book is both motivational in the why and how to do this, but also inspirational and practical for focusing on improvement over time. You will find no book that is as thorough and helpful for improving one's school on an ongoing basis.

This book helps to get the internal house in order. But it also prepares the school to deal with the outside. The future brings the need to link with other schools and levels of the system, as we have detailed in our latest book, *The devil is in the details* (Fullan & Gallagher, 2020). It should also prepare schools as they shift from the basics to more fundamental learning goals, such as global competencies (Fullan, Quinn & McEachen, 2018).

In sum, *Driving school improvement: Practical strategies and tools* provides a solid foundation for improving schools, whatever demands they face.

REFERENCES

Fullan, M. (1982). *The meaning of educational change.* New York: Teachers College Press.

Fullan, M., Quinn, J., & McEachen, J. (2018). *Deep learning: Engage the world Change the world.* Thousand Oaks, CA: Corwin Press.

Fullan, M., & Gallagher, M.J. (2020). *The devil is in the details.* Thousand Oaks, CA: Corwin Press.

Goodlad, J., Klein, M. & Associates. (1970). *Behind the classroom door.* OH: Charles Jones.

Robinson, V. (2018). *Reduce change to increase improvement.* Thousand Oaks, CA: Corwin Press.

Sarason, S. (1972). *The culture of the school and the problem of change.* Boston: Allyn & Bacon.

CONTENTS

FOREWORD — iii

FIGURES — vii

TABLES — ix

ABOUT THE AUTHORS — xi

HOW TO USE THIS BOOK — xii

THE REASON FOR A SECOND EDITION — xiii
    What's new in this edition — xiii

CHAPTER 1   THE IMPROVEMENT CHALLENGE — 1
    What makes the difference to student learning outcomes? — 2
    The difference teachers make — 3
    The difference the school can make — 4
    Changing behaviour — 5

CHAPTER 2   HOW CHANGE FOR IMPROVEMENT OCCURS — 6
    Diagnose before you prescribe — 7
    Use research wisely — 8
    Do a manageable amount — 9
    Can we only do one thing? — 11
    Carrying people with you — 11
    Stay the course — 13

CHAPTER 3   IT DEPENDS ON LEADERSHIP — 17
    Leadership for whole-school improvement — 18
    A leadership framework to consider — 22
    The detailed framework and thinking behind it — 23
    Building a strong and united leadership team — 39
    Coaching to build leadership capacity and drive improvement — 42
    What is leadership coaching in schools? — 42
    What can leadership coaching achieve? — 43
    A coaching culture for all — 43
    No coaching at your school yet? Start here ... — 44
    You have coaching at your school already? Try this ... — 45
    A coaching plan is a must — 47
    Building coaching capacity in your school — 50
    Selecting and developing coaches — 50
    The journey from unconscious incompetence to unconscious competence — 51
    Role clarity for coaches, teachers and leaders — 52
    The power of good questions — 53

CHAPTER 4   THE THREE STAGES OF WHOLE-SCHOOL IMPROVEMENT — 57
    Ensuring the preconditions are in place — 58
    Building baseline capacity — 61
    Drilling down into classroom practice — 63

CHAPTER 5	STAGE 1: THE PRECONDITIONS	69
	Overview of the four preconditions	70
	Leadership—the precondition of the preconditions	76
	High expectations for students and staff	83
	An orderly learning environment where students are well known	91
	The 'Good Standing' program	93
	Putting first things first	107
CHAPTER 6	STAGE 2: BUILDING TEACHING CAPACITY	114
	Planning good lessons	115
	Using an instructional model for consistently more effective teaching	118
	Developing an instructional model	121
	Explicit instruction	129
	Making the instructional model happen in your school	133
	Manuals to support implementation	133
	Embedding one phase at a time	138
	Review and reflection: The Queechy Alliance	142
	Monitoring implementation	147
	Structures for collaboration so more can work like the best	148
	Effective professional learning	151
	Guiding norms	153
	Phasing the introduction of PLTs: An approach to consider	163
	An effective PLT	168
CHAPTER 7	STAGE 3: IMPROVING CLASSROOM PRACTICE	172
	Effect sizes	172
	Theories of action	173
	A word on data	175
	Learning goals as the entry point	177
	Writing good learning goals	183
	Adding success criteria to the mix	190
	Quality success criteria	191
	Feedback to students	200
	What is effective feedback?	200
	The focus of feedback	202
	A note on differentiating your delivery	206
CHAPTER 8	CLASSROOM OBSERVATION TO SUPPORT THE SHIFT	210
	The purposes of classroom observation	211
	Options for classroom observation	213
	Processes and pro formas for effective classroom observation	218
	Quality of feedback	224
	Feedback from students	227
CONCLUSION		230
REFERENCES		234

FIGURES

Figure 1.1	Percentage of achievement variance	2
Figure 1.2	The difference teachers make	3
Figure 1.3	Performance of School A and School B compared to a group of statistically similar schools, 2015 to 2017	4
Figure 2.1	The normal curve for the adoption of change	12
Figure 2.2	The implementation dip	13
Figure 3.1	The work that leaders do	18
Figure 3.2	Conscious Competence Learning Model	51
Figure 3.3	Roles and responsibilities in the coaching process (AITSL)	52
Figure 4.1	Stages of sustained school improvement	57
Figure 5.1	The High-Performing Schools Roadmap	70
Figure 5.2	Student management roles and responsibilities, Kambrya College	98
Figure 5.3	Classroom rights and responsibilities	100
Figure 5.4	Hampton Park Primary School classroom observation pro forma for the orderly learning environment	102
Figure 5.5	Determining school priorities—Heads of Domain Planning Day	108
Figure 5.6	Difficulty Impact Grid	110
Figure 5.7	Illustrated Difficulty Impact Grid	110
Figure 5.8	Blank Difficulty Impact Grid	112
Figure 6.1	Victorian and Northern Territory school instructional models	119
Figure 6.2	Tasmanian and Northern Territory school instructional models	120
Figure 6.3	Noble Park Secondary College instructional model	125
Figure 6.4	Oakleigh Grammar School TLM	126
Figure 6.5	The explicit instruction lesson process at Pioneer State High	129
Figure 6.6	Hampton Park Primary School learning behaviours	130

Figure 6.7	Glen Waverley Secondary College instructional model	133
Figure 6.8	Glen Waverley Secondary College instructional model handbook extract	134
Figure 6.9	Springvale Rise Primary School instructional model	135
Figure 6.10	Springvale Rise Primary School instructional model handbook extract	136
Figure 6.11	Queechy Alliance compass points task	144
Figure 6.12	Determining strategies to trial	145
Figure 6.13	Queechy Alliance instructional model implementation rubric	148
Figure 6.14	Narre Warren South P–12 planning cycle for PLTs	153
Figure 6.15	Griffin's PLT process	157
Figure 6.16	Sample PLT planner and meeting summary	160
Figure 6.17	The role and work of PLTs in the school	164
Figure 6.18	Forms that useful data can take	165
Figure 6.19	The PLT meeting structure	166
Figure 6.20	English KLA survey: Lyndhurst Secondary College, July 2016	170
Figure 7.1	The Ladder of Inference	174
Figure 7.2	The Data Wise Improvement Process	176
Figure 7.3	Learning goals as the frame for teacher planning	178
Figure 7.4	Planning a lesson using Pythagoras' Theorem, Narre Warren South P–12 (extract)	180
Figure 7.5	Learning Intentions Survey small group questions	189
Figure 7.6	Glen Waverley Secondary College reflection and planning tool	195
Figure 7.7	Dandenong North Primary School maths statements, Level 4	196
Figure 8.1	Sample pro forma to help prepare for a classroom observation	219
Figure 8.2	Sample classroom observation pro forma	221
Figure 8.3	A sample script to inform feedback conversations	223

TABLES

Table 2.1	Evaluating our approach to whole-school improvement	15
Table 2.2	Action planning pro forma	16
Table 3.1	Leadership Behaviour 1: Diagnosing performance and prescribing for improvement	28
Table 3.2	Leadership Behaviour 2: Building teams to drive improvement	30
Table 3.3	Leadership Behaviour 3: Ensuring effective implementation of what matters most	32
Table 3.4	Leadership Behaviour 4: Leveraging the greatest source of improvement	34
Table 3.5	Leadership Behaviour 5: Ensuring progress and keeping on track	36
Table 3.6	Processing the self-assessment and planning for improvement	38
Table 3.7	Getting a fix on the team	39
Table 3.8	How effective is your leadership team?	41
Table 3.9	A sample coaching plan	48
Table 4.1	Stage 1: Getting the preconditions for whole-school improvement in place	66
Table 4.2	Stage 2: Building teaching capacity throughout the school	67
Table 4.3	Stage 3: Drilling down to improve classroom practice	68
Table 5.1	The preconditions for school improvement	73
Table 5.2	The preconditions for school improvement (sample outline)	74
Table 5.3	How do we rate on the preconditions?	75
Table 5.4	The maths of organisational relationships	77
Table 5.5	Assessing our effectiveness as a team	80
Table 5.6	Expectations of students in our school	84
Table 5.7	Using the school's values to ensure an orderly learning environment	91
Table 5.8	Learning environment/values matrix	92
Table 5.9	Extract from Darwin Middle School's Behaviour Expectations Matrix	93
Table 5.10	Creating your own expectations matrix	95

Tables

Table 5.11	Lyndhurst Secondary College Digital Technology Policy review	99
Table 5.12	An orderly learning environment checklist	105
Table 5.13	Identifying priorities for your school	109
Table 6.1	Identifying opportunities to increase student learning time	117
Table 6.2	Oakleigh Grammar School TLM implementation action plan	127
Table 6.3	Making it easier for teachers to implement the approach	137
Table 6.4	Professional learning team plan for meeting 1	139
Table 6.5	Professional learning team plan for meeting 2	141
Table 6.6	Queechy Alliance instructional model—lesson plan	143
Table 6.7	Reviewing and progressing the implementation of instructional model phases at Noble Park and the muka layna Collaboration	145
Table 6.8	Structuring your PLTs	150
Table 6.9	Evaluating the effectiveness of PLTs	169
Table 7.1	Applying the Data Wise process through PLTs	177
Table 7.2	Developing good learning goals	183
Table 7.3	Sample learning goals	184
Table 7.4	Choosing the right verb for your learning goal	185
Table 7.5	Narre Warren South P–12 College Learning Intentions survey	188
Table 7.6	Assessing our use of learning goals and success criteria	199
Table 7.7	Identifying examples of good feedback to students	202
Table 7.8	Evaluating the effectiveness of my feedback to students	205
Table 7.9	What differentiation is, and is not	206
Table 8.1	The WRSC Developmental Behaviour Management Model Student Management Rubric, 2014	211
Table 8.2	The WRSC Relationship Diagnostic Rubric, 2014	213
Table 8.3	Assessing the quality of feedback I give	226
Table C.1	Signposts for your journey	231

ABOUT THE AUTHORS

Pamela Macklin and Vic Zbar are the Managing Director and Director of Zbar Consulting respectively, which was established in 1993 to support ongoing improvement in schools. They are also both partners in G9 Education Consultancy Services.

Pamela Macklin has held a number of senior positions in Australian education, including Deputy CEO (Professional Resources) at the Australian Council for Educational Research and Deputy CEO of Curriculum Corporation. She is an experienced senior executive, coach, teacher, education consultant and writer.

Pamela has significant experience in the development and management of major community and education projects. Her interests lie in leadership coaching, the management of organisational change and improvement, educational policy, curriculum, assessment and school improvement. Her national and international work has focused on education reform and has included the development of policy and implementation strategies in areas such as ICT in education, literacy, numeracy, studies of Asia and gender equity.

Pamela is an experienced company director and has held several positions, including Chair, on not-for-profit Boards.

Vic Zbar has extensive consultancy and project management experience and is recognised internationally for his writing on education and a range of education reports. Prior to the establishment of Zbar Consulting, Vic was the Assistant Director of Human Resources in the Victorian Department of Education, having earlier been principal adviser to the Chief Executive, giving him an in-depth knowledge of the work of most aspects of the then Office of Schools. He is a widely-published author in both education and management and is the author of the best-selling *Managing the future*, and its sequel, *Key management concepts*.

More recently Vic co-edited four volumes of *Leading the education debate*, published by the Centre for Strategic Education (CSE), and co-authored *Better schools, better teachers, better results*, published by ACER. He has written numerous articles and papers, and recently authored *Leadership to make things happen in your school*, also published by the CSE.

Both Pamela and Vic can be contacted through Zbar Consulting's website, www.zbarconsulting.com.

HOW TO USE THIS BOOK

There are literally thousands of books on school improvement and how to achieve it, so let's start with the elephant in the room. Why do we need another?

The problem with most, as discussed in some detail in Chapter 2, is that they treat all schools as if they are the same. This commonly leads to a 'one-size-fits-all' approach that may work in some, but by no means all, schools. This book, like its predecessor, is designed to begin with where your school is at in its improvement journey, and then provides the strategies and supporting tools to enable you to advance. This will help you to craft your own strategic response, based on relevant research and experience in other successful schools.

We provide an outline of the stages that schools commonly go through as they pursue whole-school improvement, and hence an indication of where best to enter the process to significantly improve your school. Each stage is underpinned by leadership since all our experience suggests that whole-school improvement does not occur unless there is a united and cohesive leadership team driving it through the school.

Given this, we suggest that you read the first four chapters to understand the approach and determine exactly where your school is at. You can then complete the self-assessment to identify the stage of development of your school and hence which other chapters will be most valuable to you.

There is an apocryphal story that needs to be told at this point to give further context to this book and how it ought to be used. It concerns an English scientist who was asked to give a keynote address to an audience in China on his detailed and complex research. Since he intended to speak for an hour to an audience who did not all necessarily speak English, he arranged to meet with his interpreter to work out when he should break. The interpreter, who also was a trained scientist, suggested he speak for 15 minutes and then he would translate, a further 15 minutes, and so on until the hour was up. While unsure about the efficacy of the approach, the scientist bowed to the interpreter's expertise and agreed.

The following day, after he was introduced and spoke for the first 15 minutes, the interpreter uttered what amounted to a single sentence before signalling the scientist to proceed. Another 15 minutes and a sentence, a third that yielded the same result and then the final 15 minutes and polite applause. Somewhat flabbergasted, the scientist sought out the interpreter after his address to find out what had just transpired. In response to his query about the unfolding speech, the interpreter explained that after the first 15 minutes he told the audience, 'he hasn't said anything new yet'. After the next 15 minutes he explained that 'he still hasn't'. After the third 15 minutes he advised them that 'he isn't going to', and then at the conclusion of the speech he said 'I told you so'.

The point of the story is to illustrate that much of what we have written is not necessarily new. Not only that, we reference and at times even reproduce things we have written in earlier articles because they continue to hold true. There is nothing wrong with this, since the issue is not so much newness, as the implementation of strategies we know will work if schools are to improve. It might seem at times like stating the obvious but, as the management thinker Tom Peters is reputed to have said, 'if the obvious was so obvious, then everyone would be doing it'; and of course, when it comes to whole-school improvement, they are not.

Driving school improvement: Practical strategies and tools is designed to support you in meeting your improvement challenge in ways that can be contextualised to the circumstances of your school. The focus of this second edition, like the first, is implementation, so it contains an even broader range of tools, activities and pro formas, which have been used successfully in a range of schools (all the school materials reproduced in this book are used with permission), that you can adapt and use as appropriate to the context in which you work. Whenever possible, these are provided on a single page so you can photocopy them if you wish. We would only request that in using these, you acknowledge the source.

THE REASON FOR A SECOND EDITION

We first published *Driving school improvement: A practical guide* in 2017. So why is a second edition needed now?

The answer lies in the challenge of implementing whole-school improvement and change.

Most school leaders know what needs to be done if they are to significantly improve their schools. Teachers commonly share their views, though not always the strategies for achieving them. Where schools, leaders and teachers struggle, is in making it happen consistently through the school.

That is because it is difficult, long-term work. If it were easy, to paraphrase Tom Peters again, everyone would be doing it.

In the years since we first wrote *Driving school improvement,* we have continued to work with many committed leaders and teachers on making the changes needed to ensure consistent improvement in their schools. This means not just initiating and implementing the changes for improvement that are required, but embedding them so they become the 'new normal' of how things happen in the school. In this way, school improvement can transcend the leaders and teachers who were there at the start and become truly sustainable over time.

Along the way, we have significantly expanded the range of support materials for leaders and teachers to use, based on activities, tools, pro formas and the like that have been co-developed, tested and then refined with these schools to ensure that they work—support materials that help schools to meet the implementation challenge.

Over the same period, we have also found and learned from additional research that has gone on to inform our work with schools, and which is worth bringing to the attention of readers of this book.

If you found the first edition of *Driving school improvement* useful, then you will find even more in this second edition to inform your work. If you are coming to the book for the first time, the feedback we have received from your colleagues who have read it is that it contains a structured set of resources you can adapt and use as appropriate to the stage of development and specific circumstances of your school.

The choice of what to use and how is then a strategic one for you to make, consistent with your diagnosis of where your school is at, and informed by the approaches outlined in the remainder of the book.

WHAT'S NEW IN THIS EDITION

Peppered throughout this new edition are some additional research sources we have used that are reflected in an expanded reference list on which readers can draw.

For the most part, however, the additions are focused on further school experience and associated tools and advice for driving improvement consistently through your school. Most notable, but by no means exhaustive in this regard are:
- Some advice to support a focus on the important rather than urgent in Chapter 2, along with a new section in the chapter on carrying people with you as change for improvement is pursued.
- The inclusion in Chapter 3 of a discussion of what leadership means, two new principal case studies, and a leadership framework and associated self-assessment to consider.
- Significantly more detailed advice on coaching and examples of how it has worked successfully in schools, along with a sample plan for introducing a coaching program to your school and additional scenarios to practise in Chapter 3.
- A brief discussion in Chapter 5 on involving middle-level leaders to ensure successful whole-school improvement and a new activity for developing both the leadership behaviours to adopt and a compelling message for staff.

- An outline of a Gold Badge program in Chapter 5 to supplement the discussion of Good Standing and a pro forma and rubric to support classroom observation of the extent to which an orderly learning environment exists in the school.
- An example of the Pose, Pause, Pounce, Bounce questioning strategy in Chapter 5 that helps teachers to extend their wait time in class.
- Additional school instructional models in Chapter 6, along with an outline of the way in which the structure of most instructional models conforms to how student learning occurs.
- Significantly expanded advice and activities in Chapter 6 that will enable the school to collaboratively develop, design and then implement its own instructional model, informed by the successful experience of other schools.
- Further advice and activities to strengthen teachers' understanding of the explicit instruction component of the instructional model in Chapter 6.
- A major new section in Chapter 6 on 'Making the instructional model happen in your school', which includes the experience of a number of schools and clusters and the key implementation tools and activities they used, case studies of driving through different elements of the instructional model and a rubric to monitor its implementation.
- Additional advice on guiding norms for professional learning teams (PLTs) and a set of questions to improve the effectiveness of PLT leadership in Chapter 6.
- Samples of quality planning undertaken by PLTs in schools in Chapter 6 along with a new activity to maximise the performance of PLTs.
- A case study of 'Pre-PLTs' in Chapter 6 to ensure the successful introduction of these teams throughout the school.
- The inclusion of an illustration in Chapter 7 of how learning goals can be used to plan a lesson for students regardless of the area or year level involved.
- The provision of a work sample to illustrate success criteria in action in Chapter 7, along with a new activity for developing rubrics to inform their use.
- Additional tools to support teacher reflection on their use of learning goals and success criteria in Chapter 7.
- A new activity in Chapter 7 to help teachers determine the type of feedback to provide to students' work and further examples of differentiation in practice in schools.
- Additional school experiences and advice on how to implement classroom observation in Chapter 8.

CHAPTER 1
THE IMPROVEMENT CHALLENGE

Our schools educate a greater proportion of young people than was the case in the 1960s, which many cite as an age to which they would like to return. Government figures show, for example, that 82% of 15- to 19-year-olds participated in education and training towards a recognised qualification in 2014 (Australian Institute of Health and Welfare, 2015, p. 120), compared with 22% of the same cohort still in school in 1960 when the 'golden years' started (Le & Miller, 2002), and between 2005 and 2016, the proportion of 15-to 19-year-olds not in employment, education or training fell from 7.7 to 5.1% (Australian Institute of Health and Welfare, 2017). What is more, UNESCO reports that the literacy rate for this cohort stood at an almost universal 99% in 2004 (Forbes, 2016). But is this good enough?

While the 2015 Program for International Student Assessment (PISA) results show Australia continues to be a 'high quality–high equity' education system, with results well above the OECD average, they remain below some countries, such as Canada, with which we can reasonably be compared. For example, Australia's mean score on the reading literacy scale was 503 compared to Canada's 527, and the difference between the 5th and 95th percentiles of students was 338 compared to 305 (Thompson, De Bortoli, & Underwood, 2017). In addition, we have been experiencing a declining trend in these results over the past decade, confirmed by the preliminary results for 2018, due to a fall in the number of students achieving at higher levels and a rise in the number achieving at lower levels, with Aboriginal and Torres Strait Islander, rural and students from low socio-economic backgrounds disproportionately represented in this group. Results for PISA 2018 released at the time of writing show a further decline in the relative performance of Australian students in reading, science and maths (Australian Council for Educational Research, 2019). While Australia on average still performs relatively well, these PISA 2015 and 2018 results suggest that we are slipping backwards relative to other countries, and that we may be getting worse at preparing our students for the everyday challenges of adult life. See, for example, *PISA 2015: A first look at Australia's results* (Thompson, De Bortoli, & Underwood, 2016).

PISA is but only one snapshot of the performance of Australia's schools, but is consistent with recent National Assessment Program—Literacy and Numeracy (NAPLAN) test trends and the level of inequity in student outcomes that exists.

The challenge this inevitably presents, and which this book seeks to address, is how we support a fundamentally good system, with significant variability of performance within it, to become a truly great system with consistently better teaching and schools. And the good news is that significant experience exists within Australia's schools to show that it can be done.

WHAT MAKES THE DIFFERENCE TO STUDENT LEARNING OUTCOMES?

We know the factors that really make a difference to student learning outcomes in schools. Hattie (2003), for example, has demonstrated that, aside from what students themselves bring to school, teachers and teaching account for the greatest level of variance of any other factor operating in a school, as illustrated in Figure 1.1.

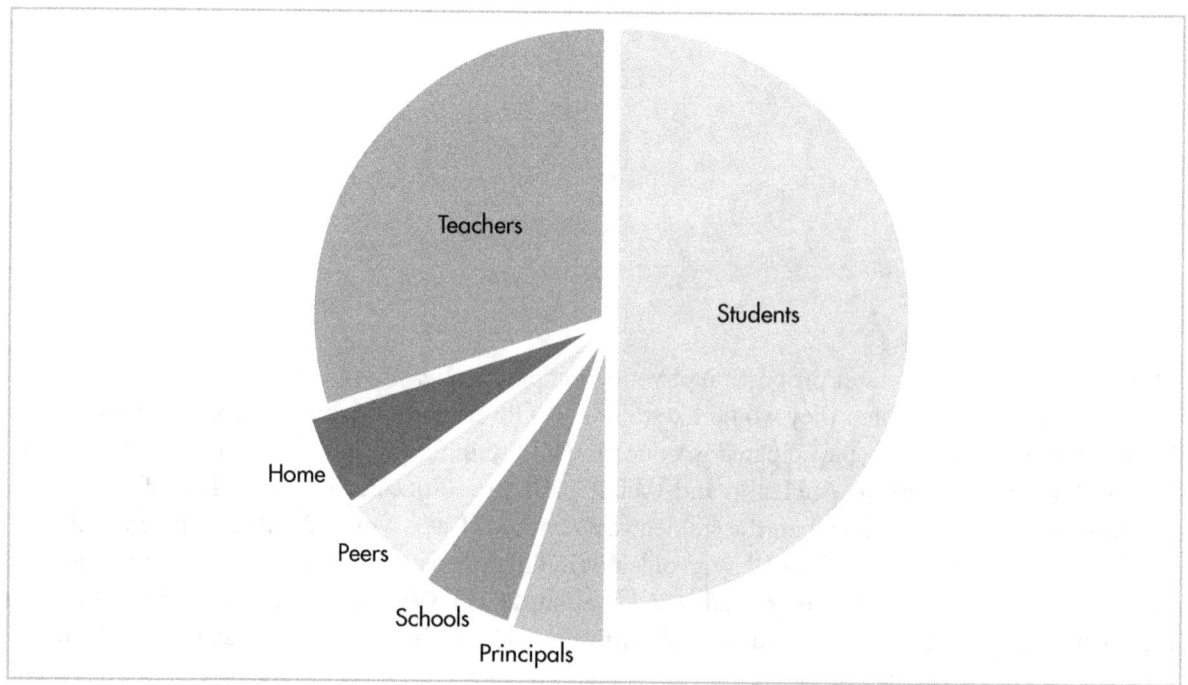

FIGURE 1.1: PERCENTAGE OF ACHIEVEMENT VARIANCE
Source: Hattie (2003, October, p. 3).

More specifically his analysis showed that:
- Students account for around 50% of the variance of achievement, which is responsive to government programs to reduce poverty or improve health outcomes, but not particularly amenable to strategies a school can adopt.
- Home accounts for only 5 to 10% because the major effects of home already are included in the attributes of the students themselves.
- Schools account for about 5 to 10%, which at first blush may appear to suggest that schools barely make a difference to achievement, until we recognise that the structure and operations of the school critically determine the effectiveness of its teachers and the quality of teaching they provide.
- Principals are already taken into account in the variance attributed to schools and, though Hattie does not make this point, experience suggests that they also come into their own when it comes to influencing the teachers and teaching variable.
- Peer effects account for a further 5 to 10% of the variance, which suggests we can make too much of the significance of the nature of the peer group at times, perhaps, even using it as an excuse for poor outcomes.

- Teachers, and most particularly what they do in the classroom, account for the remaining 30% of the variance.

This means that, as far as the school is concerned, it's the teaching that matters most.

THE DIFFERENCE TEACHERS MAKE

Despite what we have just written, we also know that not all teachers have the same effect. As far back as 1996, Sanders and Rivers used extensive longitudinal studies into teacher effectiveness in the US state of Tennessee to show the difference that teachers make to students who essentially start at the same point (Sanders, & Rivers, 1996).

As Figure 1.2 shows, an eight-year-old student at the 50th percentile in literacy performance who is placed with a low-performing teacher will, on average, by age 11 have dropped back to the 37th percentile. This should not necessarily be taken as judgment of the teacher who could, for example, be relatively new to the profession, or starved of professional development opportunities, but simply an acknowledgment of their current performance level, which could, with the appropriate support, significantly improve. By contrast, the same student placed with a high-performing teacher on average will have progressed to the 90th percentile.

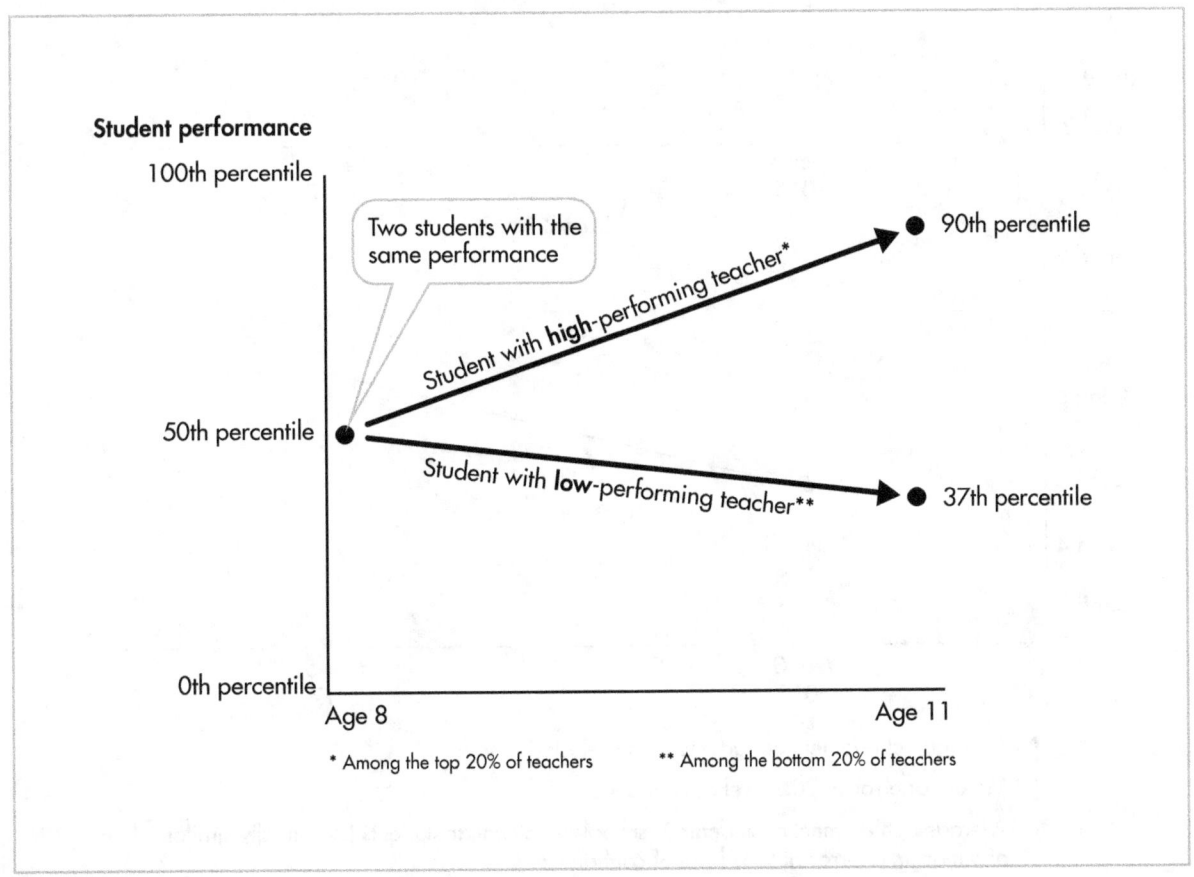

FIGURE 1.2: THE DIFFERENCE TEACHERS MAKE
Source: Sanders & Rivers (1996).
Note: This figure is created by the authors and is derived from the evidence in the text. There are many versions on the internet based on the evidence and this is one that CSE drew for the authors for an article they wrote for them.

The greatest source of improvement in any school comes from narrowing this gap by supporting more teachers to work like the best teachers in the school, with the result that consistently more effective teaching occurs in each and every class.

THE DIFFERENCE THE SCHOOL CAN MAKE

Just as some teachers perform better than others, so too do some schools.

Consider the outcomes for students in two anonymous neighbouring primary schools depicted in Figure 1.3 with an almost identical socio-economic mix. The Index of Community Socio-Educational Advantage (ICSEA), developed for the MySchool website as a measure for making meaningful comparisons across schools, is 939 for School A and 945 for School B, compared with an average of 1000, which means both are disadvantaged schools. The figure shows the performance of a cohort of students who undertook the NAPLAN reading test in Year 3 in each school in 2015 and then again in Year 5 in 2017, compared with the performance of students in a group of statistically similar schools.

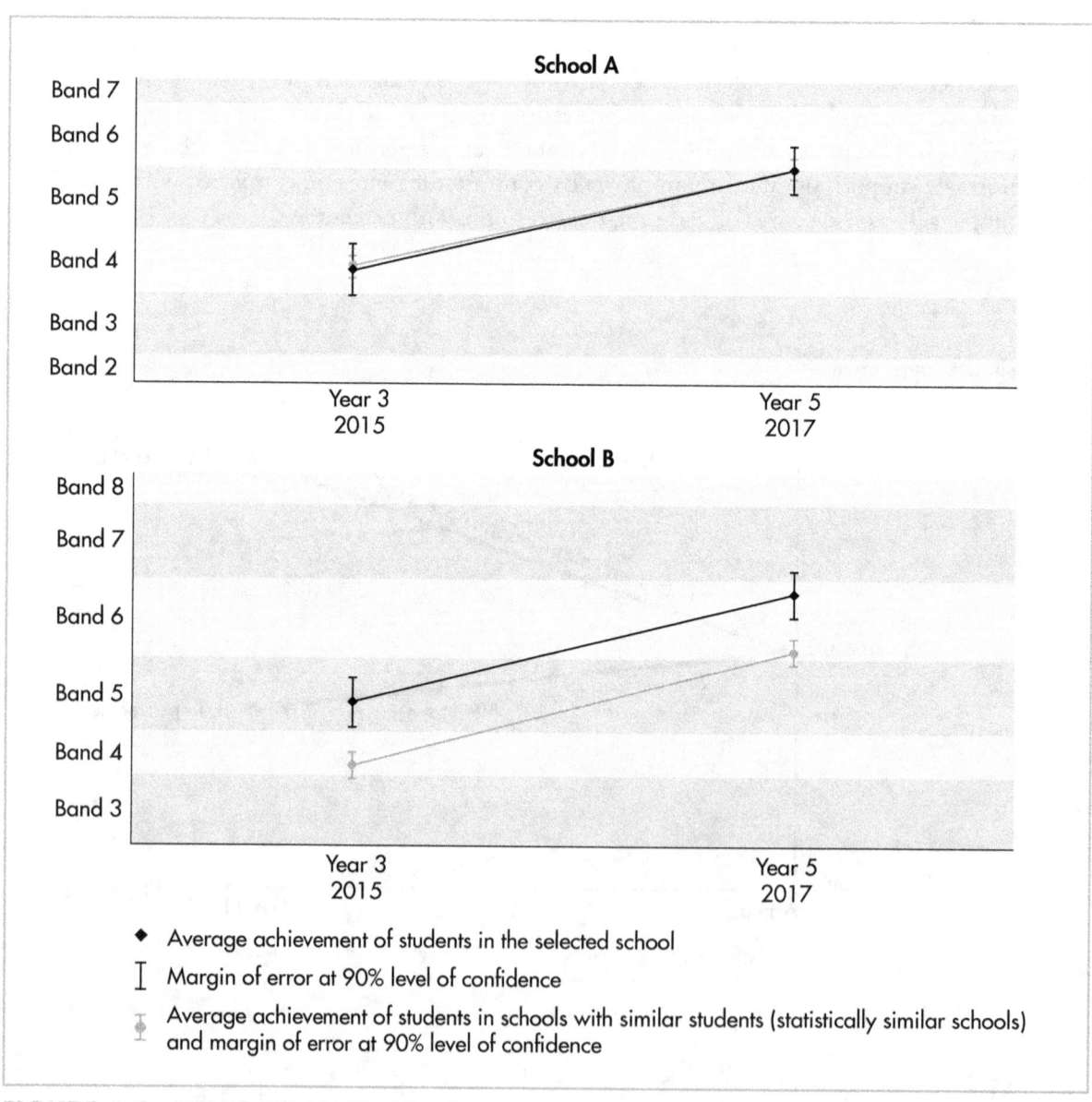

FIGURE 1.3: PERFORMANCE OF SCHOOL A AND SCHOOL B COMPARED TO A GROUP OF STATISTICALLY SIMILAR SCHOOLS, 2015 TO 2017

Note: The two components of the Figure are sourced from the MySchool website: https://www.myschool.edu.au/ More specific information cannot be provided as this would identify the schools.

Clearly School B is adding far more value than School A to its students' NAPLAN outcomes in reading, which is matched by its comparative performance in the persuasive writing, spelling and numeracy tests as well.

The challenge is to identify what schools like School B do, so that more schools, like teachers, can work like the best.

CHANGING BEHAVIOUR

Whether it is teachers or schools, supporting more to work like the best depends on changing behaviour so successful practices are more consistently used.

In a significant analysis of staff development and teacher change, Guskey (1983), explained how 'traditionally, staff development has focused first on initiating change in the beliefs, attitudes, and perceptions of teachers' on the assumption that 'these changes would lead to other specific changes in their classroom behaviours and practices' (p. 58). It's a model that he argues does not really work with experienced teachers in schools. Rather, he suggests, 'significant change in teachers' beliefs and attitudes takes place only after student learning outcomes have changed' (Guskey, 1983, p. 58), which in turn depends on changed classroom practices that teachers adopt.

In other words, we change behaviour if we want to change beliefs, rather than as is commonly assumed, the other way around.

A good example of this in Australia is community practice regarding the use of seat belts. The 1960s, a Department of Transport study explains, saw 'a sustained attempt to educate the public on the value of wearing seat belts' (Milne, 1985, p. 2). However, the publicity campaigns appear 'to have had little impact on belt wearing' (p. 5). In December 1970, Victoria became the world's first legislature to make it mandatory to wear a seat belt. This saw a rapid increase in belt usage and a marked decline in casualties with the result that other Australian states followed suit. In all states, the subsequent legislation had 'an immediate and significant effect on wearing rates' (p. 11).

Relatively soon seat belts were almost universally worn by Australian car drivers and there would not be a reader of this book who would now get in a car without doing up their belt. Put simply, the behaviour of drivers was changed and their belief about the efficacy of seat belts followed later.

The fundamental improvement challenge that all schools face is to change teacher behaviour so more can work like the best and student learning outcomes can be improved. It is a challenge that many schools around Australia are striving to meet, including all of the schools cited in this book.

CHAPTER 2
HOW CHANGE FOR IMPROVEMENT OCCURS[1]

In 1996, Vic was working with a group of colleagues on a national project that saw them all meet up in Sydney for dinner before a major project milestone had to be met.

For some time he had been feeling tired and lethargic, was off his food and consequently was losing some weight. Nothing to worry about, as he had been working really hard and not sleeping that well. In addition, he had a bad cough he couldn't shake, which his general practitioner initially treated as a cold, but subsequently, because of how stubborn it had been, tackled with antibiotics after a diagnosis of bronchitis.

Not long after, despite what was some pretty flash food that was ordered at the dinner meeting he was at, Vic found he couldn't partake, and at one stage, a colleague and friend put his hand on Vic's back and noticed that his shirt was sopping wet. He and others suggested Vic return to his doctor as soon as their meeting was finished and he returned home.

The following night, Vic was woken from his sleep by severe chest pains that he initially mistook for a heart attack, but subsequently realised was connected to everything else that was going on. Not surprisingly, he cancelled his appointments for that day and visited his GP who sent him for a chest X-ray straight away. The X-ray revealed a mass in his chest, which the GP explained, was non-Hodgkin lymphoma, or cancer by any other name.

A visit to the specialist confirmed the diagnosis and recommended a biopsy to determine the type of cancer it was and the consequent treatment required. This was because, as he explained, each cancer is individual and requires a tailored response. You cannot simply treat cancer as a generic disease, but rather you must target the specific cancer itself.

Five years later, Vic was able to say that he was 'statistically cured', which means he then had the same chance of getting this cancer again as any other member of the public.

Twenty-five years on he still sees his oncologist annually and thanks him for the contribution he made to his cure, by virtue of closely diagnosing what Vic had, and prescribing the appropriate cocktail of chemotherapies and radiation in response.

---

[1] Material in this chapter draws on Zbar (2016).

DIAGNOSE BEFORE YOU PRESCRIBE

Before proceeding to the lessons we draw from this, keen-eyed readers of the first edition will have noticed a change to the title of the chapter this time around. The change, from 'How change happens', reflects the fact we have recently read and been influenced by Viviane Robinson's *Reduce change to increase improvement* (2018). 'Change', she argues,

> is too often equated with progress and improvement, despite the fact that they are very different. To lead change is to exercise influence in ways that move a team, organisation, or system from one state to another. The second state could be better, worse, or the same as the first. To lead improvement is to exercise influence in ways that leave the team, organisation, or system in a better state than before'. (Robinson, 2018, p. 2, emphasis in the original has been deleted)

As we know from experience, not all change is desirable, and some is to be avoided at all costs. Hence it is change for improvement that we seek, by learning from how it has occurred successfully in other schools.

Let's return to our contrast between the approach of Vic's doctors as outlined in the preceding vignette, and the way in which we approach change in our schools and, in particular, systemic change where governments or departments seek change at significant scale.

What generally happens is that the system leadership, whether at the bureaucratic or political level, identifies a particular program it wants to push through all of its schools. Often the program derives from research, and is accompanied by detailed documents outlining why it should be implemented, the benefits of doing so and some strictures about how it is going to be done. Then schools and their leaders are expected to flick the switch from whatever they are doing now, to the new, much vaunted approach.

In other words, the system goes straight to prescription, and what needs to be done, without first diagnosing the problem, contextualised to the individual experience of each school. The result, not surprisingly, is that the generic cure works for some, but not all. It's the equivalent of Vic's oncologist having said, cancer is cancer regardless of who gets it, and have I got a cure for you.

When inevitably the systemic intervention does not work as planned, then it's always the schools that we blame because they didn't implement as we designed. The problem is, the design may not have fitted the context sufficiently well and may not have even been the best thing to do. It is basically a one-size-fits-all approach or, as Henry Ford famously said of his first model Ts, 'you can have any colour you want, provided it's black'.

By blaming the people who took the prescription, rather than those who prescribed without first diagnosing, we're effectively saying that the treatment was fine, but regrettably the patient has died.

However, our criticism should not be limited to those authorities who can exercise power over schools. There are also plenty of observers and commentators on schooling who are happy to prescribe what all schools should do, regardless of the stage of development in which the school finds itself and the major strategic challenges it has to face. Our newspapers are still full of articles written by experts suggesting 'our schools should do this', or 'our schools should do that', regardless of the state in which the school finds itself.

Even some unarguable propositions about schooling can be problematic depending on how they are used. The constant references to 21st century skills provide a case in point. No-one can argue against the need to develop skills appropriate to the modern world, such as critical and creative thinking, collaboration, communication, flexibility, information literacy and more; though some might contest how new some of these really are. However, there is no point focusing on 21st century skills if you are dealing with a group of students who enter school so far behind that they basically can't read and write. Until you bridge that gap, they can't even access skills, such as critical thinking or technological literacy, that you may be seeking to promote.

The experience of Hume Central Secondary College in the highly disadvantaged suburb of Broadmeadows in Melbourne helps illustrate the point. A very significant proportion of students entering this school do so with literacy and numeracy levels that are well behind the expectation for students starting Year 7. So far behind, in fact, that the school's mantra from the time of its establishment in 2009 was 'two years learning in one'. In other words, rapidly bringing students up to the expected standards in literacy and numeracy, as the entry point for being able to address the more complex 21st century skills. While inevitably this involved teaching literacy and numeracy with a focus on such skills as collaboration and creative thinking, that was a secondary focus to the more urgent task of ensuring the students can effectively read and write.

When the school was formally reviewed in 2013, after only four years of its existence, it had already achieved the equivalent of 1.6 years learning in one year for students in Year 9.

Any focus on programs to promote 21st century skills would arguably have been a distraction from this cause. In addition, the high level of progress the school made resulted from its work in using an 'explicit instruction' model it designed to plan better lessons in professional learning teams (PLTs) and not because of any systemic approach to improvement or reform.

So the message is that systemic prescriptions and global exhortations generally fail. Instead, you need to first diagnose what is most needed for the school to improve and then prescribe an approach that suits the needs of the individual school, albeit guided by things that we know can apply to more than one school.

Three overarching questions to consider in this regard that Garmston & Wellman (2016) suggest are, 'Who are we?', 'Why are we doing this?' and 'Why are we doing it this way?' Among other things, an examination of these questions can help challenge the unquestioned assumption that commonly exists that, as they put it, '(i)t's just the way we do things around here' (p. 12).

There is, however, no magic bullet for school improvement and reform, and rather, we need to look to guidelines and experiences from which we can learn, provided we first diagnose the health of the school.

USE RESEARCH WISELY

But, you might ask, isn't the whole point of a systemic approach to change to inject research into our schools and ensure that their practice is evidence based? Good point and we agree that we do. But research is sometimes uncertain, often contested and has to be contextualised to the actual circumstances of each school.

The growing focus on using open learning classrooms helps illustrate the point. In 2011, for example, the Victorian Department of Education and Early Childhood Development produced a booklet to guide schools in moving to an open learning spaces approach (DEECD, 2011). This guide, based on the experiences of a number of principals, teachers and schools, outlined how flexible spaces give teachers choices in how they interact with students and help meet students' individual and social needs. By contrast, an investigation of open learning classrooms conducted by Macquarie University in 2014 found noise levels were such that further research is needed 'to determine if they are suitable learning spaces for young students' (Mealings, Buchholz, Demuth & Dillon, 2014, p. 1). As a result, as reported in *The Age* (Cook, 2015), there are schools with open classrooms that are now spending money to put back the walls.

The two documents are clearly looking at different things in relation to open learning classrooms, each of which is relevant to whether or not the approach ought to be used. These different frames of reference can also help explain why the overall effect size of having an open as opposed to 'traditional' classroom approach is a negligible 0.01 (Hattie, 2018). Thus, any decision to adopt the approach must be a local one that is contextualised to the specific circumstances of the school, the key learning needs and challenges its students have and the capacity and experience of its staff.

The point is that research ought to be used to guide strategic thinking in schools based on an analysis of where the school is at and hence its major developmental need. Research should never be viewed as a prescription in its own right, nor the answer to all of your ills.

Just as importantly, leaders need to use research judiciously so it aligns to strategies already being successfully used in the school, is manageable and within the capacity of the school to sustain and is structured in ways that ensure staff can see how it fits.

We experienced one case where research was touted in ways that distracted and confused, rather than supported the school's efforts to improve. More specifically, the school's leaders had read some of the Visible Learning research and wanted to implement what they referred to as 'Hattie's top ten'. (see, for example, *Visible learning*—Hattie, 2009). As fans of Hattie's work, we could assure the school that this was far from how he intends his research to be used. Consider if they had adopted the approach. The top ten in order at the time were: teacher estimates of achievement; collective teacher efficacy; self-reported grades; Piagetian programs; conceptual change programs; response to intervention; teacher credibility; micro teaching; cognitive task analysis and classroom discussion (drawn from Hattie, 2015). While each one may be important in its own right, some can be difficult to introduce and implement. In addition, the ten constitute a disparate group of strategies and influences that are hard to explain in a consistent story for staff, which makes them even more difficult to adopt. Taken together they lack coherence as a strategic approach, do not in themselves address the key challenges facing the school, may be beyond the capacity of its staff at this time and would, as a consequence, simply engender chaos in the school.

The problem here is not the research, but how the school was intending it to be used. Research does not exist in a vacuum or separate from whatever else is happening in the school. That is why, as suggested earlier, it has to be used judiciously, and even wisely to inform strategic thinking and the consequent approaches we adopt.

In working with this 'top ten' school, we instead decided to focus on using learning goals and success criteria to drive through consistently better teaching in the school; and this subsequently saw a dramatic improvement in students' results.

Learning goals, it is noted, is not in the top ten. In fact, it comes in at a somewhat lowly 36. Yet many schools are finding that learning goals and associated success criteria provide one of the best entry points for improving teaching and supporting more teachers to work like the best. The reason why, is that learning goals cannot be taken in isolation and, if implemented as intended, connect to other important things, as outlined in detail in Chapter 7 of this book.

Taking this example into account, the question is not so much whether or not research should inform what we do, since the answer must always be 'yes', but rather which research should inform us and when and how should it be applied. This in turn depends on the diagnosis of your school's key developmental need and therefore the best strategies for addressing it.

DO A MANAGEABLE AMOUNT

A significant challenge in this context is for leaders to resist the temptation to try to do too much.

One of the messages that resonates most when we speak to networks of principals and other school leaders is that taking on too much is always the enemy of successful improvement and change. When schools do take this path, it inevitably means the implementation suffers and none of it is done well. This in turn breeds cynicism about, and even some resistance to change and fuels the naysayers who are quick to remind, 'we told you it wouldn't work'.

Far better for schools to tackle less, provided it is something important that has been demonstrated to support improvement in schools, and then drive it consistently through the school so it becomes the new way in which everyone works. Then, when leaders can point to 'what we've achieved', through consistently applying the new strategic approach, they can invite discussion about 'where should we seek to be more consistent next'.

Closely related to the problem of trying to push through too much, is the way in which schools add to all that they do. The default approach to change that most schools adopt is to accumulate new strategies, add them to those they are seeking to implement, and never abandon anything at all. A point that has been made forcefully by Professor Brian Caldwell—for example, in *The transformation of schools* (Caldwell, 2000). The result is that time and effort are often wasted on old approaches that no longer are worth it and existing practices take oxygen from the new strategies they are seeking to introduce.

In an approach that other schools might consider and adopt, a colleague of ours worked with one school on what they called 'an abandonment audit', whereby they examined all of their practices to determine which ones could go. A kind of Marie Kondo for schools, but well ahead of its time.

The mere fact of codifying all that you do is useful since much of it simply reflects 'what we have always done' without reference to value for the effort we expend. It then gains added traction when we ask, 'Is it still worth doing or can we benefit by getting rid of this practice to make room for something else?' If nothing else, it's a useful antidote to the legitimate but ultimately unhelpful response that 'we haven't got the time'.

It's interesting to note that when the idea of abandonment audits was raised with other school leaders, it resonated but they wondered about the term. Far more useful, one leader suggested, would be to call it a 'garage sale', where we go through our possessions to get rid of those we no longer need. The difficulty with that, another responded, is who would want to buy them if they are no use, and should we be selling them to people who ought to be abandoning these things themselves. So, the metaphor we settled on was 'a hard rubbish collection', where you can junk what you truly do not need, without foisting it on to someone else.

A particular challenge in this regard is to focus on things that are important rather than urgent, since so many of us operate the other way around. For example, think of the times when someone you are speaking with is unable to resist the temptation to look at their mobile phone to see the message that just pinged through, despite the fact that ostensibly the most important thing they are doing is talking to you. Urgency drives many people, distracting them from what matters most, but can be constrained by the processes we adopt.

One of our favourite examples is the way in which Glen Lutwyche, the Principal of Ulverstone Secondary College in Tasmania, manages his email flow. Having worked with the school, Vic sent Glen an email in the middle of the day only to receive the following automatic response—'I check my emails between 8am and 9am daily and respond asap. If the matter is urgent please contact [name deleted] at USC on [number deleted] and make her aware of your request and I will attempt to follow up prior to this.' Not only does this mean he is focused on what matters most through the day, but the upshot is that he receives fewer emails as people become more thoughtful about whether a message to him is even required.

It is appropriate too at this point to say something about meetings that schools conduct, since meetings are the bane of many a leader's and teacher's life. Despite the fact that meetings are often essential, and can support significant improvement when done well, more commonly they are, as Ludden (2018, November 30) describes, 'perceived by employees as a waste of time that could have been better spent working on their assigned tasks'.

Mroz, Allen, Verhoeven, and Shuffler (2018), who studied meetings and their effectiveness in depth, have outlined a set of what Ludden called 'common-sense' best practices for conducting effective meetings that start by asking should this meeting even occur? If the answer is yes, then the obvious questions to consider are 'How the meeting should be structured?', 'When it should be held?' and 'Who should attend?'

Starting from the premise that meetings should only be called when necessary, rather than because they are regularly scheduled in the timetable we have, the effectiveness of the meeting can then be improved if we focus on Mroz et al.'s (2018) guiding questions for the meeting of 'What can leaders do to ensure that it runs smoothly?', 'What can attendees do?', 'How should attendees interact?'; and then after the meeting, 'What are our actions from here?', 'How do we ensure follow through?', 'How do meetings impact the attendees and the organisation, (and) what are the immediate and distal outcomes?' (p. 5).

It's a matter of meeting less, but meeting better, and only when a clear purpose exists, thereby helping to do a manageable amount.

CAN WE ONLY DO ONE THING?

So, if we need to diagnose first, then be judicious about using research and avoid doing too much, does this mean that when it comes to improvement, schools can only do one thing?

The answer, we suggest, is yes and no.

Yes, because all of the experience in high-performing schools suggests that they have got there by identifying one thing to drive through the school first and then leveraging off the success of that to pursue the next big thing. For the schools that became high performing having earlier been poor performers, the one key focus invariably was to get an orderly learning environment in place where the students are known well by the staff, as discussed further in Chapter 5.

But no, because there are often things you can hang off the one big thing you are pursuing, to maximise the impact with the same level of effort from the staff. More specifically, the school first identifies the most important thing it needs to drive through for whole-school improvement to occur, and then looks for what else it can connect to this, always provided it does not detract from driving the key strategic focus consistently through the school.

For example, the implementation of an orderly learning environment can link well to a simultaneous focus on the effective use of learning goals to plan and deliver better lessons in class. This is because more engaging lessons that enable students to experience learning success inevitably means there is less scope in classrooms for disruptive behaviour and the overall culture of learning in classrooms can be built. On the other side of this coin, establishing structures that ensure students are better known by the staff, such as approaches that connect teachers to fewer students for longer periods of time, helps them to plan lessons that are more closely aligned to the current understanding of their students and hence their primary learning needs.

That said, anything that detracts from the primary focus of getting an orderly learning environment in place, if that is the key strategic need of the school, ought to be avoided. So, if a focus on learning goals is likely to distract teachers from the consistent pursuit of agreed behavioural expectations and consequences, then it ought not be pursued at this time.

Determining the extent to which the question about doing more than one thing is answered 'yes' or 'no' is a leadership challenge related to making things happen in the school. Just as physicians must use their diagnosis to determine how much and which medicines the patient can take, so too must school leaders determine how many and which set of aligned strategies the school can successfully implement.

CARRYING PEOPLE WITH YOU

Changes to practice, as is well known in schools, are not adopted by all individuals at the same time. For example, Rogers' 'Diffusion of Innovation' Theory (see Rogers, 1962 through to Rogers, 2003) posited five categories of responses to change as depicted in Figure 2.1.

More recently Gladwell, in his popular work *The tipping point*, made a similar point when he sought to describe 'the moment of critical mass, the threshold, the boiling point' when ideas spread like wildfire in an irresistible way (Gladwell, 2000, p. 12). In other words, the point at which an interesting idea for some becomes the must-have concept for all.

Carrying people with you is a prerequisite for whole-school improvement and change; and the normal curve depicted in Figure 2.1 can help us in this regard.

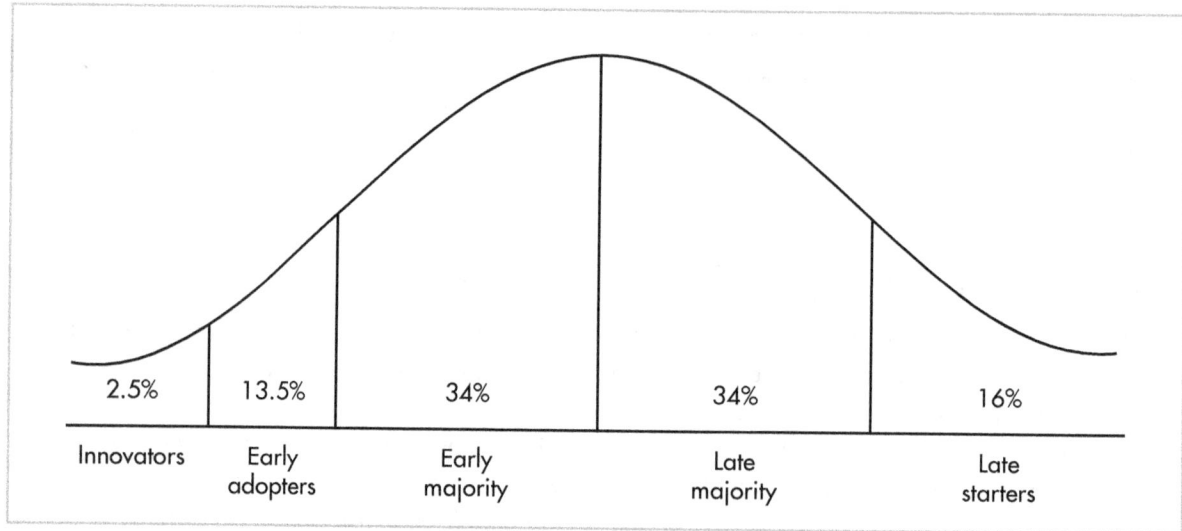

FIGURE 2.1: THE NORMAL CURVE FOR THE ADOPTION OF CHANGE

Note: A Google search will surface many versions of the normal curve from which Figure 2.1 is derived. Many refer to what we have called the 'Late starters' as 'Laggards', however, we consider this a pejorative reference that is unhelpful in schools as we strive to support more teachers to work like the best.

Often when we work with leaders in schools, we outline the curve and its categories and ask them to think of where their primary energies should go. More specifically, should they go towards:
- the innovators, who are keen to try things first and willing to take risks
- the early adopters, who are open to the need to change and willing to try a new approach
- the early majority, who won't be out in front, but will move faster than the average
- the late majority, who are sceptical of change and are waiting for the critical mass
- the late starters, who are particularly conservative and hence the hardest to shift?

Regardless of their responses, when pressed these leaders generally acknowledge that the places their energies actually go are the two ends of the curve. They pay particular attention to the innovators and early adopters because they interest them most, and to the late starters who demand it through the negative comments they make. This is despite the fact the innovators and early adopters need relatively little time, since they already are well on board, and the late starters will take plenty of leaders' energy for relatively little return.

In contrast, time can be far more beneficially spent working with the early majority to hasten the emergence of the critical mass. These are people open to new ideas, but reluctant to give them a go until they can see the signs of success. They are definitely interested in what the innovators and early adopters are doing, and eager to hear how it works; but reluctant to yet chance their arm. They also have friends in the 'top' 16 per cent who talk with them about their experiences and how it is working for them.

In one Northern Territory school we worked with, that was seeking to drive its instructional model consistently through the school, the leadership established a working group of four who determined which staff belonged in the early majority category, and where within it, and then identified two staff each to work with in order to more quickly bring them on board; thereby growing the critical mass by eight. This could then be repeated, with an impact on the late majority as well, as they saw friends in the early majority who had decided to make the shift.

It's reminiscent of the approach that Fullan describes in the successful turnaround of Benjamin Adlard Primary School in England, where Principal Marie-Claire Bretherton adopted a personalised focus on 'which teachers were going to be our quick wins, who could learn quickly and raise the bar about what's possible' (Fullan, 2019, p. 38). It both builds a sense of hope in the school and demonstrates that it can be done.

This does, of course, put a premium on the nature of support that leaders provide for teachers' practice to change. While this very much is the focus of the remainder of this book, Knight (2009) has some helpful advice on which we can draw.

The key to supporting teachers to implement new practices, he suggests, is to ask, '(w)hat can we do to make it easier' for them? And the answer to this question in his view is to ensure that the new practices are both 'powerful' (in that they can be demonstrated to have a positive effect on student learning) and 'easy to implement' (in that they are demonstrated through modelling for teachers and outlined in clear and simple steps) (Knight, 2009, p. 508).

With this in mind, the eight specific suggestions that Knight (2009) has for increasing 'the likelihood that teachers will adopt and implement proven practices' (p. 512) can be summarised in the following way. Schools and their leaders should:

- seek teaching practices that have proven successful in schools
- use data to select and then monitor the implementation of these practices
- support teachers with quality coaching to implement the practices
- balance the quest for precision of practice with the need for teachers to adapt to their particular students' needs
- foster commitment by ensuring that teachers are part of the process and have a genuine say
- focus professional learning on the few key high-leverage practices being introduced
- align all of the school's activities to this focus
- build trust which, as Covey famously observed, is 'the most essential ingredient in effective communication … (and) the foundational principle that holds all relationships'. (This is a widely cited quote. See, for example, Kruse, 2012.)

It is salutary advice for the actions that leaders take to shift teachers to the left of the normal curve in Figure 2.1.

STAY THE COURSE

Finally, it is well known from a range of research and experience that organisations, including schools, commonly experience an implementation dip as they seek to implement change. This dip, illustrated in Figure 2.2, as Fullan (n.d.) explains, reflects a 'dip in performance and confidence as one encounters an innovation that requires new skills and new understandings'(p. 6). Leaders who understand the dip, he advises, 'know that people are experiencing two kinds of problems' when they are in it—'the social-psychological fear of change, and the lack of technical know-how or skills to make the change work'(p. 6).

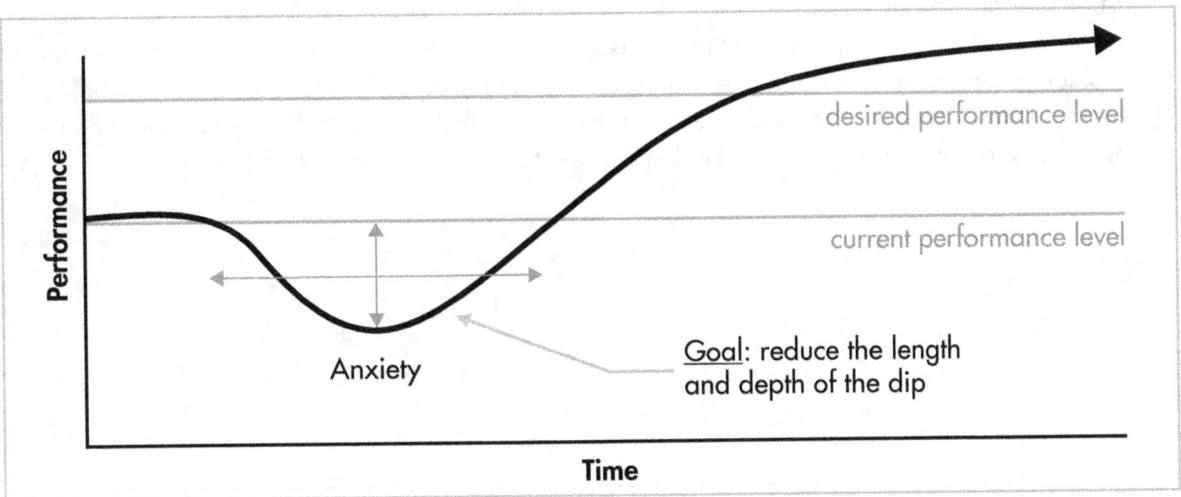

FIGURE 2.2: THE IMPLEMENTATION DIP

When schools or systems continually review direction or seek further change, and/or set too many hares running not in unison but in different (disconnected) fields, they effectively set off another dip as the same anxieties and skill shortfalls emerge, and nothing gets properly implemented as a result. In contrast, what Fullan (n.d.), drawing on a range of organisational research, recommends is that leaders maintain 'an urgent sense of moral purpose' for consistency of vision and approach, and 'still measure success in terms of results', but that they also 'do things that are more likely to get the organisation going and keep it going'(p. 6).

Put simply, schools, principals, teachers and systems need to stay the course if they are going to consolidate and implement change. Apart from anything else, time to consolidate the implementation of targeted change, is also time to develop and provide the support that those responsible for implementation require to overcome the 'social-psychological' anxieties they feel and develop the skills to make it work.

Staying the course in turn depends on an approach to leadership that Vicki Phillips termed 'gentle pressure, relentlessly applied'.[2] In other words, the sort of leadership that sustains the effort towards the outcomes the school seeks without let-up or distraction along the way. If nothing else, the approach is needed because, when it comes to pursuing whole-school improvement and change this is, as one of the principals we have worked with explained, 'work that is never done'.

ACTIVITY FOR LEADERSHIP TEAMS: EVALUATING OUR APPROACH TO WHOLE-SCHOOL IMPROVEMENT

The following self-assessment (Table 2.1) is designed to support a conversation in your school's leadership team about the improvement strategies your school has adopted and the effectiveness of their implementation. It is not a judgment as such, but a conversation starter for you to pursue.

You may notice that we have adopted a four-point scale in the assessment rather than five points, which is more commonly used. This is because we have taken away the 'safe' middle option of neither agree nor disagree, so respondents will take a more active stance. This, we believe, contributes to a better conversation than otherwise might occur and requires respondents to think more carefully about the ratings that they give. We have adopted the same approach for all self-assessment pro formas in this book.

Instructions

1 In the first part of Table 2.1, individually rate each of the following statements about how you pursue improvement and change in the school on a four-point scale where:
1 = We don't do this, 2 = We sometimes do this, 3 = We often do this and 4 = This is a routine part of how our school works.
2 Taking account of your responses to this self-assessment, then identify the strengths and key aspects of pursuing improvement and change that require development in the second part of this table.
3 When you have completed the self-assessment, share it with the colleagues in your team and see what, if any, common strengths and weaknesses exist that can be worked on together.

---

[2] Vicki Phillips was, until 2015, the Director of Education, College Ready in the United States Program for eight years, having formerly been the Superintendent of Portland Public Schools.

TABLE 2.1: EVALUATING OUR APPROACH TO WHOLE-SCHOOL IMPROVEMENT

Our approach to improvement and change	Rating (1–4)
The strategies we are pursuing for whole-school improvement are based on a diagnosis of the stage of development of our school	
We pursue a limited number of strategies so we can drive them through the school and avoid trying to do too much	
We abandon strategies that are not working effectively rather than holding on to everything we have ever done	
We link the different strategies into a coherent story of whole-school change that our teachers, parents and students can understand	
We avoid distractions from our primary purpose and rigorously pursue the key strategies we have identified	
We ensure that our strategies are informed by relevant research which is shared with the staff	
We engage teachers in co-development of the improvement strategies being implemented	
We engage all staff in ongoing school-based professional learning and other support needed to implement the strategies	
We have a customised coaching program designed to support the achievement of identified school goals	
We understand the implementation dip and seek to support staff through it and stay the course in implementing our strategies	

The major strengths our school has in the way it pursues improvement and change:	The evidence for these strengths: • • •
A key aspect of the way in which we pursue improvement and change that we really need to develop:	The evidence for identifying this area: • • •

© Pamela Macklin and Vic Zbar, *Driving School Improvement*, Australian Council for Educational Research, 2017

With a clear approach to improvement in place, the school can then turn its attention to the detailed planning it needs to undertake. The action planning pro forma in Table 2.2 provides a structure to support schools in this regard.

TABLE 2.2: ACTION PLANNING PRO FORMA

School name:

Vision for the school:

Focus of the activity	What is the current situation?	What changes are required?				How are we going to make the changes?			
		Goals	Success criteria	Status and evidence of progress		Professional development strategies	Other strategies	Who is responsible?	Due date
Curriculum (ensuring the necessary documentation in the school)									
Pedagogy (supporting more teachers to work like the best)									
Assessment (to inform and hence improve teaching)									
School organisation (ensuring a supportive structure to improve teaching and learning)									
Engagement plan (involving all stakeholders at all stages along the way)									
Human resources plan (using all staff to the best effect and building capacity)									

© Pamela Macklin and Vic Zbar, *Driving School Improvement 2nd Edition*, Australian Council for Educational Research, 2020

CHAPTER 3
IT DEPENDS ON LEADERSHIP

In a major review of the impact that leadership has in schools, Leithwood, Seashore, Anderson and Wahlstrom (2004) found evidence to suggest that successful leadership can play a 'highly significant—and frequently underestimated—role in improving student learning. At a more detailed level still, they found that:
- leadership is second only to classroom instruction among all school-related factors that contribute to what students learn at school and, as our own more recent high-performing schools research has demonstrated (Zbar, Kimber & Marshall, 2009), it is leadership that sets the conditions for teachers to perform effectively in the classroom, or not
- leadership effects are usually largest where and when they are needed most, such as in highly disadvantaged schools.

This of course begs the question of what 'leadership' actually means.[1] While there are many taxonomies of leadership that can readily be found online, they commonly are not definitions per se, but rather descriptions of different leadership styles.

Our extensive work with schools suggests to us that there are basically two sorts of leaders, albeit stylised to make a point. Put simply, there are leaders who can make things happen in their schools and leaders who can't. In fact, the fundamental difference between effective and ineffective school leaders is that effective leaders are better at making things happen in their schools. It's a point made more eloquently still by Fullan (2019) when he distinguishes between leaders who he admittedly 'unfairly' calls 'surfacers' who 'don't know what else to do … (and) treat problems as technical', and the leaders he calls 'nuancers' who 'work with key principles that lead to adjustable actions'(p. 2).

Looked at in these terms, leadership can be defined as the capacity to make things happen consistently in the school. Or even more specifically, to make the 'right' things happen consistently in the school. It is neatly embodied in the four mantras of the 2018 Australian of the Year, Professor Michelle Yvonne Simmons, who urged leaders to 'do what is hard, take risks, embrace high expectations and do work that matters' if you are to deliver positive results ('Top scientist Michelle

---

[1] Material that follows in this chapter draws on Zbar (2018).

Yvonne Simmons wins Australian of the Year', 2018). This in turn is somewhat resonant of Franklin Delano Roosevelt's advice to leaders to 'do something. If that works, do more. If it doesn't, do something else'.[2]

Where this gets complex is that it involves diagnosing and hence knowing where your school is at, knowing what to do, knowing how to do it, making it happen consistently while carrying people with you, and then knowing what to do next and so on in a cycle of continuous improvement as depicted in Figure 3.1.

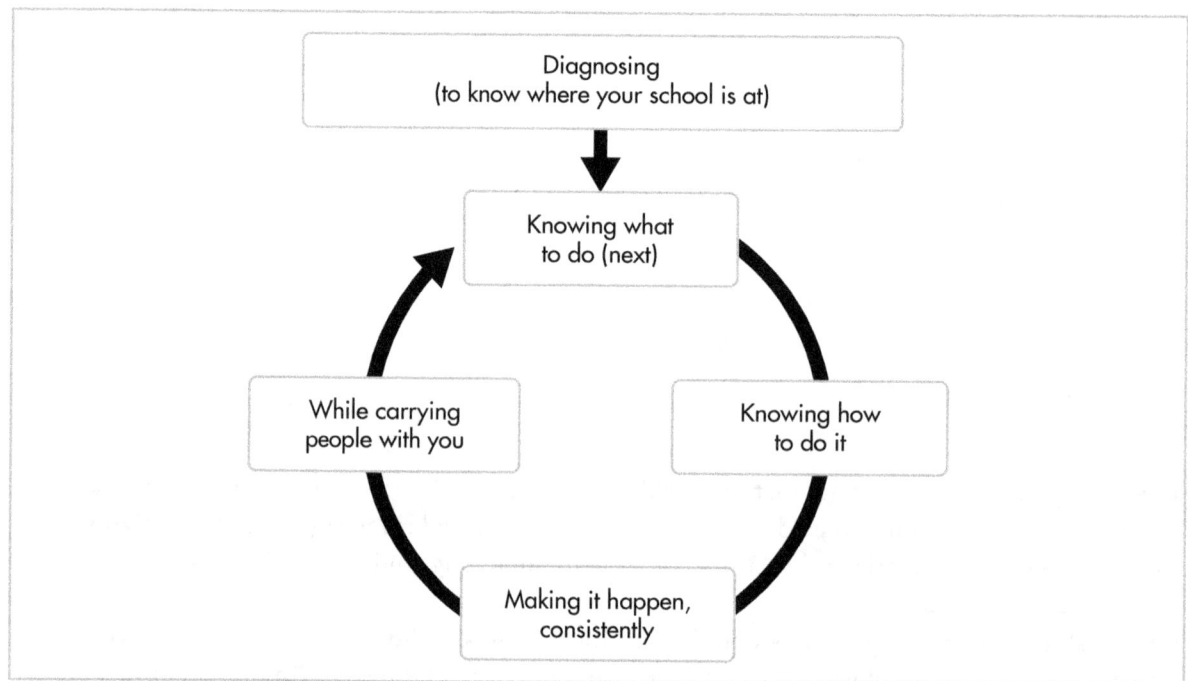

FIGURE 3.1: THE WORK THAT LEADERS DO

LEADERSHIP FOR WHOLE-SCHOOL IMPROVEMENT

Leadership, in the terms just described, is the difference between pockets of improvement in a school and whole-school improvement. In any school, there will be areas that arguably perform more effectively than others. For example, a school may have a Year 3 team that is getting excellent literacy and numeracy results, or an effective history faculty that consistently achieves senior secondary student outcomes above those in other studies in the school. However, the excellent practices these teams adopt never go whole school in the absence of a leadership team leading it, and with the necessary authority to drive it through.

In summary, the practices that leaders need to undertake to help bring substantial and sustained school improvement about involve:

- *Setting direction*: to enable every learner to reach their potential, and to translate this vision into whole-school curriculum, consistency and high expectations.
- *Managing teaching and learning*: to ensure that there is both a high degree of consistency and innovation in teaching practices to enable personalised learning for all students.
- *Developing people*: to enable students to become active learners and to create schools as professional learning communities for teachers.
- *Developing the organisation*: to create evidence-based schools and effective organisations, and to be involved in networks collaborating to build curriculum diversity, professional support and extended services.[3]

---

[2] Accessed from https://www.goodreads.com/quotes/1542488-do-something-if-it-works-do-more-of-it-if
[3] Drawn from the research of Leithwood et al. (2004) and cited in Hopkins, Harris, Stoll, & Mackay (2011).

Making things happen in schools is not so much a matter of charisma and charm, as it is of character and moral purpose, along with an awareness of what needs doing and the capacity to lead others in making it happen through the whole of the school. In the previous edition of this book, we provided case studies of two principals—Robert Lamb at Gladstone Park and Reservoir High Schools and Glenn Proctor at Hume Central Secondary College—to illustrate the strategies they used to make things happen in their schools as they focused on what matters most and a capacity to prioritise the use of resources and time.[4] While their approaches differed significantly, the case studies demonstrated how each reflected high expectations of students and staff (a refusal to accept 'you can't expect more of these kids' or that things are 'beyond my control') and a willingness to do the tough things needed in the interests of all students in the school.

This was underpinned by their work to develop their leadership teams and strategic approaches to ensure an orderly learning environment and build the capacity of staff. Each of the principals worked to show people how to do things differently, supported them to succeed, and expected them to perform as skilled professionals in all that they do.

Making things happen depends on knowing where to start and how. This required these principals and their leadership teams to first determine where their schools were at, what their major strategic challenge was, and the range of potential strategies that could be adopted in response. In other words, to diagnose the health of the school in order to then prescribe the interventions required, drawing on relevant research and successful practice in other schools.

Robert Lamb and Glenn Proctor have subsequently retired as school principals, though each continues to contribute to school improvement within and beyond their state. However, many others have followed in their footsteps and are leading successful improvement in schools, as evident in the two new case studies in Box 3.1.

Box 3.1

Two principals who made things happen in their schools

TURNING A BIG SHIP AROUND: ROB DUNCAN AT NARRE WARREN SOUTH P–12

While work already was underway to ensure an orderly learning environment at Narre Warren South when Rob Duncan became the principal in 2015, the school was still the subject of priority review[5] because of poor data, particularly at the primary level, and poor attendance throughout. This, according to Duncan, reflected an inadequate emphasis on teaching and learning and, in particular, the lack of consistency in approach.

With the support of a leadership coach (Pamela, who continues to work with the school as both a leadership coach and school improvement consultant), he worked to create a sense of urgency through the school about the importance of using an instructional model to improve the quality of teaching that all students receive. Particularly significant in this regard was the conduct of a whole-school professional learning day that, in a break with tradition, mixed up teachers across the primary and secondary divide, and surfaced the substantial degree of commonality rather than difference that exists about what matters for good teaching to occur. This then formed the basis for ongoing, customised whole-school professional learning to support the implementation of the model that was devised.

Continued...

---

[4] These two case studies were drawn from a larger, unpublished paper prepared by Vic Zbar—see Zbar (2011).

[5] A priority review is conducted by a department-accredited independent review team in Victorian Government schools when a school does not demonstrate sufficient progress or where there is other evidence of significant risk to students' achievement, wellbeing or engagement.

The judgment that Duncan made was that, although the orderly learning environment still needed attention and work, it was sufficiently in place across the school to shift the focus to building greater consistency of effective teaching practice using a common teaching and learning model that all could adopt. Developing and implementing this model has, in his view, been the most significant contributor to turning this big ship of more than 200 teachers around over the last five years, because it helped build a common understanding of good teaching and its components such as explicit instruction, feedback and the differentiation that students need. (This turnaround was recognised in Prytz, 2018.) Implementing and embedding the model continues to be an ongoing focus of both the instructional coaching and professional learning programs in the school.

Improvement as a result of adopting this approach was evident after only 12 months with a marked shift in primary NAPLAN data from a situation where around 40 per cent of students experienced low growth in reading to one where 35 per cent experienced high levels of growth. Not only has this been maintained over time, but similar results in numeracy have been achieved and around a third of secondary students are experiencing high levels of growth as well. In addition, the school has attained an all-study score for the Victorian Certificate of Education of 32.8, which puts it on par with many more advantaged, high-performing schools.

Underpinning this work was the development of a cohesive leadership team that could be a visible presence through the school and could work with staff, focusing on the things that matter most. A degree of team stability after some earlier leadership churn enabled its members to really clarify their respective responsibilities in a context where everyone is aware of who does what, and people are free to undertake their work without treading on each other's toes. Clarity, Duncan suggests, is central to avoiding the sort of 'random acts of improvement' that only confuse the staff, while stability has given teachers a sense of consistency of leadership and, together with leadership visibility through the school, has helped engender a greater level of trust.

Further contributing to clarity through the school is the conscious decision the principal and other leaders have made to focus on just three things to ensure staff buy-in and support—currently explicit instruction, feedback and differentiation to meet all students' learning needs. Limiting the focus, he suggests, also increases the potential for teachers to see the achievements that are made, while avoiding the perception that workloads are under threat. It contributes to a more consistent message about 'the way that things are done at this school', and enables leaders to monitor the implementation and take follow-up action if required.

The school has consciously sought to recruit wisely, not just its leaders but its graduates as well. Leaving other members of the team to select the new leaders to the school, Duncan seeks to recruit talented graduates who can then be paired with an appropriate mentor to induct them to the high expectations and consistent practices that apply. This includes a strong focus on its underlying values designed to ensure a harmonious school with a positive sense of purpose and commitment to everyone in the school. It is a part of reinforcing what it means to be part of the Narre Warren South community, while also providing an important management tool for ensuring an orderly learning environment in all classes through the school.

Asked to nominate what he most has learned in leading the turnaround of this school, Duncan points to the fact 'you cannot do it by yourself'. There has to be a strong leadership team with clear goal congruence and clarity about what it is seeking to achieve. Disagreements certainly can occur, but with an expectation that evidence and data inform the arguments made and the core guiding principle is always ensuring that the learning needs of all students are met.

DRIVING FOR CONTINUOUS IMPROVEMENT AND GROWTH: JOANNE WASTLE AT GLEN WAVERLEY SECONDARY COLLEGE

Having earlier worked as the assistant principal and then principal of Kambrya College, which is described in Chapter 5, Joanne Wastle was appointed principal of the socio-economically more advantaged Glen Waverley Secondary College in 2018. This required a shift in emphasis towards ensuring that an already high-performing school became even better over time, without infringing what is already working well.

In any school a natural resistance to change exists, which arguably is multiplied when the school is perceived to be doing well. At Glen Waverley, the high-level outcomes achieved to some extent masked an emerging trend where the senior school results had started to slightly decline. Hence Wastle began by sharing the data with staff in order to raise the need for some overall renewal to commence.

Of particular concern in this context was the lack of consistency between teachers about classroom practice, reflecting the high degree of autonomy teachers had and the fact that classroom visits rarely occurred. There was a whole-school instructional model in place, but no real follow-through to ensure that its common language and practices were pursued. As a result, the pockets of excellence that existed were not systematically spread through the school in order to support more teachers to work like the best.

Hence the initial focus for renewal and further improvement in the school was to ensure an instructional model that is consistently implemented through the school. Recognising the significant work that already had been done the leadership team, in consultation with staff, reviewed and tweaked the existing instructional model, rather than starting from scratch. They then worked to bolster support for its implementation with a new image that could readily be displayed through the school and a practical handbook on how it best can be implemented in class. The school's instructional model graphic and a sample of its support materials for staff are provided in Chapter 6.

Almost all of the school's professional development was directed towards ensuring the implementation of the revised instructional model, in contrast with the broad representation of topics that individuals tended to pursue in the past. In addition, more of the programs were delivered in-house.

A significant focus of Wastle's efforts in this context was developing her relatively new and inexperienced leadership team after a degree of personnel changes that had occurred. This included ensuring that all team deliberations were focused on the two school goals of improving teaching and learning, and positive relations between students and staff. This not only meant that leadership meetings were about important, rather than operational matters, but also shifted the focus from the individual's leadership role to their collective contribution to the leadership of the school. This in turn has helped build the cohesiveness of the team in pursuing the expectation that everyone is responsible for these two priority goals.

Central to her approach is Wastle's commitment to transparency and ensuring there are no surprises or secrets in the school. Consistent with the way in which she shared the data of declining VCE scores with the staff, she has continually sought to clarify what is happening and why. This included the need to develop and share a number of workplace practices and policies with staff that previously had tended to be the realm of leaders in the school. She and other leaders also demonstrated their openness to constructive feedback by undertaking the voluntary leadership add-on to the staff opinion survey in Victoria and sharing the results. The outcomes, she explains, can be 'confronting', but are essential to support her own and the team's efforts to improve. It also models a willingness to engage in open and honest communication about the direction and operation of the school.

Continued...

> As the leadership team increasingly is speaking with one voice, especially around the use of the instructional model to ensure consistently more effective teaching across the school, it has found fewer teachers working from the front of the room and a greater openness to feedback including from the students themselves. There is greater awareness of the need to gather and analyse data both to monitor the progress of key strategies in use and to inform planning of the next phase of improvement in the school.
>
> That said, Wastle recognises that the challenge of continually getting better is work that is never done. It starts with the leadership team and, in particular, ensuring that all leaders are on board and aligned around a common strategic focus that they relentlessly pursue. The instructional model has been the vehicle for this to occur to date and, as it increasingly takes hold, the focus will shift more to the feedback the students provide about their experience in class and what this means for the way in which teachers then teach.
>
> For Wastle personally, this means having the 'robust conversations' she needs to have, being open to constructive criticism and asking for help when required. Having experienced coaching herself, she firmly believes that every principal should have a coach, provided it's one who knows how improvement happens in schools. It also means starting the process in any new school by getting to know the context first, examining its data and talking to everybody in the school. There are no ready-made solutions you can import. You have to determine the best strategic response to the reality that exists in the school.

A LEADERSHIP FRAMEWORK TO CONSIDER

It is helpful in this context to have a framework for understanding leadership that can inform the actions that principals and other leaders take and also support them to improve.

In 2017, the Queensland Educational Leadership Institute (QELI) commissioned Vic to develop such a framework that can be used with these two ends in mind. The framework outlined was developed together with QELI staff, most notably its CEO, Neil McDonald and Principal Programs Officer, Kerry Major. Some of the material is also drawn from an annotated narrative Vic developed for QELI to explain how the framework was developed and some of the research on which it was based (Zbar, 2017). It should be noted that the framework has been slightly revised by QELI from what is used in this book to align it to the concepts of 'collective, mindful, agile, focused and innovative' leader that the Institute employs (QELI, 2017).

In developing any new framework, of course, it is wise to start with others that already are in play. A scan of the field revealed myriad leadership frameworks around the world, many of which were examined in depth. All of them are good and useful in their own way and helped inform the development of the framework that QELI subsequently chose to adopt. Some have even been used to develop advice to panels selecting a new principal. For example, the Victorian Department of Education uses the Australian Institute for Teaching and School Leadership (AITSL) Principal Standards (AITSL, 2019) to provide information to support the reading of applications, interviews and referee checks with a focus on the key areas of: vision and values; teaching and learning; improvement, innovation and change; management; development; and engagement.

Some of the flavour of the Victorian advice can be found in the information provided for teaching and learning, which suggests that an appropriate response to the relevant standard could include evidence of such behaviours as:
- creating a culture of challenge and support
- enabling effective teaching that promotes effective, enthusiastic, independent learners

- creating a positive learning atmosphere for students and staff and within the school community
- setting high expectations for every learner, including students, staff and self.[6]

That said, almost all of the frameworks examined fall short as far as ensuring effective leaders of school improvement is concerned. This is because they tend to focus entirely on the capacities individuals need to develop to become and remain leaders in their school, without reference to what leaders actually need to do to drive improvement through their school.

In contrast, the QELI Leadership Framework comprises five elements that bring together the range of leadership capacities—comprising knowledge, understanding, attitudes, skills and personal qualities—that enable a leader to perform to a high standard in their role and the actions they must take to continually improve their school (QELI, 2017). More specifically the five elements, or leadership behaviours of:
- diagnosing performance and prescribing for improvement
- developing leadership to drive improvement
- ensuring effective implementation of what matters most
- leveraging the greatest source of improvement in schools
- ensuring progress and keeping on track.

Taken together, these five elements which are outlined in more detail below, contribute to a shared understanding and common language for leadership and how it is successfully enacted in schools. This in turn can guide:
- the recruitment and selection of new leaders in schools
- the design and delivery of professional learning and other development opportunities for leaders and aspiring leaders in schools
- the self-assessment and reflection that leaders undertake as they strive to continually improve.

The five elements, which can also be readily mapped to AITSL's professional practices for school principals (that cover leading teaching and learning; developing self and others; leading improvement, innovation and change; leading the management of the school; and engaging and working with the community), reflect an understanding of how school improvement typically occurs, as discussed in detail in Chapter 4, and what leaders need to do as a result according to where their school is at.

THE DETAILED FRAMEWORK AND THINKING BEHIND IT

The following provides a brief outline of the thinking that underpins the detailed leadership behaviours that comprise the five elements of the QELI Leadership Framework, consistent with the work that leaders need to do as embodied in Figure 3.1. The framework is used with the permission of QELI who commissioned it.

DIAGNOSING PERFORMANCE AND PRESCRIBING FOR IMPROVEMENT

Leading a school through the stages of school improvement begins, as discussed in Chapter 2, with knowing where to start and how because, as Munby (2020) has observed, '(y)ou cannot divorce what a leader does from the context in which s/he is operating' (p. 5). This requires the leader to first determine where the school is at, what its major strategic challenge is, and the range of potential strategies that can be adopted in response. In other words, to diagnose the health of

---

[6] This is just a sample of a larger list linked to the Leading Teaching and Learning Professional Practice in the AITSL Standards (see AITSL, 2019), which suggests that 'Principals create a positive culture of challenge and support, enabling effective teaching that promotes enthusiastic, independent learners, committed to lifelong learning. Principals have a key responsibility for developing a culture of effective teaching, for leading, designing and managing the quality of teaching and learning and for students' achievement in all aspects of their development. They set high expectations for the whole school through careful collaborative planning, monitoring and reviewing the effectiveness of learning. Principals set high standards of behaviour and attendance, encouraging active engagement and a strong student voice.'

the school in order to then prescribe the interventions required, drawing on relevant research and successful practice in other schools.

Diagnosing the performance of one's school involves gathering and analysing a range of evidence primarily centred on the outcomes that students achieve. This enables the leader to create a compelling case for improvement and change as the basis of collaboratively forging a shared vision for developing an even better school.

This vision is then given meaning through a set of challenging, but achievable improvement goals and strategies for achieving them that reflect both relevant research on what works and its experience in other comparable schools.

In the Leadership Framework, this takes the form of an expectation that leaders will:
- use multiple sources of data to analyse performance and inform decision-making, innovation and change
- raise expectations of the school and everyone who works in it (leaders, teachers, support staff and students), consistent with the belief that all students can learn
- create a vision in consultation with parents, community and the staff for sustainable improvement aligned to the values of the school, and agreed priorities for achieving it
- set specific, measureable, action-oriented, realistic, time-limited (SMART) goals for improvement that gain the support of the staff
- identify key evidence-based strategies to achieve the improvement goals and a narrative that explains how they are linked.

DEVELOPING LEADERSHIP TO DRIVE IMPROVEMENT

Leadership, as noted earlier, is the difference between pockets of improvement in a school and whole-school improvement. In any school there will be areas that perform better than others. However, the excellent practices these teams adopt never go whole school in the absence of a leadership team leading it, with the necessary authority to drive it through.

Leadership in this context is more than just the principal of the school, critical as that role is. It involves the development of a leadership team that spreads its influence through the school and involves as many staff in meaningful leadership activity as it can. Important in this regard is the development of strong and effective middle, as well as top-level leadership as the conduit from the principal team to the staff as a whole; particularly since the sheer number of potential relationships in any reasonably-sized school precludes top-level leaders from effectively reaching all of the staff.

Spreading leadership through the school in turn depends on developing a climate where all can feel involved, communicate effectively and willingly provide and receive feedback designed to help them to improve, regardless of who in the school community they are.

In the Leadership Framework this takes the form of an expectation that leaders will:
- weld together a cohesive leadership team that speaks with one voice
- distribute and strengthen leadership throughout the school and foster the leadership capacity of others
- develop an overarching climate of two-way communication, participation, involvement and trust, and are open to feedback from others
- communicate effectively with all stakeholders, take account of their views and promote and support their involvement in the school
- develop and participate in networks and partnerships that contribute to one's own leadership effectiveness and better outcomes in and beyond the school.

ENSURING EFFECTIVE IMPLEMENTATION OF WHAT MATTERS MOST

It is not sufficient to simply identify priorities for improvement and include them in the annual school plan, even when they enjoy substantial stakeholder support. Just as important is the need to stick to these priorities and allocate time and resources to them, so they are privileged in the actions that stakeholders then take.

This requires leaders to ensure that the school is well-run, so it avoids the inevitable distractions from what matters most. Put simply, schools need the systems and processes that enable them to work efficiently and effectively, and generate consistently good practice by all of the staff.

Central to this is an orderly learning environment where students are well known since effective teaching and learning cannot occur unless this is the case. In addition, the pursuit and implementation of an orderly learning environment is a key mechanism for building consistent staff practice through the school.

In the Leadership Framework this takes the form of an expectation that leaders will:

- develop and manage systems and processes for a well-run school including budgets, human resource management, and a curriculum, assessment and reporting plan aligned to Australian (P–10) and Queensland (11–12) requirements (This element of the Framework can readily be applied to the curriculum expectations in any jurisdiction across Australia.)
- strategically align resources (i.e. people, money, facilities and time) to school priorities
- ensure an orderly learning environment where students are well known as a fundamental precondition for student learning to occur
- minimise disruptions or distractions from the core work of teaching and learning at school
- have the self-awareness to recognise, reflect and actively improve on their own role in ensuring and maintaining a well-run school

LEVERAGING THE GREATEST SOURCE OF IMPROVEMENT IN SCHOOLS

Research clearly demonstrates that, as far as schools are concerned, teaching is the major factor that accounts for variations in the learning outcomes that students achieve. That said, it is equally well known that not all teachers have the same effect, and the greatest source of improvement in any school comes from the extent to which it can narrow this gap and support more teachers to work like the best.

Generating consistently more effective teaching in each and every class depends on a shared understanding of what effective teaching is, based on the evidence of what works in classrooms and schools. This in turn enables the school to develop structures and supporting documentation, such as an agreed instructional model, to improve the quality of teaching across the board.

Leaders support capacity-building in this regard not only by providing the opportunity for teachers to plan collaboratively and undertake professional learning aligned to their work, but also by modelling and participating in it themselves. Classroom observation is a critical component in the mix since it provides the basis for giving and receiving objective feedback of what is seen and not simply what has been said.

In the Leadership Framework this takes the form of an expectation that leaders will:

- develop and promote a shared understanding of effective teaching to underpin the improvement of teaching and learning in the school
- promote and support the use of data and an evidence-informed approach to teaching and learning, including differentiation to meet all learning needs in classrooms across the school
- ensure the necessary structure and documentation (i.e. curriculum scope and sequence, a whole-school assessment schedule and a framework to support planning of good lessons) to enable more teachers to work like the best
- support, resource and participate in collaborative planning and professional learning to grow teacher capacity and spread good practice through the school
- promote and support mutual classroom observation and feedback to contribute to individual and collective improvement.

ENSURING PROGRESS AND KEEPING ON TRACK

Organisations have long known that what gets measured is what gets done. That is one reason why leaders set targets for improvement that are aligned to the school's shared vision and goals. These targets in turn enable the school to monitor its progress and achievements as its strategies are applied and to adjust their implementation, including abandoning unsuccessful approaches, as required.

Monitoring progress is not limited to gathering and analysing quantitative data such as student test results, attendance records or the rate of retention from one year to the next. It is supplemented by such qualitative evidence as staff and student opinion, input from focus groups and the like that leaders use to create a fully-rounded picture of the performance of the school, in order to then take it to the next stage.

Since staff and their work are central to what the school is able to achieve, leaders collaboratively develop mechanisms for improving this work as part of a process of continuous improvement in the school. Accountability throughout the school helps link people to purpose and align their work to the collective vision they are seeking to achieve. This requires leaders to have honest and open conversations with staff, and to invite such conversations themselves, to ensure that the moral purpose of lifting all students' achievement at school is reached.

In the Leadership Framework this takes the form of an expectation that leaders will:
- identify targets to monitor progress towards the achievement of the school vision, priorities and goals
- use data, including student assessment data and stakeholder feedback, to monitor progress towards these targets, and adjust the implementation of and/or abandon strategies as needed in response
- use staff performance and development systems in ways that contribute to a culture of continuous improvement and support, and reflect and consider feedback on their own contribution to improving the school
- hold people to account including oneself, acknowledge and learn from failures, and recognise and celebrate success
- have courageous conversations when needed to ensure that goals and targets are achieved.

Applying the framework, of course, is easier said than done, and arguably starts by building a strong and united leadership team.

Before pursuing this, however, there may be value in considering a self-assessment we have developed that readers can use to determine their current level of performance and consequent areas where further development is required.

ACTIVITY FOR INDIVIDUAL LEADERS: A SELF-ASSESSMENT USING THE LEADERSHIP FRAMEWORK

Use the following assessment pro formas (Tables 3.1 to 3.5) to determine your level of performance in relation to the five leadership behaviours comprising the QELI Leadership Framework (2017) and hence areas for development as you pursue your leadership aspirations and goals. You can then identify appropriate professional learning and other development opportunities to help you improve your performance and skills.

Instructions

1 Please rate each of the following statements in Tables 3.1 to 3.5 on a four-point scale where:
   1 = I have no experience in this, 2 = I have limited experience in this, 3 = I am experienced in this and 4 = This is one of my strengths.
   Note: The rating is for the entire element and not for each dot point 'I can' statement.

2 In determining your rating, consider the indicative 'I can' statements provided, which are designed to illustrate how you will know the extent to which the element has been achieved. To give added objectivity to your ratings, you could consider seeking feedback from one or more colleagues familiar with your work and effectiveness, including the principal if you do not occupy that position yourself, in the relevant elements of the Framework before deciding on your score.

3 Taking account of your responses to the self-assessment of each element of the Leadership Framework, complete the pro forma 'Processing the self-assessment and planning for improvement' (Table 3.6) as the basis for developing your own leadership improvement plan.
   You are now in a position to develop a coherent personal leadership improvement plan for the next and subsequent years.

TABLE 3.1: LEADERSHIP BEHAVIOUR 1: DIAGNOSING PERFORMANCE AND PRESCRIBING FOR IMPROVEMENT

Element	Rating (1–4)
Use multiple sources of data to analyse performance and inform decision-making, innovation and change. This is evident when I can: • use the full range of data available to the school to determine the extent to which it is meeting its goals and priorities • identify appropriate improvement strategies in response.	
Raise expectations of the school and everyone who works in it (leaders, teachers, support staff and students), consistent with the belief that all students can learn. This is evident when I can: • lead the school to set student achievement targets that are higher than just matching its group of like schools • ensure these targets are then reflected in stretch targets for individuals and teams.	
Create a vision in consultation with parents, community and the staff for sustainable improvement aligned to the values of the school, and agreed priorities for achieving it. This is evident when I can: • lead the development of a vision that is both agreed and being pursued by the school's stakeholders • ensure there are clearly identified priorities for how this vision will be achieved.	
Set specific, measurable, action-oriented, realistic, time-limited (SMART) goals for improvement that gain the support of the staff. This is evident when I can: • ensure that each whole-school priority is defined in terms of clear and agreed whole-school goals • ensure the whole-school goals are supported by specific goals for individuals and teams.	
Identify key evidence-based strategies to achieve the improvement goals and a narrative that explains how they are linked. This is evident when I can: • lead the development of a set of interrelated strategies for achieving the school's vision • provide a consistent story that ties these strategies together into a coherent whole.	
Total score	

Interpreting your score

5 to 10 You have yet to develop the key underpinning leadership skill of being able to diagnose current performance in order to determine how to strategically move the school forward to improve. You should seek opportunities to analyse school performance, including any training that may be needed, as the basis for developing a challenging vision for improvement that can galvanise staff around agreed goals and strategies to pursue. You could also seek mentoring from a leader who has demonstrated effectiveness in this regard.

11 to 15 You are developing the core skills of being able to diagnose performance and prescribe appropriately and have exercised some leadership in this regard. In order to progress to the next stage of your career you need to work with others to strengthen one or more of the sub-skills in this element of the Framework, and carry it through with the support of your staff. This could include observing successful leaders in or beyond your school.

16 to 20 Your ability to diagnose the performance of your school and then prescribe appropriate ways in which it can be improved is a strength on which you can continue to build. This may be an area where you can contribute to the development of others in your own or another school(s).

© Pamela Macklin and Vic Zbar, *Driving School Improvement 2nd Edition*, Australian Council for Educational Research, 2020

TABLE 3.2: LEADERSHIP BEHAVIOUR 2: BUILDING TEAMS TO DRIVE IMPROVEMENT

Element	Rating (1–4)
Weld together a cohesive leadership team that speaks with one voice. This is evident when I can: • develop a united leadership team • ensure the team presents a common front to staff and other stakeholders about the direction and improvement strategies of the school.	
Distribute and strengthen leadership throughout the school and foster the leadership capacity of others. This is evident when I can: • genuinely let go and allow others to lead • provide opportunities for individuals to develop their leadership skills and develop a pipeline of future leaders in the school.	
Develop an overarching climate of two-way communication, participation, involvement and trust, and be open to feedback from others. This is evident when I can: • support and encourage all school community members to fearlessly espouse their views without judgment • openly hear feedback from others about my own performance in the school.	
Communicate effectively with all stakeholders, take account of their views and promote and support their involvement in the school. This is evident when I can: • ensure that structures and processes are in place to ensure an informed school community • ensure that the community has input to the major decisions the school makes.	
Develop and participate in networks and partnerships that contribute to your own leadership effectiveness and better outcomes in and beyond the school. This is evident when I can: • commit to regularly engage in relevant networks and partnerships, including networks of other school leaders • use these networks to inform and advise on my own efforts to improve my school.	
Total score	

Interpreting your score

5 to 10 You have yet to successfully forge and lead a team that operates effectively and engages both its members and those it seeks to influence. You will need to work on team leadership and dynamics and seek opportunities to observe successful leaders and/or feedback on your own leadership as it unfolds. Targeted coaching from a successful leader with appropriate training could assist in this regard.

11 to 15 You are achieving some success through the team you lead, supporting others to develop their leadership skills and engaging stakeholders along the way. In order to progress to the next stage of your career, you need to ensure that the impact of your leadership is maximised by working with, and learning from other successful team leaders in your school. There may be a need for some targeted training in aspects of team leadership embodied in this element of the Framework.

16 to 20 You are successfully leading one or more teams in the school and achieving valued outcomes with the support of your team members, the broader staff and the stakeholders in the school. You may be in a position to provide support to other leaders who are seeking to develop their leadership capacities and effectiveness in or beyond your school.

© Pamela Macklin and Vic Zbar, *Driving School Improvement 2nd Edition*, Australian Council for Educational Research, 2020

TABLE 3.3: LEADERSHIP BEHAVIOUR 3: ENSURING EFFECTIVE IMPLEMENTATION OF WHAT MATTERS MOST

Element	Rating (1–4)
Develop and manage systems and processes for a well-run school including budgets, human resource management, and a curriculum, assessment and reporting plan aligned to Australian (P–10) and Queensland (11–12) requirements.[7] This is evident when I can: • ensure that the major systems required for school operations are clearly documented • ensure this documentation is supported by processes for their consistent implementation throughout the school.	
Strategically align resources (i.e. people, money, facilities and time) to school priorities. This is evident when I can: • package resources to maximise their efficiency and potential impact • ensure that the full range of resources available are distributed in a way that reflects the school's priorities and goals.	
Ensure an orderly learning environment where students are well known as a fundamental precondition for student learning to occur. This is evident when I can: • ensure that there are clear behavioural expectations for students that are consistently implemented by the staff • ensure structures are in place to enable teachers to get to know their students well.	
Minimise disruptions or distractions from the core work of teaching and learning at school. This is evident when I can: • ensure that teachers can teach free of interruptions during the school day • ensure that teachers can focus their energies on the core business of collaboratively planning and delivering high-quality lessons in all classes.	
Have the self-awareness to recognise, reflect and actively improve on your own role in ensuring and maintaining a well-run school. This is evident when I can: • analyse my own strengths and weaknesses in relation to my leadership role • pursue personal improvement with reference to an objective framework of what constitutes good leadership in a school.	
Total score	

---

[7] As noted earlier, this is equally applicable to curriculum expectations in other jurisdictions.

Interpreting your score

5 to 10 You have yet to successfully drive a strategic improvement consistently through the school and/or ensure the conditions are in place for teachers to focus effectively on their classroom work. You should seek feedback and mentoring on how to make things happen consistently in a school, possibly supplemented by training to strengthen your knowledge and understanding of key systems and processes for managing and leading a successful school. You should also seek the opportunity to lead and drive a targeted improvement initiative through one or more teams in the school.

11 to 15 You are effectively managing one or more key systems and processes in the school and contributing to the development of a working and learning environment where teachers can carry out their core tasks, free from significant student misbehaviour and/or other disruptions that can impede their work. In order to progress to the next stage of your career, you need to broaden the range of systems and processes you lead, thereby taking on more of a whole-school leadership and improvement role.

16 to 20 You lead a well-run school with efficient and effective systems and processes and an orderly learning environment where students are well known by the staff. You ensure that your staff can focus on what matters most and continue to improve. You may have a role to play in supporting other school leaders who are struggling to achieve similar outcomes in their schools.

© Pamela Macklin and Vic Zbar, *Driving School Improvement 2nd Edition*, Australian Council for Educational Research, 2020

TABLE 3.4: LEADERSHIP BEHAVIOUR 4: LEVERAGING THE GREATEST SOURCE OF IMPROVEMENT

Element	Rating (1–4)
Develop and promote a shared understanding of effective teaching to underpin the improvement of teaching and learning in the school. This is evident when I can: • *lead the development of an agreed whole-school statement of effective teaching and learning* • *ensure it is reflected in an instructional model that informs lesson planning in the school.*	
Promote and support the use of data and an evidence-informed approach to teaching and learning, including differentiation to meet all learning needs in classrooms across the school. This is evident when I can: • *ensure coherent sets of data are collected and used by teachers to inform their work* • *support teachers, including with any necessary professional learning, to effectively differentiate their teaching in class.*	
Ensure the necessary structure and documentation (i.e. curriculum scope and sequence, a whole-school assessment schedule and a framework to support planning of good lessons) to enable more teachers to work like the best. This is evident when I can: • *lead the development and regular updating of curriculum, assessment and pedagogical support documents and materials for teachers* • *ensure these resources are used to inform lesson planning by individuals and teams.*	
Support, resource and participate in collaborative planning and professional learning to grow teacher capacity and spread good practice through the school. This is evident when I can: • *ensure a whole-school professional learning plan is in place to develop the capacity of staff* • *demonstrate commitment to the plan by actively participating in professional learning with staff.*	
Promote and support mutual classroom observation and feedback to contribute to individual and collective improvement. This is evident when I can: • *lead the development of a culture of collaboration, including the regular formal and informal observation of each others' work* • *promote regular constructive feedback within the school, including to myself.*	
Total score	

Interpreting your score

5 to 10 You have yet to ensure that teaching and learning in the school is consistently based on the evidence of what works, a shared understanding of what effective teachers do and an underpinning culture of collaboration, mutual observation, challenge and support. You could seek training or other support, including guided reading, to develop your understanding of effective teaching and learning and how it manifests in classrooms across a school. There may be value in observing effective teaching and learning in action in a school where this consistently applies and talking with leaders about how this outcome was achieved. You may need to start your journey in this element of the Framework by leading the development of an agreed understanding of effective teaching in your school.

11 to 15 Your leadership is contributing to consistently more effective teaching and learning across the school, based on collaborative planning of lessons and professional learning in teams. In order to progress to the next stage of your career, you need to work with targeted teachers and teams to ensure that high-quality teaching and learning occurs in every classroom, and professional learning is structured in ways that genuinely support all teachers to improve. You may benefit from targeted training in particular pedagogical practices and how to ensure their adoption throughout the school.

16 to 20 You have successfully ensured an evidence-informed approach to teaching and learning across the school, based on a shared understanding of effective teaching among the staff. This is underpinned by the range of documents, professional learning opportunities and feedback processes that support more teachers to work like the best. You are in a position to contribute to the development of other leaders seeking to have a similar impact, including mentoring individual leaders and/or enabling them to observe how you lead.

© Pamela Macklin and Vic Zbar, *Driving School Improvement 2nd Edition*, Australian Council for Educational Research, 2020

TABLE 3.5: LEADERSHIP BEHAVIOUR 5: ENSURING PROGRESS AND KEEPING ON TRACK

Element	Rating (1–4)
Identify targets to monitor progress towards the achievement of the school vision, priorities and goals. This is evident when I can: • *set targets for improvement that are aligned to the school's vision, priorities and goals* • *ensure these targets are agreed by the key stakeholders in the school community.*	
Use data, including student assessment data and stakeholder feedback, to monitor progress towards these targets, and adjust the implementation of and/or abandon strategies as needed in response. This is evident when I can: • *use a range of sources of evidence to monitor the impact of the strategies the school is implementing to achieve its targets* • *adjust this implementation if needed to ensure there is sufficient progress for the targets to be achieved.*	
Use staff performance and development systems in ways that contribute to a culture of continuous improvement and support, and reflect and consider feedback on their own contribution to improving the school. This is evident when I can: • *ensure a rigorous, improvement-focused performance and development system is in place in the school* • *ensure that this system is underpinned by a focus on giving and receiving constructive feedback that applies from the classroom to the leadership team.*	
Hold people to account including oneself, acknowledge and learn from failures and recognise and celebrate success. This is evident when I can: • *ensure sufficient accountability within the school to enable it to recognise and foster individual and collective success while challenging shortcomings that exist* • *model mutual accountability through my openness to being challenged and consequent willingness to change if needed to improve.*	
Have courageous conversations, when needed, to ensure that goals and targets are achieved. This is evident when I can: • *initiate conversations with individuals whose behaviours do not accord with whole-school expectations and/or whose performance is below what is required* • *conduct these conversations in a respectful and constructive way that reflects a desire to support the individual to improve.*	
	Total score

Interpreting your score

5 to 10 You have yet to see a major project through from inception to consistent implementation, including building the capacity of staff involved and holding them to account. You could seek an opportunity to initiate, lead and follow through to full implementation a strategic initiative in the school, perhaps with the support of an experienced mentor leader. You could also consider targeted training in areas that commonly challenge people and where you may feel weak, such as using data to achieve targets or having courageous conversations where required.

11 to 15 You are experiencing some success in leading a major initiative in the school and moving towards embedding new practices in the work of staff. In order to progress to the next stage of your career, you need to consolidate your capacity to make things happen consistently in the school and, in particular, to have the sort of conversations that promote capacity and improvement and hold people to account. This could include observing successful leaders in or beyond your school and/or targeted training in such challenging areas as conducting conversations that help to ensure goals and targets are met.

16 to 20 You have successfully led and managed major projects from their initiation through to embedded new practice throughout the school. You do this in ways that strengthen staff capacity and performance, while challenging individuals when they fall short of expectations to be met. You have experience and expertise in project management to share with others in and beyond your school, including mentoring less successful leaders who are seeking to improve.

© Pamela Macklin and Vic Zbar, *Driving School Improvement 2nd Edition*, Australian Council for Educational Research, 2020

TABLE 3.6: PROCESSING THE SELF-ASSESSMENT AND PLANNING FOR IMPROVEMENT

Element
Strengths   It is important to acknowledge your existing leadership strengths. They are things you are already good at and hence the building blocks for further improvement and success.   My three leadership strengths are: •   •   •
Areas for development   At the same time as developing your strengths, you need to acknowledge and address any key weaknesses that need to be overcome.   The three areas in which I most need to develop my leadership capacities and/or performance are: •   •   •   That said, the enemy of effective improvement is when we try to do too much, because implementation inevitably suffers and nothing is done well. It is better to focus on one thing only to really develop it well and ensure it is consolidated and embedded in the way you lead. Taking account of these three areas for development, the <u>one</u> capacity and/or area of performance I most need to develop in the next 12 months is: •
Options for development   Personal capacity and performance development depends on a mix of training to fill identified skill gaps, opportunities to exercise leadership in an area of school improvement and targeted support from others within or beyond the school.   Training I need[8]:   Leadership opportunities I can pursue: Support from others I need: •   •   •   •   •   •   •   •   •
My improvement goal for the next 12 months is to: The target for achieving this goal is that I will:

© Pamela Macklin and Vic Zbar, *Driving School Improvement 2nd Edition*, Australian Council for Educational Research, 2020

---

[8] Note that most systems and sectors in Australia have a range of programs that can support leaders to develop important leadership skills.

BUILDING A STRONG AND UNITED LEADERSHIP TEAM

While the Leadership Framework outlined can help provide guidance to build individual performance and effectiveness, it is not sufficient on its own. Just as important for any program of improvement is to build a strong and united leadership team that speaks with one voice. One way of commencing the process of achieving this is to first assess how united and effective the team is. This can then provide the basis for improving its overall effectiveness and hence impact in the school.

ACTIVITY FOR LEADERSHIP TEAMS: GETTING A FIX ON THE TEAM[9]

This activity is designed to enable your leadership team to examine, in detail, critical aspects of its own practices and effectiveness to ensure that it is doing the right things and doing them in the right way. This involves examining a number of key statements about leadership team behaviours and honestly seeking a collective response, where necessary, with the involvement of a leadership coach who can bring an objective ear and voice.

While the following survey (Table 3.7) can be completed individually by members of the team and then collectively discussed with reference to the interpretation that follows, there is even more value in seeking to reach agreed scores as a whole team. Alternatively you may choose to add up each respondent's scores for each item and average them to then determine which areas ought to be the primary focus of the team.

Instructions

Please rate each of the following statements on a four-point scale where:
1 = Strongly disagree, 2 = Disagree, 3 = Agree and 4 = Strongly agree.

TABLE 3.7: GETTING A FIX ON THE TEAM

Our leadership team	Rating (1–4)
The school leadership team has a clear strategy for improving the school	
The strategy is agreed by all members of the leadership team	
The strategy is designed to build on the key strengths of the school	
The strategy is designed to address and overcome identified areas for improvement	
The leadership team speaks with one voice	
The leadership team actively engages staff in developing and implementing strategies for improvement	
The leadership team consistently mentors and coaches staff	
Members of the leadership team collaborate with staff and lead professional learning in priority areas	
Members of the leadership team are comfortable in raising differences and talking them through	
Team meetings focus on the key priorities of the school	
The team analyses its own performance and uses the outcomes to help it improve	
This is a strong and united leadership team	
Total score:	

---

[9] This activity is an adapted and extended version of the one included in the first edition, which was copyright to Vic Zbar, Ross Kimber and Graham Marshall (2010).

Interpreting your score

37 to 48 This is a strong, united and well-functioning team that is clear about its direction and is working collaboratively with staff to achieve its strategic vision for the school. The key challenge is to maintain the focus and relentlessly pursue the improvement strategies in place. It is a team that may even have expertise it can contribute to leadership teams in other schools.

25 to 36 The team is developing a degree of unity and purpose as well as its working relationships internally and with the staff. There may be one or more key areas that the instrument has highlighted that should be the focus of improvement in the team and how it works.

16 to 24 The team has some strengths it can capitalise on as it strives to develop as a strong and united team, but these are counterbalanced by some significant weaknesses that need to be overcome. There may be a need for some targeted training and/or other support in this regard, perhaps from a coach the school or its jurisdiction can identify and engage.

Less than 16 The team is not functioning to any great effect and needs to return to basics in terms of determining what its focus is and how its members work. The team may not have the capacity to do this on its own and could require a degree of systemic support and, in some cases, even intervention to bolster leadership capacity in the school.

© Pamela Macklin and Vic Zbar, *Driving School Improvement 2nd Edition*, Australian Council for Educational Research, 2020

It is important to balance the team's own deliberations with some feedback from staff about their experience of leadership as opposed to just the experience that leaders feel they provide.

The following short questionnaire can provide a snapshot of staff views to inform the ongoing discussions within the leadership team aimed at continually improving its reach and effectiveness in the school.

Note: To gain maximum value from this survey, it is suggested that you specify who constitutes the leadership team the staff are being asked to assess. There is commonly more than one team with a leadership role in the school and it is important to ensure that respondents are referring to the same leadership team.

A SHORT SURVEY FOR STAFF: HOW EFFECTIVE IS YOUR LEADERSHIP TEAM?

The leadership team is seeking your view on its overall effectiveness and impact in the school to inform its ongoing discussions about how it can continue to improve.

Your response will be anonymous and you also have the opportunity to provide additional comments at the end of the survey.

Instructions

Please rate each of the statements in Table 3.8 on a four-point scale where:
1 = Strongly disagree, 2 = Disagree, 3 = Agree and 4 = Strongly agree.

TABLE 3.8: HOW EFFECTIVE IS YOUR LEADERSHIP TEAM?

Leadership team effectiveness	Rating (1–4)
The leadership team has developed a clear strategy for improving the school	
This strategy is effectively communicated to the staff	
The leadership team has a strong and visible presence in the school	
The leadership team speaks with one voice	
The leadership team is seen as the driver of improvement in the school	
The leadership team collaborates with staff to design and implement improvement strategies	
Members of the leadership team work alongside teachers to improve teaching and learning	
The leadership team provides mentoring and coaching for staff	
The leadership team is open to feedback and alternative ideas for improving the school	
The roles and responsibilities of leadership team members are well defined and understood by the staff	
The leadership team demonstrates high expectations of themselves and others	
The leadership team models behaviours that encourage staff to contribute and take on leadership roles	
What is one action the leadership team could take to improve its effectiveness and impact in the school?	

© Pamela Macklin and Vic Zbar, *Driving School Improvement 2nd Edition*, Australian Council for Educational Research, 2020

The mere fact of discussing the data from the two surveys as a team can contribute to team unity and the development of the strong working relationships that underpin an effective and functioning team. However, it will only really contribute to improvement if it is then used to move to the next stage of developing clear and agreed strategies to pursue. Strong and united leadership teams develop by virtue of actually leading the school, rather than simply talking about becoming a better performing leadership team. In other words, the team needs to get on with the task of leading improvement in the school and developing its own capacity as a result.

That is the challenge that the remaining chapters are designed to help you to meet.

COACHING TO BUILD LEADERSHIP CAPACITY AND DRIVE IMPROVEMENT

An appropriately qualified, independent coach can help build the overall capacity and impact of the school's leadership team.

'Leadership coaching', according to Gorham, Finn-Stevenson and Lapin (2008), 'is a powerful and cost-effective means for developing school leaders, both in conjunction with other leadership development strategies and by itself. Moreover, by engaging in coaching, a school leader invests in the most important lever for school improvement available: oneself' (p. 4). This accords with the substantial experience Pamela, in particular, has working with school leadership teams around Australia to generate and drive whole-school improvement and support more teachers to work like the best.

It requires an approach to coaching that builds on the individual leaders' strengths as they pursue improvement in the specific context of their school, and not simply providing a template of leadership capacities in order to address some perceived deficits the leader may have.

In this context, it is important to distinguish between coaching and the sort of mentoring that many school leaders have experienced. A mentor is most often seen as an experienced person who will teach and provide advice to a less experienced person in an area of endeavour they are seeking to improve. There is certainly an important place for this kind of professional support for many, if not all, leaders at various points in their career.

The word 'mentor' derives from Greek mythology. In Homer's epic, *The odyssey*, Odysseus leaves his trusted friend Mentor in charge of his household during his absence. Athena, the goddess of wisdom, disguises herself as Mentor to guide Odysseus' son, Telemachus, on a journey to find his father. On this journey, Telemachus is able to learn, mature and find his own identity.

An accomplished coach does not use the 'expert' model and attempt to teach and guide a leader in a certain direction. Rather, the coach seeks to support and challenge the leader in their quest to be the best leader they can in their particular context. The direction, then, is set by the coachee and not the coach. Socrates captured the essence of this type of learning when he said, 'I cannot teach anybody anything, I can only make them think'. A successful leadership coach asks questions that stimulate thinking, reflection and creativity in others, which then leads them to plan and develop their own new pathways for personal improvement and the goals they seek to achieve.

WHAT IS LEADERSHIP COACHING IN SCHOOLS?

Given this, leadership coaching, as it applies to schools, can be defined as a strategy to support leaders in their efforts to become more effective, to develop colleagues and to improve student learning. It builds leadership and staff capacity, and uses research, theory, practice and feedback for improvement. It does not preclude the provision of evidence-based advice by the coach when that is required, but this is not the main focus of the role. The issues tackled in conjunction with the coach are those prioritised with the leader that are most relevant to their own context.

Common to all leadership coaching is the need to have a trusting and respectful relationship between the coach and coachee. Often there is a coaching contract or plan, which clearly outlines the expectations each person in the coaching relationship has, so there is a common understanding and the purpose is agreed. The coaching conversations in this context, must be strictly confidential and highly focused on the goals of the coachee. Importantly, the coach must be extremely skilled at questioning techniques to assist the coachee to gain new insights and approaches to their own development.

Attentive listening and powerful questioning are critical skills in this regard. A key factor in successful leadership coaching is the coach's skill in drawing out very clear goals and actions for the leader to take that would not have been possible without expert listening and questioning.

A great coach will only speak for about 20 per cent or less of the time they spend with the coachee, as they are listening attentively for the important messages, information and storylines that will prompt a powerful question to ask. Powerful questions lead the coachee to new insights that provide the impetus for novel solutions and actions they can pursue.

The leadership coaching conversation is simultaneously a supportive and robust conversation that leads to challenge, new thinking and action. It is particularly important, when school leaders are so often busily responding to the many demands of their role, that the time for self-reflection and leadership growth is made so a key source of improvement is not lost.

Importantly, since the leader arrives at goals and actions themself, they are committed to achieving them. This kind of focused, personalised and deep leadership development is difficult to achieve in generic leadership courses and is one of the main reasons that much of the corporate sector invests so heavily in coaching for emerging and established leaders they employ. Increasingly this is also the case in schools.

WHAT CAN LEADERSHIP COACHING ACHIEVE?

Leadership coaching outcomes vary according to the individual and their context. In our experience, typical outcomes for people who commit to leadership coaching include the following:
- more effective team leadership and change management skills
- the capacity to think and act strategically in terms of outcomes and thereby drive improvement through the school
- improved leadership skills in identified areas for growth
- the ability to effectively prioritise, set goals and manage time more effectively
- increased knowledge and insights into themselves and their organisation that allows them to become more flexible and versatile in the way they act
- more advanced communication skills, such as more effective verbal and non-verbal interactions, listening skills, capacity to provide feedback that has impact, and the capacity to effectively manage challenging communications and relationships.

If you don't think you need a leadership coach, then you probably do. We haven't yet known a leader (ourselves included) who would not benefit from working with a leadership coach at some point in their career.

Leadership coaching is not about 'fixing' people or addressing perceived deficits. It's about maximising potential and the performance of the individual starting from where they currently are. Just like great teaching.

A COACHING CULTURE FOR ALL

Many successful schools have been working consistently over a long period of time to implement a coaching culture to strengthen improvement at every level. Put simply, a coaching culture is a learning culture. It is one that openly says we are on a continuous path to being the best that we can be and we need both challenge and support to get there. A coaching culture is one that starts with the individual, has high expectations of each person, values their strengths and builds on them. The trust, respect and strong relationships engendered by coaching create an environment where robust and difficult conversations can be had without fear.

Coaching is a powerful strategy to support improvement in teaching and learning and it's a timely reminder that whatever the focus of your school improvement, leaders must be active in ensuring positive relationships are built. 'The single factor common to successful change', according to Fullan (2002), 'is that relationships improve. If relationships improve, schools get better. If relationships remain the same or get worse, ground is lost.' (para. 12).

A school with a coaching culture is a learning community where goals are clear, teams capitalise on the strengths that individuals have while supporting them to further improve, and successes are celebrated along the way.

Listening is central to developing a culture of coaching in the school; which is much easier said than done. If we are to successfully diagnose before we prescribe then we must, as Covey (1990) famously advised, 'seek first to understand, then to be understood' (p. 237). This requires us to consciously resist the natural temptation we have to not so much 'listen with the intent to understand ... (as) listen with the intent to reply' (p. 239).

Maxwell (2019) uses his own mixed leadership experience to suggest that being a better listener means that you need to listen well every day, stop interrupting, start asking questions and invite people to keep you accountable for listening. Itzchakov and Kluger (2018) take this a step further by adding the need to not judge or evaluate, not impose your own solutions, and reflect afterwards on your own listening and the opportunities for better listening that you may have missed.

Some particularly powerful strategies to use in this regard are:
- paraphrasing and repeating the content of what has been said to indicate that you are attending
- rephrasing the content to indicate that you are thinking about what has been said
- reflecting feeling so that you focus on how the other person feels about what they are saying
- in something of a combination of the previous points, trying to really understand what is being said.

However, this all will only be effective if accompanied by a genuine desire to understand the other person more than to be understood yourself.

School leaders will often seek training for themselves and others so they can develop a coaching culture and coaching practice throughout their schools. This undoubtedly is a good thing. Coaching integrates many fields of knowledge and there is a range of models from which to choose. Careful study of many models, approaches and coaching processes available indicates that there are core common features of successful models, such as the well-known GROW framework.

The GROW model is one of the most established and successful models for personal and professional learning through coaching. It uses a deceptively simple framework and process to support people to elicit meaningful goals and plan actions for change and ongoing improvement.

Whitmore (2002) provides a good overview of the GROW model, which has been used to improve individual and team performance in a range of contexts. In particular, he suggests a sequenced structure of questioning under the four headings comprising the GROW acronym:
- GOAL setting for the session as well as short and long term
- REALITY checking to explore the current situation
- OPTIONS and alternative strategies or courses of action
- WHAT is to be done, WHEN, by WHOM and the WILL to do it (p. 54).

The GROW model underpins many diverse coaching approaches and training programs used widely in the education sector. However, as is the case when considering the implementation of any major strategy for improvement in the school, it is important not to begin with solutions (e.g. training in a particular coaching program), but rather to assess your current reality as a school and use your diagnosis of that to guide what, how and when you will implement in relation to coaching in your school to best meet the needs of your context and the people in it.

NO COACHING AT YOUR SCHOOL YET? START HERE ...

If your school does not formally provide coaching for staff, convene a structured meeting of the leadership team to consider the possibility of providing coaching for teachers to improve teaching and learning through the school.

Instructional coaches can play a particularly powerful role in this regard, provided they are appropriately prepared, supported and introduced.

'Instructional coaches (ICs)', according to Knight (2018), 'partner with teachers to help them improve teaching and learning so students become more successful. To do this, ICs collaborate with teachers to get a clear picture of current reality, identify goals, pick teaching strategies to meet the goals, monitor progress and problem-solve until the goals are met' (pp. 2–3).

ACTIVITY FOR LEADERSHIP TEAMS: PREPARING FOR COACHING IN YOUR SCHOOL

Leaders should prepare for the meeting by doing some agreed professional reading[10] about coaching before discussing such agenda items as:

1. How are we currently providing professional support to staff to build their capacity to improve teaching and learning?
2. What is the evidence and any experience we can share that some form of coaching could improve teaching and learning at our school?
3. What are the reasons we currently do not prioritise coaching as a strategy to support the improvement of student learning in our school?
4. Given our school priorities and resources, is it appropriate or timely for us to consider planning to introduce coaching to strengthen teaching and learning in our school? If we are not sure, what do we need to know to help us decide? If we are sure, what are our first steps?

YOU HAVE COACHING AT YOUR SCHOOL ALREADY? TRY THIS...

We work in many schools who have some form of coaching for teachers in their school, but rarely are leaders or teachers completely satisfied with its implementation and the impact it has. We have worked alongside many school leadership teams to support them to better understand the current effectiveness of coaching in their schools and how to continually improve it, in consultation with all concerned.

We have learned that very often it is necessary to reflect on and answer some fundamental questions, at least annually, to ensure that planning and implementing coaching best meets the needs of teachers and students in the school. Sometimes these questions have not been addressed at all previously, or perhaps not in enough depth, and in some instances there has not been adequate follow through by leaders to address the issues the questions raise.

---

[10] There is a range of accessible professional readings that can be used, such as Chapters 1 and 2 of Knight (2018) or MacCrindle & Duginske (2018).

ACTIVITY FOR LEADERSHIP TEAMS: EVALUATING THE IMPLEMENTATION AND EFFECTIVENESS OF YOUR COACHING PROGRAM

It is a valuable process to work through the following questions with leadership teams to get a fix on the current reality of coaching in the school to inform future planning and to make sure your program has the best chance of success. We have found it most useful when leadership team members have been provided with the questions prior to the meeting and are asked to bring along their brief answers to inform the team discussion.

Although there is usually a broad general alignment of views about coaching in the team, the process almost always surfaces some misconceptions, areas where further clarity and shared understanding is required and, in some cases, some robust discussions are had that go to the root of the very nature of the coaching work. As is the case with all school improvement work, it is critical that the leadership team takes the time to ensure that their words and actions are thoroughly informed and aligned.

The current reality of coaching at the school—guiding questions
1 What is the purpose of coaching at the school?
2 Who coaches (i.e. position of coaches)? How many coaches?
3 Do the coaches have formal training? Which training? How do we know what their professional learning needs are right now?
4 Does the coaching include mentoring and other kinds of support in response to individual needs?
5 Who is coached? How are coachees selected?
6 How much time is dedicated to coaching? Who decides?
7 What structures, approaches and documents are used in the coaching process?
8 What is the teacher and student feedback about the coaching work and its impact?
9 How and when is the coaching program regularly reviewed and monitored?
10 How is the impact of coaching known and improved as needed?

Sometimes smaller schools can experience difficulty developing coaching plans and practices simply because there are too few teachers in the school. This is something that the muka layna Collaboration in Tasmania, for example, has sought to address as part of its broader collaborative work to engage teachers from the ground up.[11] More specifically, the Collaborative worked on developing a coaching plan that addressed the broad questions of: 'What is the best fit for the muka layna Collaboration in 2020 and why?'; 'What approach to coaching can we agree upon?'; 'Many coachees or few?'; 'How is coaching currently viewed by staff?'; 'Do they seek out coaching?; 'Why or why not?; and 'What's the consistent message we want to give staff about why coaching will be offered to colleagues and what coaching is?'

Discussing and responding to these questions enabled Collaborative leaders to consider and identify the areas where alignment already exists between current practices and the developing coaching plans, areas where there is greater diversity and hence the need for alignment to be built, and what more they need to know or do to be able to plan and collaboratively implement the next steps. In other words, to develop a clear picture of their current reality and, in particular, what is working and what is not to inform the emerging coaching plan and the way in which Collaborative teachers are engaged.

---

[11] The muka layna Collaboration comprises Bicheno Primary School, Campbelltown, St Helen's and Winneleah District High Schools and St Mary's District School. *muka layna* is *palawa kani*, the language of Tasmanian Aboriginals, with thanks to the Tasmanian Aboriginal Centre. The term *muka* (which along with *layna* is not capitalised) means salt water and layna means fresh water, reflecting the fact that water is the geographical link between the five schools comprising the Collaboration.

The guiding question the Collaborative then addressed to give focus to their work was, 'based on your current reality, what might be two important next steps for your school to take to build a culture of coaching?'

A COACHING PLAN IS A MUST

Whatever consensus is arrived at in response to these questions, a simple, clear and agreed coaching action plan is needed to guide the work. Just as great lesson planning is the key ingredient for effective lessons in class, so too does an effective coaching program depend on having a good plan.

Pivotal to success in this regard, is the early and regular engagement of staff in the process of developing and implementing the plan. Collaborating and partnering with teachers in this work, rather than taking a 'top-down' approach will ensure the best chance of success. It is something that is more likely to be achieved if underpinned by an appropriate set of principles for engagement, such as those suggested by Knight (2018), which, in summary form, comprise:
- 'equality' of all the partners involved
- 'choice' to be involved
- 'voice' so that all views matter equally
- 'dialogue' that balances advocacy with inquiry
- 'reflection' to support learning
- 'praxis' so that knowledge and skills are not just talked about, but also applied
- 'reciprocity' that sees all partners learn (p. 5).

It is not necessary in this context to reinvent the wheel when planning and implementing a coaching program in your school. Once you have identified the goals and basic parameters of the coaching support suitable for your current context, you can draw on some of the excellent training programs and resources available, which can be adapted to meet your specific needs. You can also seek the support of colleagues in schools that have successful coaching programs in place, who can provide support and advice as you develop your own plans.

Although the coaching plan for each school is necessarily unique, the sample action plan in Table 3.9 provides an indication of some of the key steps that many schools have adopted in developing their plans. It is important to note that this sample is not perfect, but rather a reflection of a robust collaborative planning process undertaken by a school team. It is an ongoing work in progress that must be regularly monitored, reviewed and reshaped. The value of the plan is that it provides a vehicle for using the questions outlined above (and your own targeted questions) to reach shared understandings, agreed goals, a clear commitment to action and shared accountability to ensure that your goals can be met.

At Springvale Rise Primary School, the manifestation of its successful coaching plan in action was the adoption of a range of strategies that included:
- formally timetabling a 'sacrosanct' hour a fortnight for collaborative (coaching) conversations for every teacher in the school
- intentionally naming this as time for 'collaborative conversations' rather than coaching to overcome some negative 'coaching' experiences some teachers had
- clearly documenting the expectations of coaches and coachees and their associated accountabilities
- providing readings and professional learning for all staff to demonstrate the value that coaching can bring
- providing underpinning professional learning for leaders on the GROW coaching approach along with research about 'personality types' to support a differentiated coaching approach[12]

---

[12] There is substantial research about personality types available on the internet from the traditional Myers-Briggs categories (see for example https://www.myersbriggs.org/) to more recent research on personality types reported in Science Daily (2018, September 17) that can be accessed at https://www.sciencedaily.com/releases/2018/09/180917111612.htm

- coaching as a key action with the school's strategic and annual implementation plans and supporting this with a specific coaching goal that was incorporated in each leader's performance and development plan
- providing staff with six-monthly feedback on the evidence of progress and impact so that stories of success and improvement, including in student outcome data, could be acknowledged and celebrated through the school.

Critical to the success of any coaching plan and the way it plays out, is the extent to which leaders and staff have 'buy in', and that the plan is regularly used and reviewed. Many schools have an existing representative school improvement team to drive the implementation of a coaching program, while some have a specially-convened coaching working group or similar to lead the coaching work.

TABLE 3.9: A SAMPLE COACHING PLAN

Our purpose: To improve student learning outcomes by creating a culture in which reflective thinking, feedback and coaching is embedded in our teaching practice.					
Draft version completed on _____ by _____					
Goal	Strategy	Who	Timeline	Success criteria	Evidence/ progress
1. Develop a shared understanding and common language regarding instructional coaching (IC).	Collaborate with colleagues in structured professional learning (PL) sessions to identify the type of coaching most suitable for our school improvement goals and context Provide professional reading and video resources to all staff about IC to support PL sessions	School improvement team (SIT) to lead staff PL All staff participate in PL	Weeks 3, 5 and 8, Term 1	All staff have shared their knowledge and experience of coaching and undertaken prescribed reading/ viewing regarding IC Staff can describe several coaching approaches (e.g. facilitative, dialogical, directive) Staff have demonstrated an understanding of key features of the action planning cycle commonly used in schools Staff have contributed to the development of draft guidelines for coaching	

2. Develop a consistent approach to IC throughout the school	Structured collaborative meetings designed to develop draft coaching processes, guidelines and documents that build on current knowledge and practice	SIT to lead staff meetings. All staff participate in developing coaching processes, guidelines and documents	Weeks 2, 4 and 6, Term 2	All staff have collaborated in teams to share coaching knowledge and practice, and develop agreed guidelines and processes for beginning to implement coaching in Term 3 Draft documents for coaches and coachees have been developed for trialing in Term 3	
	Identify resources required, including staffing, to implement the coaching approach	SIT	Week 8, Term 2	Detailed draft budget, proposed staffing and timetable for coaching complete	
	Identify process for selecting coaches and providing PL for coaches as required	SIT	Week 9, Term 2	Process for coach selection and training documented and shared with staff	
3. Trial IC for selected year levels	Middle years literacy to be the first focus of coaching in line with the School Improvement Plan. Invite middle years teachers to participate in IC Weekly coaching sessions implemented using agreed processes and documents	Coaches and middle years teachers	Terms 3 and 4	Middle years teachers engage in coaching with a focus on improving literacy teaching Coaching sessions proceed according to schedule and agreed processes.	
	Coaching effectiveness monitored and reviewed using targeted surveys and feedback tools. Coaching processes and practices refined and improved as required	SIT, coaches, teachers and students	Week 6, Term 4	Data and evidence of improvement gathered Feedback sought and used to inform commendations for future coaching work	
4. Develop Annual Implementation Plan to take IC to the next stage in the school	Implementation plan for wider roll-out of coaching developed for the following year	Leadership team, SIT, coaches and teachers	Weeks 7–9, Term 4	Annual Implementation Plan for coaching developed, agreed, scheduled and resourced	

BUILDING COACHING CAPACITY IN YOUR SCHOOL

While we have seen many successful coaching programs being implemented in schools, we have also seen some which have struggled to be effective, despite the best of intentions and a lot of hard work. Often, this has been because a sense of urgency to get the coaching work going—sometimes due to top-down system pressure, sometimes due to pressure that is self-imposed—means that there is inadequate assessment of the current situation and hence a lack of inclusive planning and preparation has occurred.

Hasty implementation can lead to steps being taken that may not best meet the needs of the school and indeed take more time to undo in the longer term. For example, in some cases there has been a rush to train middle leaders on how to coach using a particular approach, purely so the coaching can quickly start. While the coaching training that was undertaken may have been perfectly fine, the chosen approach was subsequently used with teachers almost regardless of the individual needs of the teacher or team. It reminds us of Maslow's caution that, 'if the only tool you have is a hammer' it is tempting 'to treat everything as if it were a nail' (Maslow, 1966, p. 15). In the same way that teachers need to differentiate strategies and approaches in response to the individual learners in their class, so too do coaches need to differentiate their coaching strategies rather than taking a 'one-size-fits-all' approach.

Education professionals quite correctly understand the importance of research-based practice and implementing learning strategies with fidelity and consistency, so it is often tempting to simply learn a proven technique and then follow a 'script'. We do not doubt that following a script, or a step-by-step approach does have a place. The issue is the extent to which the script or steps can become a straightjacket, rather than a helpful tool or support. There are no simple answers. Coaching is a challenging and high stakes professional practice on many levels, so the security of knowing you are getting it 'right' by adhering to a process of standard coaching steps, particularly while you are building your skill and confidence as a coach, is important. However, just as teachers build a 'toolkit' of effective teaching strategies over many years of experience and learning, coaches do the same, once they determine where to start.

SELECTING AND DEVELOPING COACHES

When leading the implementation of coaching in a school it is important, then, to have both a clear diagnosis of the current reality of the school context and the coaching support that might best promote and sustain improvement in the school. In particular, leaders must ensure that the selection and training of coaches is carefully planned, and that they each have the right knowledge and skills to enable the best 'fit' for the teachers who will be coached.

One thing to consider at this point is whether the innovators and early adopters discussed in Chapter 2 might be a good fit as coaches for targeted members of staff; especially those in the early majority who might be persuaded and supported to 'give it a go' earlier than otherwise might be the case (see Figure 2.1). It's an effective way to ensure that these self-starters do not run too far ahead of the pack and instead work to bring others on board with them provided, of course, that they have the requisite personal capacities to work with others in this way and are appropriately trained for the role. It especially can work when, as Moyle (2015) advised in her discussion of coaching and mentoring for school improvement, the early adopters 'model the approach' to other staff.

The key questions that leaders need to address in selecting and developing coaches as part of formulating the school coaching plan are:

1 What skills, experience and knowledge are required for coaches to be effective in our school?
2 How can we ensure we select the best coaches for our needs?
3 What kind of professional learning will our coaches need?
4 Is there a place for new coaches to 'learn on the job' to some extent? If so, how do we, as leaders, support and scaffold this learning?

While it is essential to answer these questions in a way that best matches your own particular context, there is plenty of sound, simple advice widely available that can help guide your work. MacCrindle and Duginske (2018), for example, cite seven qualities of an instructional coach consistent with the evidence of effective instructional coaching practice widely available from within and across schools. These include the capacity to build strong relationships, quality questioning skills, knowledge of high impact instructional practices and being student focused. They also recommend starting small, building knowledge and skills in response to emerging needs and providing professional learning that teachers can volunteer to attend.

This accords with our own experience that coaching is most successful when time is taken to slowly introduce the work, so that coaches build their knowledge and skills side by side with teachers who are keen to be coached. It is important that coaches and teachers enter the process understanding that coaching is a partnership requiring a solid relationship, genuine dialogue and mutual trust.

THE JOURNEY FROM UNCONSCIOUS INCOMPETENCE TO UNCONSCIOUS COMPETENCE

Leaders and teachers learning how to coach regularly tell us how challenging they find coaching conversations and how aware they have become of the need to build their skills in such new areas as asking powerful questions in the moment, authentically listening and setting meaningful goals. Although as educators we all know that real learning is challenging and can involve discomfort, difficulty and mistakes along the way, when confronted by the big learning curve that coaching involves, we often lack confidence in our capacity and feel concerned about the need to immediately get it 'right'.

So, while we intellectually know how learning occurs, in practice we can neglect the fact that many of us need plenty of encouragement, support, feedback and time to build our confidence and capacity to coach.

We have found the Conscious Competence Learning Model in Figure 3.2 helpful in this regard, since it supports coaches to take a longer-term view of developing their own capacity, and hence the steps they need to take along the way.

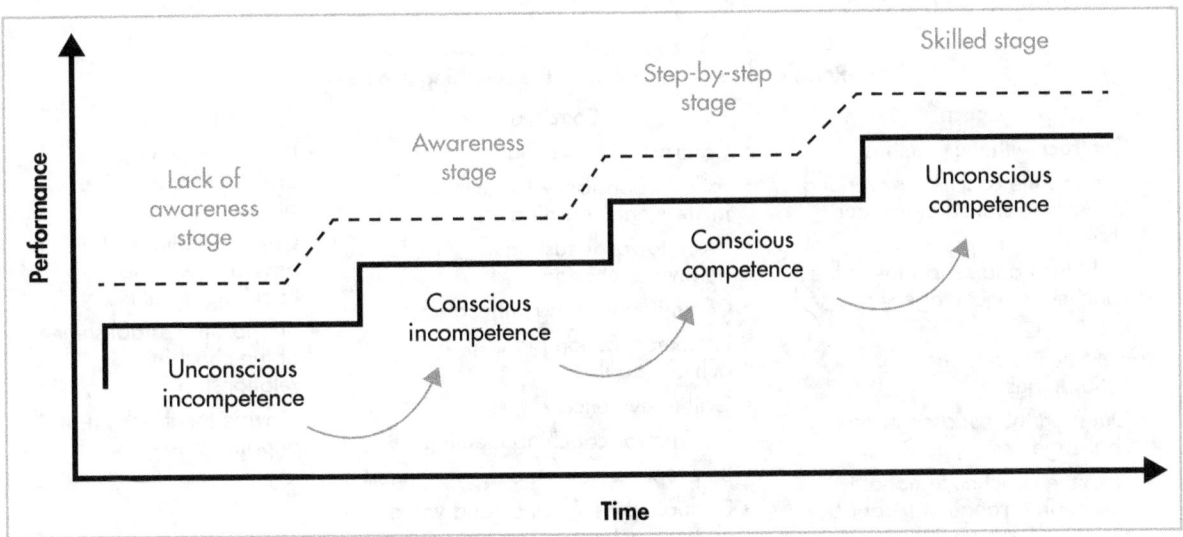

FIGURE 3.2: CONSCIOUS COMPETENCE LEARNING MODEL

Psychology suggests that the four stages individuals commonly progress through as they move from incompetence to competence in using a skill are:

1 Unconscious incompetence—where the individual does not know or understand how to do something and may not even be aware of it, sometimes denying the importance of the skill. To move forward, the individual must first recognise their own incompetence and the value of the new skill. How long this takes depends on the nature and strength of the stimulus to learn.
2 Conscious incompetence—where the individual does not yet know or understand how to do something, but they are aware of their own deficit and the value of the new skill in addressing it. Making mistakes is an important element of the learning process at this stage.
3 Conscious competence—where the individual knows or understands how to do something, but it requires significant concentration and effort to do. It may be broken down into steps at this stage, and there is a lot of conscious involvement in exercising the new skill.
4 Unconscious competence—where the individual has so much practice with the skill that it has become a matter of habit, or 'second nature', that can be performed easily when required. The skill can even be performed while doing something else, and the individual may be able to teach it to others with whom they work.

Put simply, these four stages suggest that individuals are initially unaware of how little they know, or unconscious of their incompetence then, as they recognise their incompetence, they consciously acquire a skill and begin to consciously use it, until eventually, the skill can be used without it being consciously thought through at all. The individual is said to have then acquired unconscious competence which, for many aspiring coaches, is the goal.

ROLE CLARITY FOR COACHES, TEACHERS AND LEADERS

As is the case with all school improvement work, keeping things simple, minimising the number of priorities and ensuring role clarity for all will support the development of competence and effective implementation through the school. Figure 3.3 from AITSL (n.d.) provides a helpful example of the differing roles in the coaching process and what each might involve. It is important to involve staff in developing these roles and responsibilities since the shared understanding that results can help to ensure a smoother and ultimately more successful embedding of coaching practices than otherwise might be the case.

Roles and responsibilities in the coaching process

Coach	Coachee	School leader
• Contract with the coachee	• Contract with the coach	• Play an active role in professional learning of teachers
• Support the coachee in working towards sustained behaviour change	• Take responsibility for own professional learning	• Create a culture where development and coaching is valued
• Build trust and rapport with the coachee to encourage supported risk-taking	• Work towards sustained behaviour change	• Support the establishment of the coaching relationship
• Help define clear goals and action plans	• Commit to meeting with coach	• Provide feedback on an ongoing basis
• Question the coachee in order to challenge assumptions	• Implement action plans to achieve goals	
• Help the coachee to honestly reflect on a range of feedback	• Gather evidence	
• Manage boundaries and maintain confidentiality	• Prepare for coaching meetings	
	• Be prepared to be open and honest	
	• Evaluate the relevance and value of the coaching experience	

FIGURE 3.3: ROLES AND RESPONSIBILITIES IN THE COACHING PROCESS (AITSL)

Source: AITSL (n.d., p. 11). © 2020 the Australian Institute for Teaching and School Leadership Limited (AITSL). The Content was created by AITSL. AITSL was formed to provide national leadership for the Commonwealth, State and Territory Governments in promoting excellence in the profession of teaching and school leadership with funding provided by the Australian Government.

THE POWER OF GOOD QUESTIONS

Of course, coaching-style conversations happen all the time in schools and classrooms, staffrooms and corridors because educators understand the power of great questions to stimulate learning. However, in schools where leaders are coached and a coaching culture develops as a result of carefully assessing your context and planning for coaching to happen regularly, the focus on questioning becomes much sharper, more intentional and purposeful. Explicitly practising and understanding more about how to become better at questioning to stimulate thinking and learning can be a focus for all in the school, since it is intrinsic not only to coaching, but to leadership in general.

'Questioning', as Brooks and John (2018) have observed, 'is a uniquely powerful tool for unlocking value in organisations: It spurs learning and the exchange of ideas, it fuels motivation and performance improvement, (and) it builds rapport and trust among team members' (p. 4). And the good news, they suggest, is that 'by asking questions, we naturally improve our emotional intelligence, which in turn makes us better questioners—a virtuous cycle' (p. 4).

Starting from the presumption that leaders should simply ask more questions to promote learning and the relationships on which it depends, Brooks and John (2018) suggest that the key to better questioning is to:

- focus more on follow-up questions, since they signal your desire to know more
- use more open-ended questions that invite people to talk
- think carefully about the sequencing of your questions
- use a more casual tone to minimise the risks
- take account of the group dynamics when more than two people are involved.

ACTIVITY FOR LEADERSHIP TEAMS: LEADING LEARNING CONVERSATIONS

A core component of coaching others is to pose questions for them to consider and discuss that contribute to learning and then potentially, to behaviour change. Here are two to consider:

- What is your primary purpose in working with your class right now?
- What could be your first step in working towards this?

Instructions

1 Individually, see if you can identify five further learning-oriented questions you could ask in a coaching conversation with a teacher in your school. Share your individual responses and develop a team list to inform the coaching conversations you have.
2 Here are some further coaching questions to consider that apply to your own leadership role. Think about how you would adapt these to use with the teachers you coach. The questions include:
   - What is the most important focus for your work right now? Why?
   - What changes are most needed now?
   - What would make the biggest difference right now?
   - What is your first step?
   - How are you going to ensure quality professional learning for all?
   - What will you do to support behaviour change?
   - How will you manage the nay-sayers?
   - What is the worst that can happen and are you ready for it?
   - Are you acting on intuition or evidence?
   - How do you maintain the momentum when there are set backs?
   - What is stopping you from acting?

Like all activities centred on learning, coaching and the listening and questioning on which it depends, not only requires training, but is something we get better at by practising and doing. This especially is the case when we seek to have what are often termed 'difficult conversations', which suffer from the fact that, once defined in this way, that is exactly what they will be. That is why Robinson and colleagues, for example, prefer the term 'open-to-learning conversations' (OLC), which are concerned to establish the validity of one's views rather than seeking to simply demonstrate that we are 'right'. (See, for example, Robinson, Le Fevre, Sinnema, Meyere & Pope, 2016).

They are, nonetheless, conversations that leaders have to have, and we can learn how to conduct them more effectively than often is the case.

The leadership team at Hume Central Secondary College developed an effective means of practising OLCs to build the skills of leaders in this regard. In team meetings that Vic observed while working as a critical friend to the school, leaders worked in threes to practise a coaching conversation around a scenario that could occur and which they might need to discuss. More specifically, leaders alternated in the role of coach, coachee and independent observer to model the conversation, consider feedback and discuss how it could have been improved.

Having successful conversations in this context is more likely to occur when leaders keep in mind the key components of any OLC, which in summary form, according to Robinson et al. (2016), require them to:

- describe their concern as their point of view, rather than a statement of fact—e.g. I think we could have different views about …
- describe the basis of their concern—e.g. The reason I am concerned is that, in walking through your classroom I observed that …
- invite the other's point of view—e.g. I would like to understand your perspective on this
- paraphrase their point of view and check for accuracy—e.g. What I believe I heard you say was … Have I heard correctly?
- detect and check important assumptions—e.g. What evidence do you have for that view?
- establish common ground—e.g. While we may see the cause somewhat differently at the moment, we both want to ensure that …
- make a plan to get what you both want—e.g. What would you like to know to investigate this further and what support is needed for that?

ACTIVITY FOR LEADERSHIP TEAMS: PRACTISING OPEN-TO-LEARNING CONVERSATIONS

Instructions

Working in groups of three, alternating the role of coach, coachee and observer, discuss each of the following three scenarios developed by Hume Central Secondary College for its leadership team, keeping in mind Robinson's advice. Alternatively, you may like to create one or more scenarios of your own reflecting current issues in the school.

1 The school has set an ambitious target for improving student outcomes. A colleague comes to you at the end of Term 3, with 20/25 students failing and says 'I told you this would not work, they are not capable'.

2 Each Thursday since the start of term, a teacher, who is a member of your team and teaches opposite you, has 'exited' at least one student to you. The student/s arrive without a pen, explanation for being exited—seemingly with nothing. The student/s claim that the teacher does not give them a warning or isolate them before 'exiting' them.

3 You are teaching the last class of the day. After the bell, you walk outside and see students from your school leaving out of uniform and you can hear them swearing. A teacher nearby is aware of this but ignores it.

More recently still, Sanderson Middle School in the Northern Territory developed the following scenarios with a stronger focus on the classroom itself, which can be practised in the same way:

1. You and a teacher being observed have agreed on the importance of using success criteria in a lesson. During the lesson, the learning intentions were present, but there were no success criteria to which students could refer. In the feedback conversation, the teacher said that the success criteria 'were met', but did not feel it important to share them on the board.
2. You have observed a class where the teacher seems unaware that several students are disengaged—e.g. they are talking about social activities and reading an unrelated text.
3. You were being observed by a colleague, having agreed on the focus for observation. Halfway through the lesson, the observing teacher (uninvited) began instructing and interacting with the students.

We subsequently have also added the following scenario reflecting the fact that many of the schools with which we work are in the process of developing their professional learning teams (PLTs):

> Since the start of the year, PLTs in the school have been focused on planning lessons collaboratively on the basis of learning goals. It has come to your attention that a member of one team is not really engaging with the task. Aside from regularly coming late to PLT meetings, he does not do the pre-work the team expects and does not contribute when the team meets. This inhibits the consistent and effective implementation of lesson planning and delivery in the school.

We have spent significant time discussing open-to-learning conversations in a context where 'difficult' things need to be said. That is because so many principals and other leaders we meet nominate this as one of the areas where they struggle most and hence feel in need of support. However, 'difficult' conversations are only a small part of the coaching conversations that occur in the schools with which we work.

Far more prevalent are the ongoing coaching conversations that leaders and instructional coaches (ICs) engage in to support individual teachers to gain and implement an important new teaching skill or technique. In other words, the coaching conversations that support more teachers to work like the best. This is part of the structured work undertaken to pursue the school's overall coaching plan, as outlined earlier and in the sample plan in Table 3.9, aimed at driving through one or more agreed high-impact teaching strategies that have been demonstrated to significantly improve student learning outcomes through a mix of research and experience in a number of schools.

Simply having a plan, of course, is not sufficient to guarantee success. Equally important is the way in which the plan is enacted, in particular to ensure that coaching is not something done 'to', as done 'with' the teacher(s) concerned. It requires the coach to work side-by-side the teacher in and outside the classroom to collaboratively build their teaching effectiveness and skills.

It arguably starts by developing a common understanding between the teacher and coach of the prevailing reality in their class. For example, classroom observations, including video observations, may have surfaced that a significant proportion of students are clearly disengaged from class, with the result the teacher is only teaching to the front of the room. It is important to reiterate here that developing this shared understanding needs to be consistent with the advice provided in this chapter that the coach does not assume this is the case, nor impose their view. Rather, the coach works with the teacher to jointly identify what is going on including, as recommended earlier, by seeking first to understand before seeking to be understood.

Questioning, as also already discussed, is essential in this regard, with a particular focus on what the teacher themselves experienced and, in the case of videos, observed, using such prompts as:

- How would you rate the effectiveness of the lessons observed on a four-point scale from highly ineffective to highly effective?

- How would you rate the level of student engagement using a similar scale from highly disengaged to highly engaged?
- What do you think worked really well in the lessons observed?
- What would you need to have done differently to move each of your scores towards a 4?
- Are there any strategies you are aware of that might help in this regard?

It is then a matter of developing an agreed improvement goal to take things to the next stage. Setting a challenging yet achievable goal for improving student learning focuses the mind on the instructional strategies that will realise the goal and makes it more likely that the strategies will become embedded in the teacher's work. Goals, according to what Knight and colleagues (2018) describe as the 'most important finding' from their instructional coaching research, 'are essential for coaching success. When teachers partner with coaches to set and meet measurable student goals, coaching improves instruction. When there is no goal, there is a real danger that coaching will have no lasting impact'(p. 65).

So in the context of the shared reality of disengagement identified in the hypothetical example of this teacher's class, the goal that could emerge from detailed discussion between teacher and coach could be that 'by the end of the year, 95 per cent of students in the class will be engaged in classroom learning and activities for at least 90 per cent of each lesson'. Important questions to address at this point would include: 'How will we know when this goal has been achieved?' and 'What would it look like?'

Having established the goal and the level of evidence we will be gathering, attention can shift to next steps and, in particular, the identification of one or more strategies that the teacher and coach can work together to introduce in order to achieve the goal. It is often the case at this point that teachers will be bereft of strategies to use, otherwise they already would have been using them. Hence this is where the coach can provide some evidence-informed advice, albeit in the context of options the teacher can consider rather than something they must adopt. Staying with our example of student disengagement, the coach might raise the Lemov strategies outlined later in Chapter 5 and, in particular, the 'no opt out' approach since a number of students clearly have opted out.

It is not sufficient, though, to just make the teacher aware of the approach. One of the things teachers regularly say to us when something new is introduced, is that too often they are told of the new techniques when really what they want is to be shown. In the case of our example, this could involve such things as: the teacher and coach jointly viewing and discussing videos of the strategy in action[13]; modelling of the strategy by the coach whether in the teacher's class or one of their own; co-teaching; and viewing someone else in the school who is known to do it well.

It is then a matter of teacher and coach continuing to work side-by-side as the new technique is progressively implemented, with appropriate monitoring, including through classroom observation, so any necessary adjustments are made, until it ultimately becomes embedded as the new way in which the teacher works. This success should then be cause for celebration as the prelude to collaboratively identifying the next area on which the teacher and coach can work together, as they strive for continuous improvement in accordance with the whole-school coaching plan.

Regardless of the focus of coaching undertaken in the school—from leadership coaching that includes conversations about 'difficult' issues that arise, to classroom coaching where ICs work side-by-side with teachers to develop their pedagogical skills—coaching is not something we innately are good at, but something we need to practise and learn. It's a case where we get better by doing it, and reflecting on what we have learned. And it is something we must continue to practise within the school, since coaching is intrinsic to the collaborative learning and problem-solving that is at the heart of all of the school and classroom improvement strategies outlined in the remainder of this book.

---

[13] There is a range of videos on the *Teach like a champion* website including a series of 'no opt out' videos that can be accessed at https://teachlikeachampion.com/blog/?s=no+opt+out

CHAPTER 4
THE THREE STAGES OF WHOLE-SCHOOL IMPROVEMENT

We have made much to date of the need to diagnose the stage of development of your school, before you prescribe the suite of strategies for improvement, to ensure you are on the right curative path. Diagnosis is not something that occurs in a vacuum, or in circumstances entirely unique to your school. Just as doctors use their knowledge of similar symptoms and the illnesses they portend, so too can schools draw on the experience of others that have been through similar events.

Through a combination of learning from school improvement research and working intensively with schools to generate significant improvement over time, we have developed a framework for school improvement that helps you to undertake the diagnosis of where your school is at. (The remainder of this chapter draws on Zbar, 2013.)

While change is never linear, and always involves some twists and turns, our experiences suggest a progression of improvement through the three stages included in Figure 4.1, underpinned by quality leadership at each stage for the reasons outlined in Chapter 3.

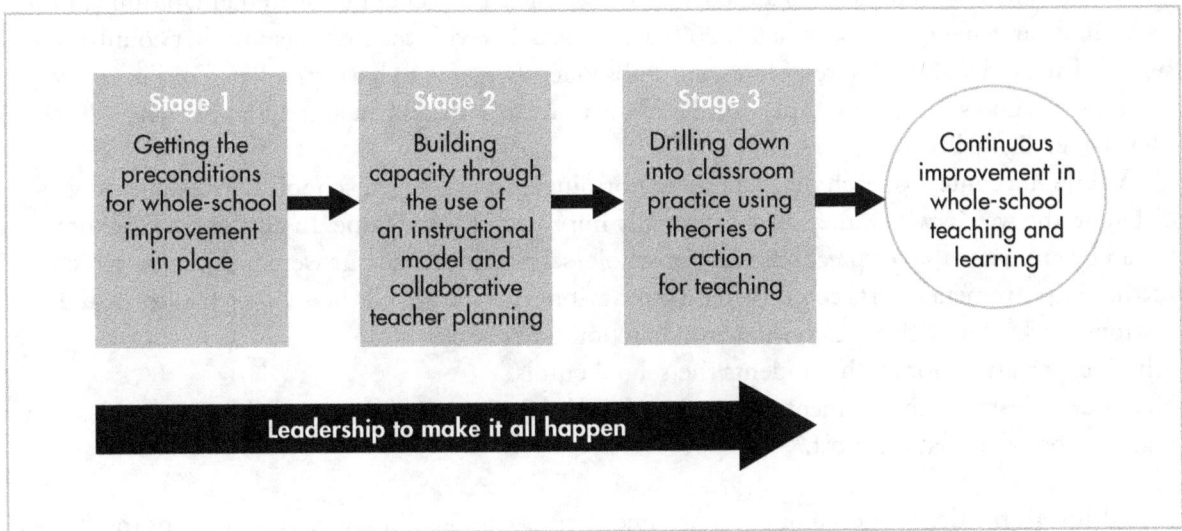

FIGURE 4.1: STAGES OF SUSTAINED SCHOOL IMPROVEMENT

Interestingly, this resonates with the work of McKinsey & Company on 'How the world's most improved school systems keep getting better' (Mourshed, Chijioke & Barber, 2010), which demonstrates how systems that moved from fair to good performance, and then to great performance and sustained excellence, all appeared to 'adopt a similar set of interventions … appropriate to their stage of the journey'(p. 11), regardless of their context to start. While context certainly does matter, their analysis revealed that it ultimately 'is secondary to getting the fundamentals right' (p. 11).

Put simply, whether it be the systemic approach that Mourshed, Chijioke and Barber (2010) defined, or the stages of development embodied in Figure 4.1, the process almost always involves:
- identifying where the school or system currently is at in performance terms
- determining the set of interventions needed to get to the next performance stage
- adapting these interventions to the particular context that exists.

Experience then suggests, as Mourshed and her colleagues observed, 'that each performance stage is associated with a dominant cluster of interventions' that are implemented in ways appropriate to the context of the system or school (2010, p. 18). This is a key leadership challenge and task, as evident in the following discussion of improvement strategies relevant to each stage in Figure 4.1, and the more detailed outline of each of the stages provided in Chapters 5 to 7.

Before proceeding, it is important to note that the three case studies provided in this chapter were all written at the time that the framework in Figure 4.1 was devised and put into the public domain. They were included in the first edition of this book and are retained in this one to outline the thinking that underpinned the development of the approach. They were snapshots at a particular point in time several years ago (September 2013 was when they were first published). All three schools have subsequently continued to progress and have moved well beyond the descriptions provided to generate even better outcomes for the students they serve.

ENSURING THE PRECONDITIONS ARE IN PLACE

Our work on school improvement started in earnest when Vic, along with his colleagues Ross Kimber and Graham Marshall, was commissioned by the Department of Education and Early Childhood Development in Victoria to examine eight high-performing, socio-economically disadvantaged schools with a view to determining the sources of their success. Since all the schools involved were not initially high performing, but became so over time, they not only could specify the characteristics they all shared, but also the means by which their improvement had been achieved.

This enabled them to develop a theory of action for whole-school improvement, outlined in detail in Zbar, Kimber and Marshall (2009), which accords with the findings in other countries such as England and the United States, and subsequently seems to have struck a chord in many Australian schools (see for example: OFSTED with Matthews, 2009a and 2009b; Haynes, 2009; Herman et al., 2008).

While the context of each of the high-performing, disadvantaged schools they examined was different, the way in which they all substantially improved was the same. In all cases, the schools began by ensuring a set of preconditions for whole-school improvement were in place on which further improvement efforts could then be built. More specifically, all the schools had to ensure:
- strong leadership with a clear vision and direction for the school
- high expectations for all the students the school enrols
- an orderly learning environment throughout the school where students are well known by the staff
- a focus on what matters most.

Although the detail of each of these preconditions is explored in Chapter 5, some of the flavour of the approach common to all the study schools, and which has been replicated by many other improving schools since, can be gained from the case study of Braybrook College provided in Box 4.1. A case study was written of each school as part of the more detailed report on which the occasional paper referenced earlier was based—see Zbar, Kimber and Marshall (2008).

Box 4.1

Turning around performance at Braybrook College

Strong leadership was key

Turning around significant enrolment decline and sustaining a strong and growing school is a task that the college has pursued for the last 20 years or more. It commenced with the arrival of a new principal who brought a clear vision and sense of moral purpose which, according to one school leader who effectively spoke on behalf of others, 'made us believe that every kid is entitled to the best we can give and, in particular, access to quality teaching to get the best outcomes'.

Initially adopting what was described as a 'commanding style of leadership blended with strong consultation', this principal then worked through this guiding belief, starting with the leadership team. Unlike some schools where significant turnover occurs with a change of leader at the top, the leadership team at Braybrook remained intact and was supported to embrace and espouse this vision as they took it out to the rest of the staff. This is not to suggest there were not 'resistors' in the college, but rather that it was able to build sufficient critical mass for the notion, as one leader simply put it, that 'it's essentially the kids first, get the pedagogy right, and how can we help you to do that?'

Leadership, it should be noted in this context, is widely distributed, and there are conscious and focused efforts to build the capacity of the 17-member leadership team. More specifically, the college has developed its own, 'homegrown' leadership development program [that] includes lots of tools that individual leaders use with their teams, as well as feedback to the leaders themselves to inform their own professional and personal improvement over time.

The leadership team meets fortnightly for 90 minutes where it generally spends the first half hour on some theory and analysis of what's going on around it, the second thirty minutes in focused discussion on an issue of importance to the college. The remainder of the time is spent sharing intelligence on things that are happening within the college, in part drawn from the connections that team leaders have with other members of staff through ongoing mentoring roles.

In effect, the college has sought to develop its leading teachers as leaders who promote the vision and priorities of the school, reflecting the belief of the three principal class members that, to keep the school strong, it is necessary to build the capacity of its middle-level leaders, and hence the effectiveness of their teams.

High expectations and demands

Implicit in the espoused vision of the college are high expectations for what students should do and achieve.

Having had what was described as a 'poor' approach to teaching and learning, whereby the quality of teaching depended on the individual teacher, the college learned it had to be clear about its mapping and sequencing of work to ensure it is coherent within and across the years, and prepares students for the Victorian Certificate of Education (VCE).

Continued...

This in turn led to a more structured set of learning experiences through which the students all progress, and which teachers and students know in advance. It also is reflected in whole-school programs the college has chosen to adopt to meet students' specific learning needs, such as the Drop Everything and Read program aimed at improving literacy in Years 7 and 8.

The shift in emphasis described represents, what one leader typically referred to as, 'a culture shift from a welfare school to one that still values welfare, but strives for academic excellence as well'. Previously, this interviewee felt that they 'shielded kids and sought to keep them happy, but without challenging them to really achieve'. By contrast, all now feel the expectations are high and they 'have structures and supports to help the kids achieve'. In other words, the oft-expressed belief that 'you can't expect more of these kids' is severely challenged in this school.

Getting the preconditions in place

For all the leaders interviewed, the precondition for achieving the learning culture that now exists was a concerted effort by successive school principals and other key leaders, which has been sustained for almost 20 years, to ensure an orderly learning environment in the school.

'You can't teach unless the kids are sitting, orderly, willing to listen, to work and to learn'. That, according to all who were interviewed, is the mantra of the school, which continually is reinforced.

While a conscious effort is made to get the 'right' teachers with the students, the primary focus is on what one leader described as 'creating coherent structures where kids feel comfortable and teachers can manage them'. A clear expectation exists in this context that students are always on time and equipped for their work, with a set of consequences that are known in advance. These rules are consistently applied, in part because the teachers wanted them in the first place to contribute to a better-functioning school.

There is little doubt in the minds of all leaders interviewed that discipline and order is one of the key reasons for the college's success. It is mixed with a strong sense of caring, most clearly enacted in the way that year level coordinators move through the school with their students to ensure they all are well known.

Teachers are very clear in the direction and processes to be pursued, and there are clear protocols and procedures that everyone knows. The result is a very stable environment, where there are clear expectations, a great deal of consistency and a strong sense of connection, which has generated a positive image within the community to the point where Braybrook College is the community's secondary school of choice.

Building on this base

Having initially focused heavily on order in the classroom and through the school, Braybrook College now is really working to improve the curriculum, pedagogy and assessment it provides, along with professional learning that underpins success in this regard.

There is an awareness in this context, however, that teachers often become overwhelmed if too much change is pursued. Thus, the college only introduces change when it thinks, as one leader put it, the change is 'appropriate and relevant to our structure, rather than jumping on every bandwagon that comes along'. Key approaches, such as a focus on standards, the core subject structure and student management, are always maintained as the framework in which change then occurs.

It is hard then to disagree with the analysis of one key leader who observed that when it is all boiled down, Braybrook College is a school where 'you feel there is a leader, a direction, a structure, a chance to try new things provided you gain the support and have done the research, and, though we may not always agree, we really value the certainty'.

BUILDING BASELINE CAPACITY

Ensuring the preconditions for improvement are in place can only take schools so far. Inevitably they will hit a plateau of improvement if it is only the preconditions they address. This reflects the fact that although they are needed for the improvement journey to commence, they do not really ensure that teaching capacity is built and improved classroom practice results.

That is why the second stage of sustainably improving a school involves building the baseline capacity of teachers to plan more effective lessons and work together in ways that open up the classroom door.

We have learned much here from our involvement in the Achievement Improvement Zones project (AiZ) implemented across the whole of the (former) Northern Metropolitan Region in the state of Victoria[1], which saw significant improvements in the educational outcomes for the region compared to other regions in the state. Suffice to say, the improvement was such that the region became something of a role model for improvement in other regions and schools, and was subject to detailed analysis in *Powerful learning: A strategy for systemic educational improvement* edited by Hopkins, Munro and Craig (2011).

Core to the AiZ, and the better student outcomes it generated in schools, was the use of an instructional model to support teacher planning and coaching in professional learning teams (PLTs) to open the classroom door; each of which is explored in detail in Chapter 6. Hume Central Secondary College provides an interesting case study of a school that fitted firmly in Stage 2 of Figure 4.1 and, as will be seen from the case study in Box 4.2, was moving to Stage 3.

Box 4.2
Building on the preconditions at Hume Central Secondary College

Strong leadership was key

Hume Central Secondary College, located in the City of Broadmeadows, is a three-campus, coeducational college established in 2009 out of the Broadmeadows Schools Regeneration Project, which merged the former Hillcrest, Broadmeadows and Erinbank Secondary Colleges into a single entity.

According to the My School Website[2], 75% of College enrolments are in the bottom quarter of the Index of Community Socio-Economic Advantage, compared with 25% for Australia as a whole, while only 1% are in the top quarter again compared with 25%. The same site reports that in 2015, 75% of students at the College came from a language background other than English.

Beyond this, the City of Broadmeadows, according to the Brotherhood of St Lawrence (2016), was one of the top 20 youth unemployment 'hotspots' in Australia with a rate at the start of 2016 of 16%. This constitutes a significant challenge to the College and the students it enrols.

The College vision in this context is 'to develop and encourage in our students a love of lifelong learning while equipping them with the skills and qualifications and personal attributes they need for a purposeful and fulfilling life beyond school'. The vision is given real

Continued...

---

[1] In 2012, the Northern Metropolitan and Loddon Mallee Regions were merged to form the North Western Victoria Region.
[2] www.myschool.edu.au

life through the College mantra cited earlier of 'two years learning in one', which challenges teachers to really improve student learning outcomes across the College, and highlights the need for a differentiated teaching and learning approach built on a consistent model of what good teaching actually means. It is something that the College leaders, in particular, continually return to as the compass for all College work.

Consistent with this vision and mantra, the College has sought over the last four years to build a comprehensive strategic approach to whole-school improvement and change, predicated on ensuring the preconditions for improvement are in place across each of the College campuses.

So clear is the focus in this regard that the College even prepared regular audits of progress against the preconditions, which were shared with the broader school community and staff. And central to achieving all this, has been a relentless effort to build the capacity of the College leaders and staff.

The College has comprehensive strategic and annual implementation plans that are supported by detailed, rigorous action plans for leaders and teachers that ensure that the high expectations for students flow through to the staff, and an impressive array of documentation that supports improved performance throughout the College. Central to this is a 'Roadmap for 2 in 1' depicting how classroom learning plans will be enhanced through a focused set of whole-school activities related to:

- implementing an orderly learning environment
- improving attendance
- building a coaching culture through the school
- implementing an explicit instructional model within the College along with guided reading for targeted ability groups
- leveraging off the literacy and numeracy approaches promoted through the Achievement Improvement Zones project
- adopting a whole-school satisfactory completion policy
- developing whole-school teaching, learning and assessment approaches through Curriculum Development Teams.

The College's explicit instruction model has been particularly important in this regard, since it supports teachers to adopt a common lesson planning approach based on what has been proven in practice to work. This in turn supports peer observations of classroom practice, through triads the school established, and from 2011 on the expectation that peer coaching, which is part of all job descriptions in the school, will include around 15 observations a year.

Use of the model in classes throughout the College is underpinned by the systematic use of data to enable teachers both to know their students well and to know what and how to teach. Data is used to inform meetings of the leadership team, including data that illustrates how each student has performed in relation to NAPLAN and other tests and analyses of how different students performed against expected levels in the VCE. Data is also used to identify and target students who are especially at risk due to poor attendance at school and thereby enable the teachers responsible for these students to develop an appropriate response.

All staff are involved in developing and shaping the curriculum through Curriculum Design Teams that meet twice a week after school and bring together teachers from each learning area on one common site. These teams are primarily charged with the task of building teacher capacity for the differentiated teaching that is needed to ensure two years of achievement in one. The teams also develop common assessment tasks for use across the College and ensure a common understanding of what satisfactory completion means so that high expectations are applied by all teachers in the College.

> Coaching, as outlined earlier in Chapter 3, is central to the role of leaders and teachers in the College. The College increased the number of teaching and learning coaches in literacy and numeracy whose work initially focused on Year 7 to then progressively flow through the College. Beyond this, all members of the leadership team were trained in coaching techniques, and work with their teams on instituting the behaviours that have been identified as leading to better teaching and learning for students at Hume. They also model the peer observation approach that teachers use by going into each other's classes to observe their teaching and provide feedback using the explicit teaching model the College chose to adopt.
>
> It is an approach that reflects an underlying belief that 'nothing changes unless behaviours change', which first requires leaders to change the behaviours they use, and hence model it to others in the College. Professional reading has an important part to play in this regard, and leaders are periodically provided with practical books and articles that provide the tools, the resilience and the confidence to act in ways that will make a difference to the College as a whole.

DRILLING DOWN INTO CLASSROOM PRACTICE

Building capacity along these lines can help transcend the improvement plateau that is reached if only the preconditions are addressed. However, another plateau inevitably awaits that can only be breached by systematically working to improve the quality of teaching, and hence learning in all classes in the school.

This involves drawing on theories of action, discussed in detail in Chapter 7, that are aligned to research and enable more teachers to work like the best teachers in the school, thereby ensuring that high-quality teaching occurs more consistently throughout the school.

Such theories of action provide a means by which schools and teachers can systematically examine their practice, and then collectively work to ensure it is improved. This is particularly the case when they are linked to regular classroom observation where constructive feedback is provided to enable the research-based improvements to be made.

There is arguably less systematic practice on which to draw in relation to Stage 3 where schools drill down into practice using the theories of action, though there is a growing number of schools where important initiatives similar to these have been introduced.

One that is particularly interesting is Dandenong North Primary School, which not only was one of the group of high-disadvantage, high-performing schools cited earlier, but which also subsequently was featured by the Australian Institute of Teaching and School Leadership (AITSL) for the positive professional learning culture it has forged. Some of the initiatives that were underway at Dandenong North are outlined in Box 4.3 as indicators of action that are relevant to moving towards sustained excellence in Stage 3.

> **Box 4.3**
>
> ## Ensuring continuous improvement at Dandenong North Primary School[3]
>
> The school long recognised the need to help teachers to improve their performance, with classroom observation as a central plank, and has worked to develop its approach for more than 15 years.
>
> In the first instance, the school established a small observation room with a two-way mirror in a larger classroom to enable volunteer teachers to watch each other teach. So positive and valued was the experience that it quickly spread, with the result that teachers at Dandenong North now regularly observe each other's classes and visit one another without a second thought. Teachers, and for that matter students, are sufficiently comfortable with the presence of others, that for some time now, the principal has been capturing snippets of classroom practice on video to demonstrate effective teaching techniques for sharing with all of the staff.
>
> The school's approach to performance and development builds on the culture of observation it developed, and includes a mix of oral feedback from mentors, peers and students who observe the teacher in class, followed by formal written feedback from either school leaders or mentors. Assessments of teacher professional growth are 'triangulated' using both a 50-item self-assessment 'snapshot' and an individual and collective efficacy assessment tool developed by the school, along with a broader global assessment of classroom performance, using the categories unsatisfactory, good, very good and outstanding. The positive effect of classroom observation and feedback on teacher performance is such that all teachers within the school have now been judged as very good or above.
>
> This whole approach, in turn, is linked to the development of a teacher performance plan using a pro forma the school devised. A particularly noteworthy feature of the pro forma is the inclusion of an 'aspirational plan for achieving continuous performance improvement in the literacy and/or numeracy goals' as outlined in the school's strategic and annual implementation plans.
>
> Welded on to this approach is a growing focus within the school on coaching for individual and collective efficacy so performance is spurred by the realisation that we together can make a difference for the students we teach.
>
> The school has progressively been training all leaders and teachers how to coach others with whom they work, and mutual coaching in teams increasingly sits alongside the classroom observation as the key means for generating improvement in the school. In this way, it has truly established a culture where teachers do expect to observe and be observed, and to provide each other with constructive feedback to ensure that the quality of teaching is continually improved. The school has further bolstered this by using a structured survey to gain student feedback, that then informs professional discussions in teams and the strategies that teachers use.
>
> The school has worked to determine a measure of efficacy it is fully comfortable with, starting with an innovative approach it used to promote discussion among the staff. This involved asking the staff to line themselves up along an efficacy continuum, which was then recorded to monitor shifts from one year to the next.

---

[3] Some of the material in this vignette has been extracted and adapted from a case study Vic Zbar prepared for AITSL on the school, which is accompanied by a video clip that can be viewed at https://www.youtube.com/watch?v=QkKMVLu3TJM

This focus on building a strong professional learning culture in the school underpins a conscious focus on using research-based practices to improve the quality of teachers' work. For example, a few years ago a school project team tackled the theory of action that assessment for learning contributes to better student learning. They did this by developing statements of what students ought to be able to do at different levels of numeracy performance, in student-friendly language that supported teacher-student discussion about the standards and helped students to take more responsibility for their own learning and work.[4]

This in turn further lifted the expectations of students that the teachers had, and hence positively impacted on the learning intentions they devised and the level of challenge for students that was set.

It serves as a good reminder of the way in which tackling one theory of action in a school almost inevitably leads to others also being addressed.

Beyond this, it is worth noting that the school's leadership team has for several years regularly worked with one or more critical friends (including Vic) to bring an independent, research-based eye to their work, and willingly shares its experiences as a high-performing school with others, thereby contributing to broader systemic improvement as well.

A SELF-ASSESSMENT ACTIVITY FOR LEADERSHIP TEAMS: DETERMINING THE STAGE OF IMPROVEMENT OF YOUR SCHOOL

This activity is designed to enable leadership teams to determine where their school is up to in its improvement journey to inform the key strategies it chooses to adopt. It has been used by many schools since its inclusion in the first edition of this book, and has proven successful in guiding leadership thinking and action to consistently improve the school.

The activity is not designed so much to make a judgment but to inform a conversation among members of the team and subsequent action as a result. It is recommended that leaders individually complete the checklist before discussing it as a team to ensure all views are considered.

While leadership underpins all of the stages (see Figure 4.1), it is included in Stage 1 for this activity to reflect the fact that a functioning leadership team is required for any whole-school improvement to occur.

It is recommended that you start the activity with the checklist for Stage 1 (Table 4.1) and work your way through, rather than make assumptions about the stage you think the school is in. Once you have identified the appropriate stage, there is no need to complete the other checklist(s) (Tables 4.2 and 4.3) until the team feels it is ready to move there.

Instructions
Fill in the checklists below using a four-point scale where:
1 = Not evident, 2 = Sometimes evident, 3 = Often evident and 4 = Always evident.

---

[4] It is worth noting, that the team subsequently wrote the experience up to share with leaders and teachers in other schools—See Colaci, Saraikin & Hilton (2013). A sample of their work is provided in Chapter 7.

TABLE 4.1: STAGE 1: GETTING THE PRECONDITIONS FOR WHOLE-SCHOOL IMPROVEMENT IN PLACE

Features of the stage	You know it when you see	Rating (1–4)	Evidence for your rating
Strong leadership that is shared	• A clear vision and direction for the school • Passion and commitment • Improvement focused leadership • A culture of learning and collaboration for students and staff to establish the conditions for high-quality teaching • A cohesive and effective leadership team • A team that is willing and able to build and spread leadership		
High levels of expectation and efficacy (staff and students)	• High expectations of students—challenge the argument 'you cannot expect more from these kids' • Higher aims and targets than matching equivalent schools, characterised by medium to high levels for all students in the school • High expectations of staff and a shared belief 'we can make a difference to the students we teach' • Programs designed to ensure all students are challenged to improve learning outcomes		
Ensuring an orderly and supportive learning environment	• Clearly documented expectations and processes for student wellbeing, behaviour and discipline • Consistent implementation of these by teachers to ensure an orderly and supportive learning environment • Structures to ensure that students are well known by the staff • Encouragement of student involvement and opportunities for student voice		
A focus on what matters most	• Relatively few priorities focused on core strategies for improvement • A clear sense of how to prioritise and put first things first • Resources are directed to the priorities		

Interpreting your score

To obtain your score, tally the rating scores you provided for each feature and find your score below:

4 to 8 You have significant further work to do to ensure the preconditions are in place for whole-school improvement to take hold. Your work will tend to focus on building the effectiveness of your leadership team as it strives to ensure an orderly learning environment is in place where students are known by the staff. This in turn will help to raise expectations in the school.

9 to 12 You are progressively getting the preconditions in place and, provided you maintain the focus, can begin to work on building teaching and learning effectiveness in the school as you transition to Stage 2.

13 to 16 The preconditions for whole-school improvement are firmly in place in the school. While this is work that is never done, your focus will shift to building capacity and ensuring effective teaching and learning practices consistently apply across the school.

© Pamela Macklin and Vic Zbar, *Driving School Improvement*, Australian Council for Educational Research, 2017

TABLE 4.2: STAGE 2: BUILDING TEACHING CAPACITY THROUGHOUT THE SCHOOL

Features of the stage	You know it when you see	Rating (1–4)	Evidence for your rating
There is a shared view of effective teaching	• Whole-school discussion and agreement on what effective teachers do • The agreed view of effective teaching used to inform teacher planning and delivery in all classrooms		
An instructional model is used to guide teacher planning of lessons	• The agreed view of effective teaching codified into a whole-school instructional model • The instructional model shared and displayed throughout the school • Teachers using the instructional model to plan more effective lessons individually and in teams		
Structures are in place to support collaborative planning	• Teachers participating in structured professional learning teams • Regular meetings of professional learning teams that are privileged in the school's meeting schedule		
The focus of planning is improved lessons in all classrooms	• Professional learning team meeting agendas centred on collaboratively planning more effective lessons • Feedback on lessons that have been delivered so they can be improved in future		

Interpreting your score

To obtain your score, tally the rating scores you provided for each feature and find your score below:

4 to 8 You need to develop a shared sense of more effective teaching to underpin the design and use of an instructional model that is used by teachers individually and in their teams to ensure the planning and delivery of consistently more effective lessons throughout the school.

9 to 12 Your lesson planning is based on an agreed view of what constitutes more effective teaching and the challenge is to drive this consistently through the school. You can begin to use this to drill down into the repertoire of strategies that teachers use in class as you transition into Stage 3.

13 to 16 Your instructional model is underpinned by a shared view of more effective teaching and collaborative planning in teams ensures it is consistently used throughout the school. You can really focus on ensuring that evidence-based approaches are used to generate better student learning outcomes.

© Pamela Macklin and Vic Zbar, *Driving School Improvement*, Australian Council for Educational Research, 2017

TABLE 4.3: STAGE 3: DRILLING DOWN TO IMPROVE CLASSROOM PRACTICE

Features of the stage	You know it when you see	Rating (1–4)	Evidence for your rating
Data and evidence are used to inform teaching	• Data gathered on student learning and progress towards learning goals • Reteaching as needed in response to the data on student progress		
Learning goals provide the focus for all lesson planning and delivery	• Learning goals used to frame success criteria, teaching and learning activities, assessments, questioning and feedback in class • Students engaged in assessing their own progress towards achieving the learning goals		
Feedback is used to inform teaching and improve student outcomes	• Mechanisms in place to gain student feedback on their own learning and participation in class • Teaching adjusted as needed in response to student feedback • Formal and informal feedback to students on strengths, weaknesses and ways in which they can improve if they are to achieve the learning goals • Regular feedback to teachers which informs their overall approach		
Lessons are differentiated to meet the full range of student needs	• Content, processes, products and/or the learning environment appropriately differentiated to enable all students to achieve the common learning goal • A strategic approach to grouping students to ensure all participate effectively and experience success in the class		

Interpreting your score

To obtain your score, tally the rating scores you provided for each feature and find your score below:

4 to 8 You need to develop a stronger focus on evidence-based teaching practices and how to apply them consistently in classrooms across the school. Using learning goals to structure the planning of more effective lessons can provide a key strategy to use in this regard.

9 to 12 A range of proven, effective teaching practices are being driven through the school and your challenge now is to ensure they are used by all teachers as appropriate to their classes at the time.

13 to 16 Your school is strongly focused on ensuring consistently more effective teaching and learning in all its classes. You may have strategies and processes to share with other schools as part of your contribution to supporting more schools and teachers to work like the best.

© Pamela Macklin and Vic Zbar, *Driving School Improvement*, Australian Council for Educational Research, 2017

CHAPTER 5
STAGE 1: THE PRECONDITIONS

During 2008, Vic, along with his colleagues Ross Kimber and Graham Marshall, undertook a major research project for the Victorian Department of Education and Early Childhood Development (DEECD) to identify the secrets behind the success of eight high-performing, disadvantaged government schools (Zbar, Kimber & Marshall, 2008). The report they wrote not only was included on a number of DEECD websites but was summarised in the Centre for Strategic Education Paper, *Schools that achieve extraordinary success: How some disadvantaged Victorian schools 'punch above their weight'* (Zbar, Kimber & Marshall, 2009).

As noted in Chapter 4, the lessons they identified from the study schools resonated with the sorts of factors commonly identified as being associated with effective and/or improving schools. What did emerge as new, however, and seems to have subsequently struck a chord in many jurisdictions and schools, was the distinction they found between those lessons that constitute the preconditions for substantial improvement to occur (and arguably provide a place for the school and/or system to start) and other lessons that then enable the school to build on these preconditions and sustain improvement over time.

This is not to suggest that the lessons they identified are entirely separate and discrete. They all inevitably overlap and interact as leaders and teachers work in an holistic way to continuously improve their schools. However, it is to suggest, based on the experience of these high performing schools, that the foundations must be in place before a whole-school program of improvement can be built.

This contrasts with much of the effectiveness and improvement research that stops at listing the factors associated with an effective school, with the result being that schools can be left wanting in terms of determining exactly how to improve, or even where to begin.

The value of distinguishing between the two different sorts of lessons outlined, is that it provides schools with a theory of action they can pursue based on an analysis of how a critical mass of high performing schools progressively transformed themselves over time. In other words, it provides the basis of a strategic approach to improvement, as illustrated in Figure 5.1, that can be replicated across schools.

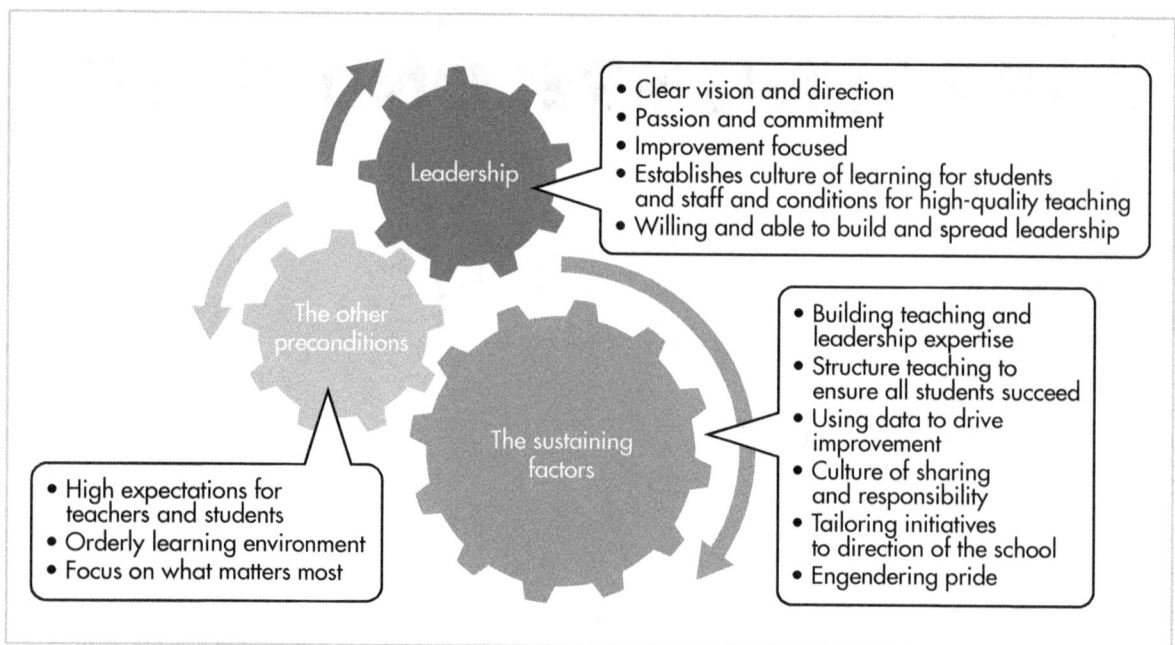

FIGURE 5.1: THE HIGH-PERFORMING SCHOOLS ROADMAP

Note: This diagram was jointly developed by Ross Kimber and Vic Zbar.

OVERVIEW OF THE FOUR PRECONDITIONS

Four preconditions for whole-school improvement to take hold were identified through the Zbar, Kimber and Marshall research mentioned above.

PRECONDITION 1: STRONG LEADERSHIP THAT IS SHARED

There is a need for strong leadership with a clear vision and direction for the school and a high degree of leadership stability over time. Central to this is a principal with a passion to lead and make a difference in the interests of students in the school, and one who is also willing to build and spread leadership throughout the school. In general, the principal initially focuses their efforts on building the leadership team and ensuring they all act according to a common vision and shared views.

Put simply, a principal and leadership team that knows how to use the resources and expertise available to them in ways that maximise the outcomes students can achieve is a key determinant of the success of the school and, in particular, the extent to which teachers can deliver high-quality teaching to each and every class. Instances of good teaching undoubtedly exist in schools where the quality of leadership is weak, but high-quality leadership is a prerequisite for this to be spread throughout the school.

In a very real sense, leadership is so central to school performance and improvement, that it almost amounts to a precondition for the preconditions, and hence constitutes the place where schools must start if significant advances are to be achieved. That also means that in cases where a requisite degree of leadership capacity does not exist in a school, then systemic intervention, such as coaching or mentoring support, may be required to ensure it is in place.

PRECONDITION 2: HIGH LEVELS OF EXPECTATION AND TEACHER EFFICACY

Improvement is predicated on having and promoting high expectations for all the students the school enrols and, in particular, challenging the belief that 'you can't expect more of these kids'.

This then is made manifest by setting higher aims and targets than simply matching equivalent schools, which often just condemns students to fall further behind their higher performing peers rather than narrowing the performance gap.

High expectations for students in turn can be used to build a feeling among staff that they have the capacity to make a difference for the students they teach. This is important, because teachers' beliefs and understandings about their professional efficacy, combined with a belief that virtually every student can learn given the right support and pace of instruction, has been demonstrated to make a difference to how the teacher, and hence their students, actually performs. Jerald (2007), for instance, found that teachers with strong perceptions of efficacy put more effort into planning lessons, are more open to new ideas and persevere in the face of new challenges. What is particularly promising about this research, however, is that efficacy perceptions are not immutable, and hence are open to the actions of school leadership teams.

PRECONDITION 3: ENSURING AN ORDERLY LEARNING ENVIRONMENT WHERE STUDENTS ARE WELL KNOWN

The existence of an orderly learning environment throughout the school—established through positive rather than negative means, whereby there are high levels of teacher consistency about how it is 'enforced' and structures in place to ensure that all students are known well by at least one adult in the school—is a fundamental precondition for improved teaching and learning to occur on which the subsequent improvement in student learning outcomes can be based.

It is interesting to note in this context that the absence of an orderly learning environment is usually the first thing noticed in an under-performing school, and the major impediment to improvement and change. And the establishment of such an environment, and the consistency of staff behaviour on which it depends, is commonly the key initial strategy for the leadership team in turning the school around. Aside from the fact you cannot have effective teaching and learning in a disorderly classroom or school, developing an orderly learning environment also provides a mechanism for getting teachers working more consistently and towards a common end. That in turn creates the basis for further united action within the school, particularly to the extent it is linked to knowing the students well, and hence developing a more personalised teaching and learning approach to ensure their needs are met.

PRECONDITION 4: A FOCUS ON WHAT MATTERS MOST

If a school is to seriously improve, then it needs to have relatively few priorities that are focused on the core things students need, which in turn constitute the basis for the resource decisions the school makes, such as the way in which staff are allocated and used.

Beyond just limiting priorities to what matters most, schools need to have a very clear sense of where to start and focus their energies on what the management literature calls 'putting first things first'. The point here is as much about the fact the school does prioritise and shape its allocation of energy and resources accordingly, as the nature of the priorities that are set. This in part reflects the premium placed on leadership as outlined in precondition one, since focusing on what matters most requires the leadership capacity to weigh up the current situation in the school, know where the school needs to head and know what is needed to get it there, and then clearly identify the entry point for commencing the improvement journey and associated incremental steps that need to be taken along the way. Focusing effort on what matters most is central to the strategic planning of any successful school, and hence should be a key focus of building leadership capacity throughout the school from the principal team down. It also brings the associated challenge of being prepared to abandon those activities that effectively have less 'bang for our buck', so the effort, resources and time they involve can instead be directed to higher leverage strategies that will genuinely improve the school.

ACTIVITY FOR SCHOOL STAFF: UNDERSTANDING THE PRECONDITIONS IN YOUR SCHOOL

Note: These activities were developed together with Ross Kimber and Graham Marshall and have been used extensively with principal networks and individual school staffs.

The following activity can help build understanding of the preconditions among the staff and the extent to which they are perceived to exist. This in turn can be used to determine the next steps to ensure the preconditions are firmly in place.

Instructions

1 Work in teams to complete Table 5.1. Then share your findings as a whole staff and compare them to the sample outline provided as Table 5.2.

2 You can take this a stage further still by using your completed table to rate where your school is at, using Table 5.3. Provide evidence for your ratings and, as a whole staff, begin to identify what you will need to do in order to move beyond where you currently agree you are at.

3 Fill in Table 5.3 using a four-point scale where:

1 = Not evident, 2 = Sometimes evident, 3 = Often evident and 4 = Always evident.

TABLE 5.1: THE PRECONDITIONS FOR SCHOOL IMPROVEMENT

Preconditions	The school will have this in place when we see
Strong leadership that is shared	
High levels of expectation and efficacy (staff and students)	
Ensuring an orderly and supportive learning environment	
A focus on what matters most	

© Vic Zbar, Ross Kimber and Graham Marshall, 2010

TABLE 5.2: THE PRECONDITIONS FOR SCHOOL IMPROVEMENT (SAMPLE OUTLINE)

Preconditions	Description
Strong leadership that is shared	<ul><li>A clear vision and direction for the school</li><li>Passion and commitment</li><li>Improvement focused leadership</li><li>A culture of learning and collaboration for students and staff to establish the conditions for high-quality teaching</li><li>A cohesive and effective leadership team</li><li>A team that is willing and able to build and spread leadership</li></ul>
High levels of expectation and efficacy (staff and students)	<ul><li>High expectations of students—challenge the argument 'you cannot expect more from these kids'</li><li>Higher aims and targets than matching equivalent schools characterised by medium to high levels for all students in the school</li><li>High expectations of staff—'we can make a difference for the students we teach'</li><li>Programs designed to ensure all students are challenged to improve learning outcomes</li></ul>
Ensuring an orderly and supportive learning environment	<ul><li>Clearly documented expectations and processes for student wellbeing, behaviour and discipline</li><li>Teacher consistency in implementing these and ensuring an orderly and supportive learning environment</li><li>School structures that ensure students are well known by the staff</li><li>Encouragement of student involvement and opportunities for student voice</li></ul>
A focus on what matters most	<ul><li>Relatively few priorities focused on core things students need</li><li>A clear sense of how to prioritise and put first things first</li><li>Resources are directed to the priorities</li></ul>

© Vic Zbar, Ross Kimber and Graham Marshall, 2010

TABLE 5.3: HOW DO WE RATE ON THE PRECONDITIONS?

Preconditions	Rating (1–4)	Evidence for your rating	Moving beyond (what needs to be done to ensure the precondition is fully met)
Strong leadership that is shared			
High levels of expectation and efficacy (staff and students)			
Ensuring an orderly and supportive learning environment			
A focus on what matters most			

© Vic Zbar, Ross Kimber and Graham Marshall, 2010

ACTIVITY FOR LEADERSHIP TEAMS: IMPROVING OUR RATINGS

Note: The set of questions is an extended version of one developed by Pamela that has been used to inform discussions with leadership teams in a range of schools, including Narre Warren South P–12 and Warracknabeal Secondary College in Victoria and middle schools in the Northern Territory.

Instructions
Use the following questions to guide a leadership team discussion on how to ensure the preconditions for whole-school improvement are consistently driven through your school.

Strong leadership that is shared

1 What have been the challenges to building strong leadership that is shared?
2 In what ways have we been successful in building strong leadership with a clear vision?
3 What would it take for us to raise our score to a 4 in this area?
4 What are the first two actions we should take as a leadership team to move towards achieving this?

High levels of expectation and teacher efficacy

1 What is the evidence that we have high expectations in our school?
2 Identify one area where expectations need to be raised immediately?
3 What does the leadership team need to do to ensure that expectations are raised consistently in this area? How would we measure success?
4 How could we further improve teachers' belief in their capacity to make a difference to student achievement?

Ensuring an orderly learning environment where students are well known

1 What have been our successes in creating an orderly learning environment?
2 What would we need to see across the whole school to give ourselves a score of 4?
3 How can we practically start working towards that now?
4 How likely is it that all students in the school would say yes to the statement, 'There is an adult in the school who knows and cares about me'? How do we make it more likely that their answer will be 'yes'?

A focus on what matters most

1 How well do we identify a few core priorities and focus on these? What are our core priorities?
2 What are the core things across the school that students need that we are not addressing?
3 What do we need to do to ensure that we are more consistently focused on what matters most for our students?
4 What do we need to abandon to strengthen this focus?

LEADERSHIP—THE PRECONDITION OF THE PRECONDITIONS

Leadership, as already noted, is the difference between the pockets of excellence that exist in any school and whole-school improvement. As Michael Fullan elegantly observed, 'I know of no improving school that doesn't have a principal who is good at leading improvement'(2001, p. 141). That is why leadership underpins all of the stages of whole-school improvement and pervades the whole of this book.

That said, we are addressing it here, as well as in the broader way already outlined in Chapter 3, because the absence of an effective, functioning leadership team will stop improvement before it even starts. It is, as we said, the precondition of the preconditions and in fact, the entire approach to improvement that your school adopts.

Leadership in this context is more than just the principal of the school, critical as that role is. It involves the development of a leadership team that spreads its influence through the school and involves as many staff, in meaningful leadership activity, as it can.

It is worth noting that many of today's schools are medium- to large-sized organisations that, in some cases, have a population to rival a small country town. In any such organisation, myriad relationships exist, which are beyond the capacity of any one person to manage. A simple algorithm of expanding relationships illustrates the point in Table 5.4.

TABLE 5.4: THE MATHS OF ORGANISATIONAL RELATIONSHIPS

Number of people	Number of potential relationships
2	1
4	6
10	45
20	190
30	435
100	4950

While things are never as neat and mathematical as this, it does demonstrate the complexity of managing relationships within a school of any size, and the consequent importance of engaging more staff in a range of leadership roles. In addition, leading in this way helps to reduce the vulnerability that any school has to the loss of a key member of the leadership team, since one or more ready-made replacements already exist. It's a case, as Fullan (2019) puts it, of individual leaders becoming 'more dispensable because the school has collaborative leaders who can carry on after the original leaders leave' (p. 31).

Of particular importance in this regard, is the development of strong and effective middle- as well as top-level leadership as the conduit from the principal team to the staff as a whole; especially since the maths precludes top-level leaders from effectively reaching all of the staff.

Middle-level leadership is commonly where the implementation of change for improvement breaks down; which is not a comment on the middle-level leaders themselves. Rather, it reflects the default way in which organisations operate when preparing for change. What generally happens is that the senior leadership gets energised and spends many hours crafting the vision and strategies for change, sometimes even going away for the task with an expensive consultant in tow. Having done so, they then go straight to a full staff meeting to sell what they have made.

The step that is missed is the engagement of middle-level leaders who have to make it happen through their teams. This is important in two respects. First, because these leaders are closer to the action and hence can signal where tweaking is required to ensure that the envisaged strategies will work. They can, for example, advise on the likely reaction of staff, or the range of supports they will need. Second, it is needed to ensure that all staff receive the same message, sense of urgency and support to drive the improvement through, which means that their leaders (the middle managers) must be engaged and prepared for how it all will unfold.

The importance of this is only magnified by Buck's finding that, although 'the evidence from a number of studies does show that senior leaders in organisations do have a significant effect on the effort made by staff, the single most influential factor determining discretionary effort in an individual member of staff is their relationship with and respect for their direct line manager' (Buck, n.d., para. 5). Which leads him to conclude that 'middle leaders really are the engine room of any school' (para. 6).

This strongly suggests that successfully pursuing improvement in the school depends on developing the sort of cohesive teams under the direction of their middle managers in which individual teachers will want to invest.

It is helpful in this context to understand the characteristics of effective teams so these can be nurtured and built as you engage in the process of leading improvement in the school.

ACTIVITY FOR LEADERSHIP TEAMS: IDENTIFYING THE CHARACTERISTICS OF AN EFFECTIVE TEAM

Instructions
1 Individually think of a time when a team you belonged to, or observed, worked really well. What were the factors that contributed to its effectiveness?
2 Work in pairs/threes to identify these factors and see if you can codify them into some characteristics to guide the work of your leadership team.
3 Compare this with the list of characteristics included in Box 5.1.
4 Discuss the key behaviours your team will need to change and/or adopt to be more effective in future.

Box 5.1
Characteristics of effective teams

A quick search of the internet will reveal many taxonomies of the characteristics of effective teams. While they all differ slightly, they all tend to have the following features of teams that work well in common.

Clear purpose and goals
The team agrees on where it is headed and its members are fully supportive of its goals.

Defined roles and responsibilities
Each team member understands their roles and responsibilities within the team and the school, and work is fairly distributed taking account of each member's skills and the contributions they can make.

Open and clear communication
There is effective communication within the team, built on active listening and vigorous discussion of ideas.

Active and balanced participation
All team members contribute to its deliberations without dominating discussion at any point. All views are welcomed and people feel confident in voicing their ideas. Leadership is shared depending on the circumstances, relevant expertise and the needs of the team.

A comfortable, relaxed and trusting atmosphere
Team discussions are conducted respectfully, in a relaxed, almost informal way free of obvious tensions or hidden agendas. Team members support and trust each other, invest in developing their relationships and have fun.

Constructive conflict
Disagreement is seen as a positive and is dealt with openly and constructively to achieve the best outcome for the team and the school.

Effective decision-making
Decisions are made based on carefully weighing up the pros and cons of each approach to deal with the issue at hand. It is not simply a matter of gaining a simple majority.

Acceptance of decisions
All team members accept and implement the agreed decisions of the team, regardless of the stance they took when the issue was discussed.

Highly organised
The team works efficiently and uses consistent procedures (e.g. agendas, minute keeping, follow-up protocols, etc.) to guide its operations.

Monitoring performance
The team has clear targets and regularly assesses its progress towards these, as well as any changes that may be required to ensure they can be met.

These characteristics can also be used to assess team effectiveness to supplement 'Getting a fix on the team' included earlier in Chapter 3.

ACTIVITY FOR LEADERSHIP TEAMS: ASSESSING OUR EFFECTIVENESS AS A TEAM

Instructions

Consider the following characteristics of an effective team in Table 5.5 and their accompanying explanation in Box 5.1 and rate your team on a four-point scale where:

1 = Does not characterise our team, 2 = Sometimes characterises our team, 3 = Often characterises our team and 4 = Almost always characterises our team.

TABLE 5.5: ASSESSING OUR EFFECTIVENESS AS A TEAM

Characteristic	Rating (1–4)
Clear purpose and goals	
Defined roles and responsibilities	
Open and clear communication	
Active and balanced participation	
A comfortable, relaxed and trusting atmosphere	
Constructive conflict	
Effective decision-making	
Acceptance of decisions	
Highly organised	
Monitoring performance	
Based on these ratings, the area we most need to develop to become a more effective leadership team is:	

© Pamela Macklin and Vic Zbar, *Driving School Improvement*, Australian Council for Educational Research, 2017

Developing positive characteristics for team effectiveness is best done in the context of leading the school. For teams focused on ensuring the preconditions for whole-school improvement are in place in Stage 1 of the school improvement continuum, this means raising the expectations of both students and staff, building an orderly learning environment where students are well known, and ensuring there are relatively few, high-order priorities that are pursued and implemented over time.

Before proceeding to examine these other preconditions in more detail, however, there may be value in the team looking beyond just the characteristics for effectiveness, to an evaluation of its own performance to date. Pamela has found the following discussion questions for the principal team and broader survey for leadership team members to each be useful in stimulating thinking about a team's current performance and how it can be improved; particularly when the team exhibits the characteristics for effectiveness outlined above.

ACTIVITY FOR PRINCIPAL TEAMS: EVALUATING OUR PERFORMANCE AS A TEAM

Instructions
As a team, consider and respond to the following questions:
- What do we do well as a leadership team?
- What have been our successes and disappointments?
- What would others say are our strengths and weaknesses?
- How could we be a more effective team?
- What are the priority areas where we need to put our focus and energy?
- What are the most critical aspects of effective teamwork that we need to get right in the coming months to achieve our goals?
- How can we work effectively with middle-level leaders to engage staff in working collaboratively towards our common goals?

ACTIVITY FOR LEADERSHIP TEAMS: SURVEY OF MEMBERS' GOALS AND PROFESSIONAL SUPPORT NEEDS

Note: Pamela has also used these as coaching questions that are completed confidentially by each member of the team and submitted to her to inform her work with individual leaders in schools.

Instructions
Team members, individually complete the following short survey related to your own contribution and performance in the team. Then collate the responses to inform a discussion about the professional learning needs of individual team members as well as the team as a whole.

Survey of members' goals and professional support needs

1 What are your key leadership strengths?
2 Thinking about your role and responsibilities this year, what are the major goals you would like to accomplish?
3 What will help you achieve these goals?
4 What might get in the way of you achieving these goals?
5 How will you work with colleagues at all levels to collaboratively achieve our whole-school goals?
6 What do you see as your major management challenges in carrying out your role and responsibilities this year?
7 What do you see as your major leadership challenges this year?
8 What kind of support would help you to meet your management and leadership challenges?

One effective way in which leaders can improve their leadership skills, and thereby contribute more effectively to the performance of the leadership team, is to look at others who have been successful, or even unsuccessful in the role and use this to inform the behaviours they adopt.

ACTIVITY FOR LEADERSHIP TEAMS: IDENTIFYING LEADERSHIP BEHAVIOURS TO ADOPT

Instructions

Consider and respond to the following questions:
- *Leadership behaviours that engage*—Think about leaders who engage and motivate you. What behaviours do they demonstrate in their demeanour and work that are engaging? Write these down and share them with a colleague. Decide on the three that you think are the most valuable.
- *Leadership behaviours that do not connect*—Now think of leaders whose behaviour fails to engage you. List these behaviours.
- *Leadership behaviours that make things happen*—Think of leaders who make things happen in the school. Describe their behaviours. Which of these behaviours are engaging and how? Which could you comfortably use?

You then need a really compelling message for why teachers should join you in your quest.

ACTIVITY FOR LEADERSHIP TEAMS: DEVELOPING A COMPELLING MESSAGE TO SUPPORT YOUR IMPROVEMENT EFFORTS

Note: This activity is adapted from one developed by our colleague Ross Kimber and is used with his permission.

Instructions

Consider the following scenario and respond to the challenge posed:

1 You are standing at the coffee station in the staff room and a colleague asks you, as a leader, 'What are we actually doing for the rest of the year, why and how?' You know that you only have about 60 seconds before they move on because their coffee has brewed. What are you going to say in the minute that you have? (This can be worked on individually or in pairs.)
2 Then try to refine this into a common message in the team for all of the teachers in your school.
3 What do you think that this teacher and other teachers you work with would say in response? And how would you answer them?
4 How can you get staff feedback on the message you have crafted so it really will resonate?
5 Finally, you need to make it easy for people to do. What can you do to make the implementation easier for the members of your team(s)?

HIGH EXPECTATIONS FOR STUDENTS AND STAFF

It is well known in education that a so-called 'Pygmalion' effect applies whereby the expectations that teachers have of students has an impact on the outcomes that they achieve.

Aside from the George Bernard Shaw play with that name, there is the influential study by Rosenthal and Jacobson (1963), effectively replicated by others since, which demonstrated the impact that teachers' expectations can have. More specifically, the study examined several Grade 1 to 6 classes that were given a nonverbal intelligence test that the researchers claimed would measure the students' potential for intellectual growth. Twenty per cent of the students were randomly selected and their teachers informed that these were the 'intellectual bloomers' in the class. When the students' IQ was tested later in the year, these students on average showed considerably greater gains during the school year than other students, particularly in the younger grades. They were also rated by their teachers as being more interesting, curious and happy, and generally more likely to experience success later in their lives.

The sting in the tail of the study was that the randomly-selected 'bloomers' were not more likely to experience success, and, in fact, were as likely to experience intellectual growth as any other student in the class. However, the fact the teachers thought they were, resulted in them making greater progress over the year. The different expectations the teachers held affected everything they did with these students compared with others they taught. They talked to them differently, using more challenging words. They posed different questions, provided different feedback and involved them in different ways. One group of students lived up to the higher expectations teachers had for them, and the others lived down to the lower expectations that applied to them. Interestingly, the same is arguably true of teachers who will either live up or down to the expectations that their leaders set.

Since expectations can constitute a self-fulfilling prophecy for many students, it not only is important to share this understanding with staff, but to evaluate their current expectations and then discuss whether they are sufficiently high.

ACTIVITY FOR STAFF: EXPECTATIONS OF STUDENTS IN OUR SCHOOL

It is suggested that the survey in this activity be conducted anonymously and the outcomes consolidated by the leadership team to inform a whole-staff discussion in the school.

The discussion can be given added value by focusing on the question, 'How do we communicate high expectations to our students and ensure they inform the work of all teachers in the school?'

An interesting exercise that teachers can also be invited to undertake every once in a while, is to consider Marzano's (2008) invitation to mentally review the students in their class they have high expectations for versus those for whom the expectations are low. Then most importantly, do they treat them any differently as a result?

Instructions
Individually rate each of the statements in Table 5.6 on a four-point scale where:
1 = Strongly disagree, 2 = Disagree, 3 = Agree and 4 = Strongly agree.

TABLE 5.6: EXPECTATIONS OF STUDENTS IN OUR SCHOOL

Individual assessment	Rating (1–4)	Collective assessment	Rating (1–4)
I believe that all students can learn with sufficient time and support		Staff in this school believe that all students can learn with sufficient time and support	
I set challenging goals for what my students will accomplish		Staff in this school set challenging goals for what students will accomplish	
I seek to convince my students that they can achieve these challenging goals		Staff in this school seek to convince students that they can achieve these challenging goals	
I promote the importance of hard work and effort for achieving challenging learning goals		Staff in this school promote the importance of hard work and effort for achieving challenging learning goals	
I take full responsibility for moving students towards achieving their challenging learning goals		Staff in this school take full responsibility for moving students towards achieving their challenging learning goals	
I always expect the most of my students		Staff in this school always expect the most of their students	
I encourage all students to strive to achieve their learning goals		Staff in this school encourage all students to strive to achieve their learning goals	
I differentiate appropriately for all students in the class		Staff in this school differentiate appropriately for all students in the class	
I provide appropriate opportunities for high- and low-achieving students to participate in class		Staff in this school provide appropriate opportunities for high- and low-achieving students to participate in class	
I pay high- and low-achieving students the same attention in class		Staff in this school pay high- and low-achieving students the same attention in class	

© Pamela Macklin and Vic Zbar, *Driving School Improvement*, Australian Council for Educational Research, 2017

In conducting this survey, we have commonly found a mismatch between individual teachers' ratings for themselves and those they give to other staff. Put simply, teachers tend to judge their own expectations as being higher, and sometimes significantly higher, than those of their colleagues, and hence the school.

Since many, if not most teachers are making this same judgment call, a fruitful conversation can be had around why this might be the case. This in turn can inform a whole-staff discussion about whether our expectations of students are sufficiently high and, most importantly, what we can now do to raise and communicate even higher expectations to all of the students we teach.

One question that does arise in this context is how you know high expectations when you see them, and hence, are our expectations high enough?

High expectations are not just a matter of what teachers say they believe, but what they actually do in class and more broadly through the school. High expectations are demonstrated to students in the learning goals and success criteria that teachers design, based on high standards in the curriculum, and the consequent instructional decisions they make.

Teachers with high expectations promote excellence in the form of challenging learning goals that they pursue relentlessly with their class. Schools with high expectations set ambitious targets for student achievement, along the lines of Hume Central Secondary College's 'two years learning in one', and structure the school to enable them to be achieved.

A good example of how high expectations for student engagement in challenging learning is promoted and sustained can be found in the daily assemblies at Auburn North Public School outlined in Box 5.2.

Box 5.2

Promoting effort and achievement at Auburn North Public School

Auburn North Public School in Western Sydney, like many schools, has a whole-school assembly each morning attended by a significant number of parents in the school.

Each time that Vic has worked with the school, he has been asked to come to the assembly first to present certificates to students that reward particular learning behaviours known to contribute to better student outcomes and results. The students come to the front of the assembly to receive their certificate and are encouraged to shake his hand and say, 'Thank you Mr Zbar'.

Vic is by no means the only presenter of such awards, which are given each day on a rotating basis to different grades within the school. The names of students receiving these awards, along with the reasons, are also printed in the fortnightly newsletter for parents in the school. Examples of the type of awards given at each year level are the certificates for:

Kindergarten
- Demonstrating excellent comprehension by retelling the stories she reads in great detail
- Trying her best to complete all learning activities
- Always working collaboratively and respectfully with her peers.

Year 1
- Being a role model to his peers by showing focus, enthusiasm and respect during all learning activities
- Reading a variety of stories with fluency and expression
- Always being kind and caring towards others.

Continued...

Year 2
- His diligent work in using arrays to share a collection of objects equally and with the correct amount of leftovers
- Trying her best to create a story map that included two animal characters who embarked on a journey in order to find a missing object
- Demonstrating high expectations through his consistently well-presented bookwork.

Year 3
- Taking a more active role during guided reading sessions
- Trying his best to achieve the success criteria in geography lessons
- Having a focused approach to improving his reading by enthusiastically participating in reading groups.

Year 4
- His excellent collaboration and communication skills when working in small groups during science and PDHPE
- Always clearly communicating her mathematical thinking during maths groups
- Demonstrating character and the value of respect at all times.

Year 5
- Beginning Term 3 with a diligent and focused approach towards her learning
- Demonstrating outstanding collaboration skills to make a simple circuit
- Consistently demonstrating the school values of respect and responsibility.

Year 6
- Her outstanding contribution and critical thinking skills during maths lessons
- Writing a well-structured, detailed information report about Auburn North Public School
- His improvement in attitude to learning and trying to achieve his learning goals in maths.

Good behaviour is also expected, recognised and rewarded at the assemblies through the granting of class points, for such practices as attentive listening and sitting up straight, that then can be redeemed for a small reward at the end of each week and a principal's morning tea when 60 commendations has been reached.

LEMOV'S FIVE CONCRETE STRATEGIES

Some particularly useful advice for communicating higher academic expectations in the classroom, which resonates with teachers every time we discuss it, is provided by Doug Lemov, in *Teach like a champion (2010)* and its follow-up, *Teach like a champion 2.0 (2015)*, books that have influenced practice in many Australian schools.

This advice depends, of course, on first having an orderly learning environment within the school as outlined below. Otherwise teachers are too busy battling order and discipline to focus on raising expectations for students in their class. Hence, there must be high expectations for student behaviour at school and consistent implementation of these by the staff.

With this precondition in place, Lemov describes five concrete, actionable ways in which teachers turn their high expectations into specific actions in class, which we have briefly summarised below.[1]

---

[1] A deeper understanding of these short summaries of the five actions can be gained not only from Lemov's books, but also through a wide range of video clips available via the *Teach like a champion* website, or online video portals.

No opt out

In any classroom, there are one or more students who have adopted a strategy that enables them to opt out of work. The strategy is that when a teacher asks them a question, they simply say 'I don't know'. After several 'I don't knows', what commonly happens is that the teacher stops asking them questions, with the result they have successfully opted out of work in this class. The strategy that Lemov proposes in response is, having probed a bit and determined that the student really doesn't know, the teacher should ask exactly the same question to another student who is likely to know the answer in this case. Having elicited the answer, the teacher should then return to the original student who said they did not know, and pose the same question again, with the expectation they will answer this time. The student may not understand the answer yet, and that is something for later work, but the teacher has clearly established that you must have a go in this class and cannot simply opt out. The teacher has also established the likelihood that this and some other students will now be more attentive in class, since a question that previously would have gone away, now might come back.

Right is right

Sometimes teachers accept from students answers that are not so much right, as half right, and then the teacher rounds the answer up to what it should have been. This particularly occurs when they get an answer from a student they are just happy to get an answer from. There are two significant problems with this. The first is that it sets a low bar on what constitutes a right answer in this class, and lowers the expectations as a result. The second is that, even though the teacher has rounded the answer up, as soon as they indicated it was 'right', regardless of what then was said, the student who gave the answer along with some others heard nothing after the 'right', and hence have an incomplete understanding of the point. Most importantly, though, it misses the teachable moment and the consequent strategy to adopt whereby the teacher might say, 'Mohammed has given an answer that is partly right, and I wonder if Bess could help us to make it completely right'.

Stretch it

The argument here is that correct answers to questions that teachers ask should be the trigger for more questions. Often they are not, and the teacher simply moves on to something else. Asking follow-up questions is an important strategy for differentiation since the questions can be tailored to where different students are at, and they can then be invited to explain their answers so that the whole of the class understands. The sorts of follow-up questions that teachers can ask include: 'Can you provide some evidence for what you just said?', 'Can you use a better word than …?', 'Why did you say that …?' and 'Can you link this to what we looked at yesterday when we …?'

Format matters

In the same way as teachers sometimes accept answers that are not so much right as half right and then round them up, so too will teachers accept product in a format that doesn't really meet high expectations for students, especially when it comes from someone who commonly does not submit any work. For example, a teacher may ignore regular references to 'youse' by a student in an oral presentation because they haven't really given one before. Once again it sets a low expectation for work in this class and is the sort of thing that will come to define the student as they progress through school and even more so into work. This is not to suggest the proverbial red pen should be drawn through every mistake the student makes, so much as to signal there are important grammatical and other formatting conventions that need to be met and eventually will harm the student if they are not.

Without apology

Sometimes what teachers will do is apologise for either the students themselves or the content they are about to teach. They apologise for the students when they say something like, 'I know you may find this difficult …'; in which case they almost certainly will. They apologise for the content when they say something like, 'You may find this boring, but we have to do it because …'; in which case it will be. The challenge of teaching is always to make it interesting and achievable with sufficient effort, time and support. We have heard of one primary school teacher who said that, 'these students cannot learn fractions and how to divide three by four'. It is hard to imagine having four of her students in a room with three chocolate bars only for them to give them back after 50 minutes saying, 'too hard, can't be done'.

It is important to emphasise at this point, consistent with our earlier advice in Chapter 2, that the enemy of effective change is when we take on too much. Schools we have worked with on this choose one or two of Lemov's strategies to introduce and drive consistently through the school. Having done so, they can then consider others, secure in the knowledge they are able to make it happen on a whole-school basis, rather than trying to do five things that are beyond the capacity of teachers to do at one time.

ACTIVITY FOR STAFF: IDENTIFYING STRATEGIES TO ENACT HIGH EXPECTATIONS IN CLASS

Instructions

Ask staff to consider the summary outline provided above of Lemov's five concrete strategies for communicating higher expectations in the classroom, or even better read the relevant chapter in his book, and then:

1 Work in small groups to share any successful strategies you have used to ensure high expectations in your classrooms.
2 Identify any of these that could constitute an adjunct to the five strategies Lemov has proposed.
3 Share the outcomes of the small group deliberations as a whole staff and identify one or two key strategies for communicating higher academic expectations that could be adopted and driven through the school, whether it be one of Lemov's or one of your own.
4 Consider how you will monitor the uptake of each strategy and know when it has become embedded.
5 How will you decide when to move on to the next high-impact strategy?

One issue that commonly emerges in this context, which is equally relevant to all of the strategies for improvement outlined in this book, is the lack of follow-through that often occurs, and subsequently detracts from the long-term sustainability of the approach. This is something that schools can address by ensuring that, in the case of implementing a Lemov strategy for example, they:

- agree on a timetable and specific actions to follow through and record these in a public action plan
- schedule follow-up on both the uptake and impact of these strategies in classrooms (e.g. by scheduling time in staff and/or team meetings for examples of evidence of teachers' work with students to be shared in order to determine the effectiveness of the approach)
- document the strategies in ways that are accessible to all of the staff
- reference the strategies in professional learning and all relevant forums and teams.

THE USE OF WAIT TIME

The five actions Lemov outlines are all examples of teaching tactics that have big impacts, with little or no cost. That said, they are far from easy to implement, requiring as they do that teachers are far more conscious about what they do in class and can monitor and adjust their own behaviours as required.

Another much-neglected, high-impact teaching tactic teachers can adopt is the use of 'wait time' after a question has been asked in class.

Vic will often ask in his workshops for participants to call out the answer to the following question if they feel they know it—'How long on average do you think teachers wait from the time they ask a question of a student in class and, having had no answer do one of three things: either ask the same student another question, ask the same question to another student, or answer the question themselves?' Most commonly he then hears two seconds, three seconds and five.

He then asks, 'How long did it take you from the time I asked that first question before you were prepared to venture an answer to it?' This is generally met by silence because of the deliberate complexity of the question he asked. People thought they either knew the answer to the first question or not, and called out accordingly. They had to think in order to make sense of the second question, thereby explaining the silence in the room.

Research conducted by Rowe (1986) at the Department of Childhood Education in the University of Florida, and replicated since, found that teachers typically only wait one second or less from the time they ask a question and get no answer to it, to the time they adopt one of the three actions included in Vic's first question above.

We think there are two reasons for this: one grounded in the research about questioning, and the other which is entirely our own view.

Research cited by Cotton (n.d.) shows that on average, 60% of the questions that teachers ask are seeking recall of things already taught, which requires a relatively speedy response. Twenty per cent of questions asked are procedural questions related to the running of the class, such as 'why are you doing that?', which expects quick compliance as a result. This means that only 20% of questions are higher order ones requiring more in-depth thought. If 80% of the questions asked expect virtually instant feedback, then a habit develops where the wait time is very short.

What also is relevant, in our view, is that most people, teachers included, are scared of silence because they don't know how it will be filled. If you doubt this, think back to a time recently when you attended a dinner party and all went quiet for a while. You almost certainly felt a bit uncomfortable, since everyone does, and someone was sufficiently uncomfortable to quickly fill the silence whether with comments relevant to what was being discussed or a new topic designed to get you talking again.

However, there are sizeable positive outcomes if we can learn to sit with the silence and give students more time to think. When Rowe and her colleagues worked with teachers to extend their wait time from one second to three they found that:
- a broader range of students volunteered answers and they were more likely to be correct
- student achievement on academic tests tended to increase
- teachers asked fewer and better questions and generally became more thoughtful about this key teaching technique
- reflecting the nature of questions asked, the length of answers given by advantaged students increased by around 500% and those of disadvantaged students by 700% from what were previously very short answers indeed.

Wait time is a particularly high-leverage strategy that sounds easy, but is quite hard to do. When Vic worked with the leadership team at the high-performing Serpell Primary School in the eastern suburbs of Melbourne some years ago and made them aware of this approach, they readily agreed to try it out. After two weeks, they acknowledged it was much harder than they thought. It requires learning to manage silence and the fear it may be filled in unproductive ways.

As an adjunct to this research, it is interesting to note that Stahl (1990) more recently advocated the concept of 'think' rather than 'wait' time because it names the primary academic purpose and activity of the recommended period of silence and points to other times where silence is valuable apart from just waiting for responses to a question that has been asked. 'Think time' in this context is defined as a distinct period of uninterrupted silence by the teacher and all students so that they can both complete appropriate information processing tasks, oral responses and actions. As such, it helps further reinforce the efforts that teachers can make to communicate high expectations to students in their class.

Pose, Pause, Pounce, Bounce is a no hands-up questioning strategy that makes effective use of wait time (refer to the the UK Teacher Toolkit at www.teachertoolkit.co.uk/2011/11/04/pose-pause-bounce-pounce/; McGill, 2019). The Principal of Richmond Secondary College, Dr Lars Andersson, in his previous role as Assistant Principal at Glen Waverley Secondary College, developed the example provided in Box 5.3 for staff in that school that can readily be adapted to other subjects and year levels in other schools.

Box 5.3

Pose, Pause, Pounce, Bounce in action: A secondary school example

1 **Pose** a question.
2 **Pause for reflection.** This is what in the research is called *wait time 1*. The average teacher waits for 0.9 seconds before allocating the question to the student. If you can extend that to 3 seconds, then all students will think more deeply about the topic. It also has a positive impact on behaviour and engagement in the classroom. A trick is to silently count to yourself ('one thousand and one,…').
3 **Pounce on a student.** If you randomly select which student to ask—for example by using icypole sticks with students' names—then students are unable to opt out of the learning. When that student has given their answer, *wait for another three seconds*. This is called *wait time 2*, and it has even more of an impact on student learning than wait time 1.
4 **Bounce the question on to another student.** Try to avoid positive or negative judgments about what the first student said. We're trying to avoid playing the 'guess what's in the teacher's head' game. Instead, give a neutral response ('hmm … interesting') or no response, instead bouncing the question on to another (randomly selected) student.

Here's what it might look like:
Teacher: So, what do you think Shakespeare is suggesting about the character in this line?
Teacher: [waits 3 seconds, then randomly chooses a name]
Teacher: … Jake?
Jake: I think he's suggesting that Macbeth is too greedy.
Teacher: [silence]
Jake: I mean, the language is very strong, and the imagery is showing someone who is really just thinking of himself.
Teacher: [silent for 3 seconds]
Teacher: I see … Do you agree with Jake's comment, or do you have a different view of this line?
Teacher: [waits, then randomly selects a name]
Teacher: … Julia?
Julia: Well, I don't really read it that way. I sort of get what Jake means, but I think Macbeth is really vulnerable in this scene.
Teacher: [waits 3 seconds]

Teacher: Okay, so Jake sees the character as greedy, but Julia thinks that Shakespeare reveals the character's vulnerability. So we have some interesting readings of this scene [etc.].

> Professional learning about the use of the approach was provided to learning specialists in the school to help promote the approach, supplemented by a video of Andersson demonstrating it in his own class. The specialists then practised and filmed themselves using it, to inform a team discussion and critique prior to introducing it to the staff, who were invited to observe the specialists modelling the approach.

The range of strategies outlined in this discussion of high expectations are an important accompaniment to the broader efforts a school can undertake to markedly improve the capacity and performance of its staff as discussed in more detail in the remaining chapters of this book.

AN ORDERLY LEARNING ENVIRONMENT WHERE STUDENTS ARE WELL KNOWN

A school can neither be effective nor improve if it does not have an orderly learning environment, since this is the foundation on which high-quality learning is built. This in turn depends on developing the sort of teacher–student relationships that ensure each student is connected to school and feels there is an adult in the school who knows and cares about them.

The starting point for developing an orderly and supportive learning environment is to seek and reach agreement about the school's overall approach.

This can commence with the values that schools commonly espouse. Staff can work to define the ways in which the agreed school values are reflected in behaviours and practices in the school, and then linked to clear expectations and rules they will commit to consistently uphold. Table 5.7 provides an illustration of how the common school value of 'tolerance, understanding and respect' might be reflected in practice throughout the school.

TABLE 5.7: USING THE SCHOOL'S VALUES TO ENSURE AN ORDERLY LEARNING ENVIRONMENT

Value	Reflected in ...			
	School practices	Curriculum programs/ activities	School rules	Consequences
Tolerance, understanding and respect	• Valuing each student and differentiating instruction as a result • Promoting the use of respectful and tolerant language in the school etc.	• Teaching about different cultures and histories and what can be learned from them • Team-based approaches to learning, problem-solving and the completion of tasks etc.	• Students must address teachers and each other respectfully and without abuse • Students will refrain from interrupting their teacher or other students in class etc.	• Counselling for a first offence • A formal meeting including parents where the student is expected to apologise and take responsibility for breaking the rule a second time etc.

ACTIVITY FOR STAFF: ENACTING THE VALUES OF OUR SCHOOL

Note: This activity was first included in Zbar, Kimber and Marshall (2010).

Instructions

1 Work together initially in teams, and then as a whole staff to complete Table 5.8, aligning the school's values to processes and practices that will contribute to the maintenance of an orderly learning environment in the school.

2 Once the table is completed and agreed upon, it can then be discussed with students and parents to gain their input along with any suggestions for how it can be improved. The mere fact of engaging them in this way not only helps bring them on board with the approach, but makes it more likely that the final matrix is something that all of the school community understands and is likely to support.

TABLE 5.8: LEARNING ENVIRONMENT/VALUES MATRIX

Our school values	Reflected in ...			
	School practices	Curriculum programs/ activities	School rules	Consequences
Value 1				
Value 2				
Value 3				
Value 4				

© Vic Zbar, Ross Kimber and Graham Marshall, 2010

THE 'GOOD STANDING' PROGRAM

An alternative to consider, or possibly even a complement to this approach, is the use of the 'Good Standing' program that has been implemented in a number of Australian schools. The program can be adapted to suit any school context, but in general terms encourages the development of such positive qualities in students as effort and hard work, punctuality, self-discipline and respecting the rights and responsibilities of others and themselves. Satisfactory attendance, punctuality, participation in learning and appropriate behaviour place students in 'Good Standing'. Loss of 'Good Standing' can result in students being refused permission to attend non-curricular events or access to rewards.

The notion of 'good standing' is outlined in a behaviour expectations matrix that the school collaboratively devises and then teachers consistently implement. By way of example, Darwin Middle School, which pioneered the use of 'Good Standing' in the Northern Territory after viewing it in Western Australia where it is widely used by schools, has developed a comprehensive matrix of expectations for different physical areas in the school as evidenced by the extract for classrooms provided as Table 5.9.

TABLE 5.9: EXTRACT FROM DARWIN MIDDLE SCHOOL'S BEHAVIOUR EXPECTATIONS MATRIX

Setting	Expectations			
	Respect for self	Respect for others	Respect for environment	Respect for learning
Classroom	• Attend all classes and be on time. • Enter classroom in an orderly manner. • Remain positive and put forth your best effort.	• Listen carefully to your teacher and follow their instructions. • Be courteous and respectful of others. • Use appropriate language and volume. • Be helpful and supportive of others. • Be respectful of other people's property.	• Keep classroom clean and organised. • Respect others' belongings by not touching anything that does not belong to you. • Respect the facility by not defacing desks, walls, etc. • Finish food and drinks before entering the hallways and classroom	• Attend all classes. • Be on time. • Put forth your best effort in class. • Bring all necessary equipment/resources. • Do your homework. • Ask questions when you are unsure. • Be responsible for the time you miss from class.

This matrix is supplemented by clear structures and processes the school has devised to ensure that students are 'caught' doing good things rather than bad, and acknowledged and ultimately rewarded for this. The school has established an Office of Good Standing where students take citations from teachers for positive behaviour to be logged, and which awards bronze, silver or gold certificates after a set number have been attained. The awarding of a gold certificate comes with a key ring for the student's parent to inform them of what has been achieved. While the office also logs negative behaviours, which can lead to time for the student in an adjacent 'reflection room', the school advises that it is rarely used, and positive affirmations outrun negative notices at least four to one.

In a somewhat similar vein, Auburn North Public School operates both a tiered cumulative awards program and a Gold Badge program that encourages students to 'do the right thing and be in the right place, at the right time'. The tiered award program gives students the opportunity to move from an entry-level of green to the highest level gold as a result of being awarded a requisite number of commendations for demonstrating the school values of Respect, Honesty, Fairness, Friendship, Responsibility, and Kindness. Through this program, students work towards achieving the highest level of reward, which is a morning tea with the principal, their parents and their teacher.

The Gold Badge program recognises students for their 'demonstrated citizenship, attendance and punctuality, wearing of uniform and consistent effort at school'. Gold Badges are presented to students at special assemblies, attended by their parents, twice a term. Gold Badges, which are worn throughout the year but which can also be lost, are awarded to students who meet criteria aligned to the school values. They are keenly sought by students and constitute an important incentive for good behaviour within and beyond class and are linked to periodic rewards such as morning teas, pizza parties and an annual movie excursion. Speaking to students reveals that the rewards themselves are not the motivators for good behaviour and effort in the school, but rather the 'icing on the cake' that accompanies the valued certificates and recognition they receive.

In addition, as indicated in Box 5.2, classroom and community language teachers nominate students each week to receive a principal's award at a morning assembly for either their academic, social, emotional, physical, creative or technological development and achievement, as well as the effort they have made. The school expects that all students should receive at least one award through the year, and Vic's experience in the school is that these are valued and appreciated by the students involved.

ACTIVITY FOR STAFF: CREATING YOUR OWN EXPECTATIONS MATRIX

Instructions

1 Taking account of the Darwin Middle School sample provided in Table 5.9 and the information provided on Auburn North, complete the following table (Table 5.10) for different areas in your school.
2 As was suggested from the previous activity—'Enacting the values of our school'—a subsequent discussion with students and parents will help to improve the matrix and gain greater commitment to it than otherwise might be the case.

A sample expectation from Darwin Middle School is provided in the first row for 'all settings' to get you started.

TABLE 5.10: CREATING YOUR OWN EXPECTATIONS MATRIX

Setting	Expectations			
	Respect for self	Respect for others	Respect for environment	Respect for learning
All settings	Dress appropriately in school uniform	Be courteous and respectful of others	Keep all facilities clean, place rubbish in the bins provided	Listen to and learn from others
Classroom				
Specialist rooms (e.g., computer lab)				
Hallways and front office				
Oval				
Canteen				
Toilets				
Bus				

© Pamela Macklin and Vic Zbar, *Driving School Improvement*, Australian Council for Educational Research, 2017

CONSISTENCY

The effectiveness of a values/behaviour matrix and/or good standing approach then depends on the consistency with which they are applied; especially since one of the defining differences between high- and low-performing schools is the degree of consistency that exists among the staff. The importance of consistency is readily evident in the experience that many a teacher has had where, on trying to implement an agreed school rule, a student tells them they are being unreasonable because another teacher down the corridor allows them to get away with the same thing. This not only undermines their authority in the class, but also sends a mixed message to students about the school's rules and what they really mean.

Gaining consistency, in part, comes from the process of involving teachers in the completion of the sort of pro formas included in the two preceding activities for staff. But it also depends on the quality and strength of leadership embodied in precondition one. In one of the Zbar, Kimber and Marshall study schools, for instance, lateness was a concern, and hence a priority for the leadership team. Having enlisted the formal agreement of staff to pursue it in a concerted way, the school's leaders became aware that some of the problem of lateness belonged with some members of staff. In response, the entire leadership team became highly visible throughout the school at the start of each period, ensuring students were on time to their class and, whenever a teacher was late, entering the classroom themselves both to settle the students for class and greet the teacher when they arrived. Suffice to say, it wasn't long before teacher lateness disappeared and flowed through to improved student punctuality as well.

While developing and maintaining high levels of consistency in the school requires an ongoing and relentless approach led by the leadership team, it can also be helped by some quick wins to build momentum from the start. These will often come from a highly visible symbolic problem the school has unsuccessfully sought to address, such as uniform, which is discussed in the Kambrya College experience outlined in Box 5.4. The turn-around of Kambrya College, which was the subject of the documentary *Revolution school* screened on the ABC in 2016, is outlined in detail in Zbar, Macklin, Muscat, Naidu and Wastle (2016). The approach outlined in Box 5.4 has subsequently been adopted by a number of other schools with which Pamela works.

Box 5.4

Driving the uniform policy through Kambrya College

School uniform was the initial entry point for action to ensure an orderly learning environment and build teacher consistency at Kambrya College, underpinned by the establishment of vertical sub-schools to ensure students were taught by stable teams of teachers who got to know them well.

Kambrya tackled the breakdown in implementing its uniform policy that prevailed in 2009 through a mix of improved documentation, procedures and a simple red bag. More specifically, the school, for some time, had a policy that prohibited the wearing of hoodies or facial piercings, but inconsistent application by teachers meant they remained rife in the school. Whenever the issue was discussed by the staff, it tended to stall at the point where individuals said they had no means of managing confiscated clothes, studs, rings and the like, and hence tended not to go down that path. Given this the school leadership, acting on the advice of its coach, decided to purchase sufficient red bags for every member of staff to serve as repositories for confiscated items during the day, revamped the administrative documentation required and established a set of procedures about how it was implemented across the school, such as when an item is confiscated, for how long and the consequences of each offence. Students and parents were advised before implementation commenced, and then all staff were expected to take the bags to class and enforce the rule that was agreed.

Apart from the symbolism of the bag as a means of enforcement, the obviousness of the colour red made it easier to ensure that staff complied with the expectation they had agreed. It only worked, however, because the principal team was out in the school reinforcing it each and every day. The principal and assistant principals would spend every morning confiscating items that infringed the uniform policy, weathering some very difficult conversations with belligerent students and parents, and regularly visiting home groups to support the sub-school leaders and double check that the policy was being driven through the school.

All of this activity contributed to maintaining the approach over time, rather than having a blitz that then disappeared, with the result that students, who Pamela interviewed as part of her coaching role in the school, acknowledged that things were 'different' this time. They pointed in particular to the fact that this 'crack-down' did not go away, and some even felt that it resulted in better behaviour in class; in part, perhaps because increased teacher consistency meant that individual teachers felt more empowered to implement behavioural expectations in each class, clear in the knowledge they would be supported by the principal team and not be undermined by what someone else did in their room. The school estimated that a compliance rate of 40 to 50% with the policy it espoused at the time grew to more like 90 to 95% because of the relentlessness with which it was pursued, and has only improved further since.

It's an approach the school was then able to leverage off to build consistency in other fields, most notably around the use of a common instructional model to inform teacher planning and the subsequent delivery of lessons across the school.

CLASSROOM RIGHTS AND RESPONSIBILITIES

Leveraging these quick wins and ensuring consistency of their implementation depends on clarity about the roles and responsibilities of different leaders and teachers in the school.

In Figure 5.2, the flow chart of roles and responsibilities for the management of student behaviour at Kambrya illustrates how the school was able to build on the success of its red bags quick win and further drive consistency through the school.

Role	Responsibilities
Teachers	• Manage Level 5, 4 and 3 behaviours in line with the Behaviour Management Policy (BMP) • Refer level 2, 1 and 0 behaviours to Assistant Sub School Leader (ASSL), Sub School Leader (SSL) and Assistant Principal (AP) as required • Maintain an orderly learning environment • Support Sub School (SS) detentions as per roster
Assistant Sub School Leader	• Investigate incidents relating to Level 1 and Level 0 behaviours and refer to SSL/Student Wellbeing • Manage Level 2 behaviours in line with BMP • Maintain and support an orderly learning environment • Maintain communication between relevant parties • Develop detention roster
Sub School Leader	• Manage Level 1 and Level 0 behaviours in line with the BMP and refer to AP and Student Wellbeing • Investigate Level 1 and 0 behaviours and make recommendations for suspension to Assistant Principal • Conduct suspension meetings • Maintain communication between relevant parties • Ensure orderly learning environment
Student Wellbeing Coordinator	• Make recommendations for alternative settings • Mandatory reports • Liaise with outside agencies as required • Referrals to Student Support Services Officer (SSSO)
Assistant Principal–Student Management	• Oversee implementation of Student Engagement Guidelines • Develop behaviour management processes • Accept recommendations for student suspensions • Parent and student complaints (liaise with Principal team as required) • Oversee alternative setting placements • Liaise with outside agencies as required • Policy development
Principal	• Expulsions • Policy development—Student engagement • Parent and student complaints

FIGURE 5.2: STUDENT MANAGEMENT ROLES AND RESPONSIBILITIES, KAMBRYA COLLEGE

Note: The flow chart has been adapted by the authors to spell out acronyms that are used in the original.

Greater clarity of roles and responsibilities enables the school to more effectively plan its student management and wellbeing policies and their implementation through the school. Table 5.11 provides an outline of how Lyndhurst Secondary College, in the south-eastern suburbs of Melbourne, used the clear lines of responsibility it had established to review its digital technologies policy in order to make it more effective and ensure its consistent implementation through the school.

TABLE 5.11: LYNDHURST SECONDARY COLLEGE DIGITAL TECHNOLOGY POLICY REVIEW

Task	Responsible party	Timeline	Status
Review the Digital Technology Policy Identify the current concerns with the policy: • Listening to music in class—educational research supports the view that this does not support students in their learning • Appropriate use of digital devices			
Seek feedback • From Leadership • From staff • From students—focus groups—at the same time as getting feedback from vision statement • From parents—random mail out			
Identify appropriate consequences for breach of policy and ensure these are clearly stated in the policy			
Make adjustments to the policy as a draft			
Send final draft to Leadership Executive for final feedback			
Once adjustments made—send final document to be approved by Executive			
Send final Digital Technology Policy to school council			
Implement the policy Communication of changes to the policy to: • Students • Staff • Parents • Website • In letter to families in January • Intranet page • Positive visual signs in each Learning Environment (e.g. learning requires listening)			
Monitor the implementation of the policy			

Note: The responsible parties and timelines have been deleted since they are specific to the school. A similar planning approach was used to develop and/or review the detention and uniform policies implemented in the school.

The existence of an orderly environment in schools is not limited to corridors and playgrounds, and extends to classrooms as well. That is why we consistently refer to it as an orderly learning environment in which all students are able to learn. Thus, any whole-school approach, in the terms outlined above, needs to be paralleled by clear and consistently applied rules and consequences in each and every class.

One means of achieving it that has proven successful in many schools, and was widely adopted as part of the Achievement Improvement Zones (AiZ) project cited in Chapter 4, is a classroom rights and responsibilities approach predicated on clearly specifying the rights and responsibilities to apply in all classrooms as the basis for more consistent teacher and hence student behaviour in class.

Figure 5.3 provides a pro forma developed by Professor Ramon Lewis of La Trobe University that AiZ project schools used to specify the expectations to apply across all classrooms in the school.

In this classroom …

1 Students and the teacher have the right to do as much work as possible.
Therefore:
- students should bring (encourage others to bring) all their equipment to class
- students should listen (encourage others to listen) when students are speaking
- students should be on time (encourage others to be on time)
- students should attempt (encourage others to attempt) all work
-
-
-

2 Students and the teacher have the right to feel comfortable and safe in the classroom.
Therefore:
- students should pass (encourage others to pass) all objects hand to hand
- students should speak (encourage others to speak) to others politely
- students should keep (encourage others to keep) their hands to themselves
-
-
-

If students make the **effort** to respect the rights of others their behaviour will be recognised by giving them:
-
-
-
-
-

If students don't make the **effort** to respect the rights of others, the following will occur (in order):
1.
2.
3.
4.
5.

Student's signature: _____

Parent's signature: _____

Teacher's signature: _____

FIGURE 5.3: CLASSROOM RIGHTS AND RESPONSIBILITIES
Note: The pro forma was included with permission in Zbar, Kimber & Marshall (2010).

Some of the figure is complete, since it constitutes the fundamental rules of behaviour in any functioning and respectful class, but the school can add to the list to ensure a comprehensive approach to meet its particular circumstances and needs. This is best done by the year level or professional learning teams that exist in the school, working individually at first, and then together, to ensure consistent expectations and approaches throughout the school. This also may reveal any areas where teachers need additional support and hence where targeted professional development or other input is required.

The pro forma is given even further meaning and impact by having the student and their parent(s) sign it as a measure of their agreement and commitment, to which the teacher's signature is added as well. Once the pro formas are completed and agreed upon, they also provide the basis for continued monitoring of progress and improvement in the learning environment of the school through such questions as:

- What are our most significant outcomes to date?
- To what extent have we achieved our desired ends?
- How consistently are we implementing the approach?
- Where do we need to do more?
- Do we have the capacity to go to the next steps?

Such monitoring is even more effective when accompanied by classroom observation to ensure consistent implementation through the school. Hampton Park Primary School has developed the pro forma in Figure 5.4 to support observations of the orderly learning environment in the school. It is accompanied by a rubric for judging the degree of proficiency with which different elements of its behaviour management approach are applied, in order to support teachers to exhibit them more 'constantly' in class.

While consistent classroom expectations are essential for an orderly learning environment in any school, the experiences that each teacher and their students then have crucially depends on the behaviour management strategies that the teacher adopts.

There is a range of strategies that have been demonstrated to be effective in running what might be referred to as a 'well-disciplined' class. All of them, however, are predicated on developing strong teacher–student relationships. As a meta-analysis undertaken by Marzano, Marzano and Pickering (2003) found, the quality of teacher–student relationships is the keystone for all other aspects of classroom management. This in turn depends on knowing your students well, as discussed in more detail below.

This should not be interpreted as having to develop 'friendships' with students as sometimes teachers may think. The teacher is always the adult in the room and needs to fulfil this role. They are the trained professionals whose role is to guide and support their students to learn. This requires them to provide clear purpose and strong guidance about both the academic learning and student behaviour in class.

This is also, interestingly, the approach that students prefer. In a study involving interviews with more than 700 students in Grades 4 to 7, Chiu and Tully (1997) discovered that they had a clear preference for strong teacher guidance and control rather than a more permissive approach. This, it is noted, most commonly manifests in teachers establishing clear expectations for student behaviour and learning goals that are relentlessly pursued for all students in the class. Learning goals are discussed in more detail in Chapter 7.

This sort of authoritative teaching approach ought not be confused with an authoritarian one, which sometimes is used to lesser effect. Students, Lewis (2001, cited in Lewis, Romi, Qui and Katz, 2005) found in a study of Australian student perceptions, tend to characterise their teachers as having two distinct discipline styles: what he called 'coercive' discipline, comprising punishment and aggression in the form of yelling in anger, sarcasm, group punishments and the like; and 'relationship-based management' comprising discussion, hints, recognition and punishment.

OLE / Classroom Behaviour Management Observation Template	Proficient This behaviour was exhibited constantly in the session	Consolidating This behaviour was exhibited multiple times in the session	Emerging This behaviour was exhibited once in the session	Not Evident This behaviour is not currently exhibited to an acceptable level
Students are met in line by the second bell				
Visual evidence of class expectations of student behaviour				
Reference made to class expectations of student behaviour				
Classroom space is neat and organised				
Floor is clear creating pathways for student movement within classroom				
Visual evidence of ADM (Assertive Discipline Model)				
Reference made to ADM (Assertive Discipline Model)				
Teacher's personal mobile phone is turned to silent and out of sight				
During classroom teaching and learning times hot drinks and food are not consumed				
Students enter the classroom and transition to session in a timely and orderly manner				
Student seating plan is set where appropriate and regularly monitored				
Students are seated on mat / at desks in a timely and orderly manner				
Juno Sound Field System is used to support student learning				
Students listen attentively when teacher is speaking				
Teacher talk kept to an appropriate length of time				
Student movement within the classroom is managed effectively				
Classroom resources are organised and easily accessible to students				
Teacher fosters an atmosphere of positivity where positive behaviours are recognised				
5:1 positivity ratio demonstrated				
Inappropriate behaviour is redirected using ADM (Assertive Discipline Model)				
Teacher's voice is not raised loudly for a significant amount of time				
Learning activities are differentiated to meet the needs of the students				
Maintain awareness and control of what is happening in the class at all times				

FIGURE 5.4: HAMPTON PARK PRIMARY SCHOOL CLASSROOM OBSERVATION PRO FORMA FOR THE ORDERLY LEARNING ENVIRONMENT

Note: The development of this pro forma was informed by the work of William Ruthven Secondary College provided as Tables 8.1 and 8.2.

Students experiencing a more relationship-based approach tended to be more disciplined when teachers dealt with their misbehaviour and acted more responsibly in that class. In contrast, the use of coercive discipline seemed to result in higher levels of student distraction from work and less responsibility on their part.

There are proven strategies that teachers can use to ensure the adoption of the more caring and effective relationship-based approach. Central to all, however, is the need to distinguish between the student behaviour at issue and the students themselves. Labelling the student will only lock them into that approach and limit your capacity to support and stimulate positive behaviour change.

The mindset the teacher brings to the task is relevant in this regard since, as already noted, they are the trained, professional adults in the room.[2] At the very least it is incumbent on teachers always to seek to maintain their composure and calm and, where necessary, try a different approach. A lot of behaviour issues can be dealt with relatively easily and effectively nipped in the bud. This often is as simple as reminding a student of the relevant rule, moving towards a group that is causing concern, or simply asking the students to refocus attention on their work.

As Dahlgren (n.d.) helpfully observes, 'Conflict is inevitable, but combat is optional, and with prompt attention paid to emergent misbehaviour through early intervention strategies, up to ninety percent of minor, pesky behaviour problems can be eliminated in the classroom' (p. 1).

Other strategies that can successfully be used in this context include:
- rewarding positive behaviour as well as punishing individual misbehaviour to reinforce the behaviours that are sought
- developing and using classroom routines, such as entering the room, stopping to listen to the teacher and forming groups, to maximise the efficiency of classroom operations and minimise the opportunities for disruptions to occur
- ensuring that 'the punishment fits the crime' and is not disproportionate, by having the sort of agreed and understood classroom rules that were outlined above
- using silence and waiting where appropriate to signal you are forming a significant response and will not be rising to the bait
- defusing the situation by redirecting it to a more productive place, such as acknowledging that 'I hear your concern; however we are continuing now with our important work'.

One of the keys to having a well-disciplined classroom, of course, is to ensure that effective instruction occurs. It stands to reason that the more that students are engaged in productive and appropriately challenging learning work, the less likely they are to misbehave. As Barbetta, Norona and Bicard (2005) have cogently observed, 'The first line of defense in managing student behaviour is effective instruction ... when teachers demystify learning, achievement and behaviour improve dramatically' (p. 17).

This puts a premium on developing teachers' capacity to deliver more effective lessons for all of the students they teach, which is why it is a major focus of the remaining chapters in this book.

KNOWING YOUR STUDENTS WELL

Designing and delivering more effective lessons, encouraging and supporting better behaviour in class, and meeting the full range of students' needs depends on teachers knowing their students well. This is not simply an issue for the teacher to address, since the school itself can either support or limit the extent to which students can become well known through the structures it adopts. For example, a teacher in a secondary school whose allotment is with a wide range of classes for one subject only each week is less likely to know their students as well as a teacher in a school that seeks to match them to classes for more than one subject, and hence more time each week.

---

[2] We are aware there may be many times where there is more than one adult, or even trained professional in the room, but this does not alter the point about the overarching mindset the teacher adopts.

Some years ago, Vic worked with a secondary school that was struggling with student behaviour and the speed with which teachers avoided responsibility for it by sending recalcitrant students to someone else. The approach the school was advised to adopt, which is outlined in Box 5.5, focused on getting all teachers involved in a way that made them more responsible for a defined group of students in the school. While it was not adopted in full because of logistical issues involved, it did inform the school's subsequent approach which, together with a focus on building a more effective leadership team, has seen the decline in student enrolments the school was experiencing reversed, to the point where it will need to find more teaching spaces for students within the next two years.

> **Box 5.5**
>
> ## A structure to enable secondary students to be well known
>
> All staff with a teaching qualification (whether timetabled for teaching or not) could be expected to serve as a 'tutor' with a consistent group of students for the whole of the year. The term 'tutor' is preferred to home group teacher, since it signals the role is as much about learning as it is about the wellbeing of the students involved.
>
> All students are then allocated to a tutorial group which, with prevailing staff/student ratios, would mean that each group would comprise no more than around 15 students each, by the time the principal and some others who might not be able to guarantee regularity of their presence are taken out. While the groups can be structured in a variety of ways, it is suggested that they be based on year levels, in part to support the development of stronger year level teams. This also has the advantage of enabling year level coordinators to become real leaders of teams. They then can focus on strategically determining how best to meet the needs of students at that year level, rather than being swamped with individual behavioural issues and concerns, as commonly occurs when structures of responsibility for students either lack clarity or do not effectively exist.
>
> Each tutor would be expected to establish a strong 'pastoral' relationship with their group and, most importantly, would be the first port of call for any issues that arise either from the students themselves, their teachers and/or their parents.
>
> The tutor would be responsible for the wellbeing and academic success of the students in their group and work with their students to develop appropriate individual learning improvement plans. Such plans not only provide a means of catering for each student's individual learning needs, but also create a mechanism for ensuring that each student is appropriately challenged and thereby progressively raising expectations in the school.
>
> The school would need to identify blocks of time in each week for these small tutorial groups to meet and where relationships can be forged. These weekly blocks could also potentially be supplemented by some longer sessions, such as an afternoon each term, for activities undertaken by the groups individually or together, planned in advance by the students in their groups.
>
> While a number of logistical challenges are associated with the approach, such as identifying the time in a busy school week, it does constitute a means of systematically connecting students to at least one teacher in the school. Thus, depending on the context and current stage of development of the school, the benefits ultimately would outweigh the costs, particularly in a school that substantially needs to improve, and ensure that an orderly learning environment is in place.

We realise that the approach outlined in Box 5.5 would be a considerable stretch, if not a bridge too far for many schools. That said, it depends on how big the behavioural issues may be in the school and hence how dramatic the solution required. Suffice to say, however, that the key imperative in terms of developing a school climate where students do generally say 'yes' to the statement 'there is an adult in the school who knows and cares about me', is to evaluate the structures the school does have in place, to ensure they do sufficiently connect teachers to the students they teach. This is an area where the students' views should also be sought.

ACTIVITY FOR LEADERSHIP TEAMS AND/OR STAFF: AN ORDERLY LEARNING ENVIRONMENT CHECKLIST

The following checklist is to be completed by leadership teams and/or staff as appropriate to the school, and can help inform discussion about the overall state of the orderly learning environment in the school. In particular, any significant disagreements that emerge can signal areas where whole-school consistency is weak, and discussion around the ratings can be used to identify whole-school strengths on which to build, and any key areas of weakness that need to be addressed. As with each of the checklists or surveys in this book, their major value resides in the conversations they promote and subsequent actions that result rather than simply completing the ratings they contain.

Instructions

1 It is recommended that respondents complete the checklist individually first, so all views are considered, and then share the outcomes to identify the key commonalities and differences that may exist.
2 Discussion around these outcomes will help build consistency of practice in the school. A whole-team/school discussion can then occur around the three concluding statements arising from the ratings to identify what next.
3 Rate each of the statements in Table 5.12 on a four-point scale where:
   1 = Strongly disagree, 2 = Disagree, 3 = Agree and 4 = Strongly agree.

TABLE 5.12: AN ORDERLY LEARNING ENVIRONMENT CHECKLIST

The orderly learning environment	Rating (1–4)
The school has a policy for promoting positive student behaviour	
The policy is agreed and understood by the staff	
Students and their parents know and understand the policy	
Students know the reasons behind the rules	
Behavioural issues are dealt with effectively in the school	
There is an appropriate balance of sanctions and rewards to reinforce desired behaviours in the school	
There is collective responsibility for behaviour management in the school	
Staff roles in relation to behaviour management are clearly defined and understood	

Continued...

Table 5.12 (continued)

There is consistent implementation of the school's behaviour management policy	
Staff discuss concerns with each other and, where needed, seek advice	
Procedures are in place to deal with any behavioural emergencies	
Staff feel supported by leaders in ensuring an orderly learning environment in the school	
Structures are in place to enable staff to get to know the students they teach	
Parents are clear about which teacher(s) to approach about an issue concerning their child	
Parents know that their children are learning and behaving well	
Most students would feel known and cared for by at least one adult in the school	
Staff clearly understand and implement their responsibilities in breaks (i.e. before and after school, recess and lunch)	
Appropriate routines are in place to ensure the efficient operation of classes in the school	
Strategies are in place to promote students' interpersonal skills and relationships	
Adults in the school model the desired student behaviours	

Based on our ratings:
- The key strengths on which we can build are:

- The main weakness we need to address is:

- Addressing this weakness will require us to:

© Pamela Macklin and Vic Zbar, *Driving School Improvement*, Australian Council for Educational Research, 2017

PUTTING FIRST THINGS FIRST

IDENTIFYING PRIORITIES

Schools in Australia are good at identifying priorities to include in their annual plans. These priorities are commonly worded well and understood by key stakeholders in the school. What schools are less good at, however, is sticking to these priorities and allocating time and resources so they are privileged in the actions they take.

It is often said that improving a school is like turning around an aircraft carrier—long, tedious and slow. That's an analogy, however, that we don't think really works. When an aircraft carrier is turned, that is basically all that is done at the time. In contrast, changing a school happens while doing all of the other daily work that needs to occur. Perhaps a better analogy, if a sea-going one is required, is scraping the barnacles off the bottom of a boat, not in dry dock, but while it continues to sail.

The point is that much of the logic of schools is determined by the fact the students arrive at the start of each day. They need to be timetabled and taught in classes, supervised in breaks, disciplined and counselled, engaged in extra-curricular activities and more. This accounts for 90 per cent or more of what the school and its personnel do, and means that resources that can be devoted to improving the school are only available 10 per cent or less of the time.

Setting clear priorities for school improvement should determine the way in which this discretionary time and resources are used. That said, the priorities we espouse are not always the priorities we enact. If you want a gauge of what your real school priorities are, analyse how you spend your discretionary (that is, non-teaching, non-required administrative, etc.) time and any discretionary dollars you have. You may find, as many schools we work with have, that this time and money does not flow to the priorities that ostensibly drive planning and action in the school. That is because we get overwhelmed with the day-to-day, and the urgent, at the expense of what really matters for making a difference in the school.

This, it should be noted, is not an uncommon phenomenon in the business literature and hence is not unique to schools. As far back as the 1970s, the business theorists who pioneered a focus on organisational development and learning organisations, Chris Argyris and Donald Schön (1974) distinguished between what they called our 'espoused theory' and our 'theory-in-use'.

Our espoused theory is the world view and values we believe are the basis of our behaviour—essentially, what we say—while our theory-in-use is the world view and values that our behaviour actually exhibits—what we do, regardless of what we say.

Establishing clear priorities and sticking to them, as all the Zbar, Kimber and Marshall study schools did, is the means of reconciling our espoused theories and theories-in-use, so that what we say is also what we do.

One approach that Pamela uses with domain heads in planning days in schools is to evaluate the range of potential priorities under consideration using a ranking for both urgency and importance in order to agree on the top three. Figure 5.5 provides a sample from one of the schools she works with, using the priorities being discussed at the time.

What are our most important priorities for inclusion in our action plans for this year?	
Thinking about the work in your Domain needed to embed these priorities in your planning and implementation over the coming year, in your teams of 3 agree on a score for each of the 10 priority areas using the following scale for urgency and importance:	
2 points	**1 point**
Extremely urgent Very important	Urgent Important
Priority Area	**Score**
Curriculum development	
High-impact strategies	
Differentiation	
Assessment and reporting	
Use of data	
Moderation	
Peer observation	
Student feedback	
Reading/comprehension	
Effective Professional Learning Teams	

Consider each item you have scored as 4 (i.e. Extremely urgent and Very important) and identify the three that you feel the school is best able to pursue at this stage. Provide reasons for your choice.

1

2

3

FIGURE 5.5: DETERMINING SCHOOL PRIORITIES—HEADS OF DOMAIN PLANNING DAY

© Pamela Macklin and Vic Zbar, *Driving School Improvement*, Australian Council for Educational Research, 2017

ACTIVITY FOR LEADERSHIP TEAMS: IDENTIFYING PRIORITIES FOR YOUR SCHOOL

Instructions

1 List the full range of priorities under consideration by the school and record them in the 'Priority area' column in the table below (Table 5.13).
2 Evaluate and score each of the priorities listed in terms of its importance (1 point for important, 2 points for very important) plus its urgency (1 point for urgent, 2 points for extremely urgent), up to a maximum score of 4.
3 Consider all items scored as 4 (that is, very important and extremely urgent) and work in small groups to identify the three that you agree the school is best able to pursue at this stage. Provide reasons for your choice. Share the outcomes of the separate group deliberations and seek agreement on a whole-team set of priorities to pursue.

TABLE 5.13: IDENTIFYING PRIORITIES FOR YOUR SCHOOL

Priority Area	Score

© Pamela Macklin and Vic Zbar, *Driving School Improvement*, Australian Council for Educational Research, 2017

WHICH STRATEGIES TO ADOPT?

Having identified appropriate priorities for the ensuing year(s), the school needs to ensure that the strategies it develops for implementing these are strategies worth having, and will have a positive effect. Schools have a range of tools for achieving this including the use of a Strengths, Weaknesses, Opportunities and Threats (SWOT) analysis or the more recent Strengths, Opportunities, Aspirations and Results (SOAR).

One approach we have found fruitful in a number of schools with which we have worked is the Difficulty Impact Grid depicted in Figure 5.6. The grid, which is similar to a range of other tools such as the Impact Effort Matrix developed by Andersen, Fagerhaug and Beitz (2010, pp. 19, 146–147.) for the healthcare sector, helps identify those strategies that are easiest to achieve, while still having the greatest effect as well as those that deliver the long-term results.

It achieves this by constructing a grid that matches the effort needed to pursue the strategy on the horizontal axis to the impact it can be expected to have on the vertical axis, to help inform discussion and subsequent decision-making about the strategies to adopt.

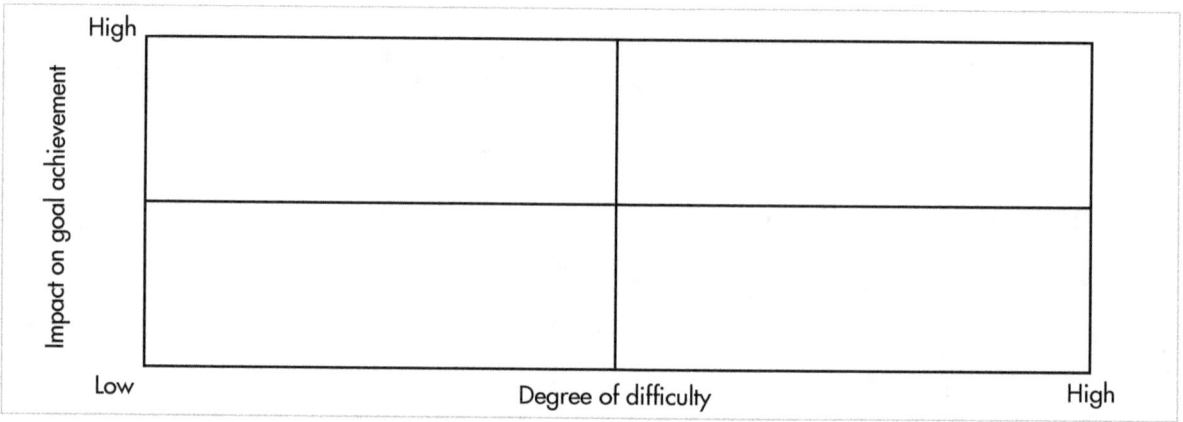

FIGURE 5.6: DIFFICULTY IMPACT GRID

Further substance can be given to this grid by labelling each of the quadrants and considering examples of the type of strategies that might fall into each, as depicted in Figure 5.7.

	Low — Degree of difficulty — High
High Impact on goal achievement	**1 First priority** • Easiest to do, with fewest risks • Provides good results	**3 More work needed** • Important but harder to achieve and involve more risk • You will need to start planning for these strategies
Low	**2 Bells and whistles** • Shows something is being done but little effort is required • Valuable, but not enough on their own	**4 Don't do** • Frustration builders and time wasters

FIGURE 5.7: ILLUSTRATED DIFFICULTY IMPACT GRID

Taking this a stage further still, here are some examples of specific strategies that each quadrant might contain based on our experiences in several schools.

First priority

These are really the quick wins on which to build. A good example is the way in which the newly appointed principal to an under-performing school responded to noticing the poor state of furniture on visiting the school prior to taking up his appointment the following year. During the long end-of-year break, he approached local businesses and used existing school funds to have all the furniture in the school replaced with new and better chairs, desks and the like. The effect on staff arriving on day one of the new year, and on the students the following day was profound, and signalled that something was different in this school.

Bells and whistles

These are the things we do to give the impression of action, and which may add some value provided we are doing other important things. In one school suffering from severely declining enrolments, the leadership established the position of Marketing Director in the hope of turning things around. In the absence of a clear program for improving the school, however, this prompted the question of what it could market and amounted to really running on the spot. It could add value to a clear program of improvement in the school, but not as a strategy in its own right.

More work needed

These are the strategies that really make an impact, but require significant planning, time and implementation to take effect. One school sought to embed a culture of coaching to significantly improve the quality of teaching in the school. It began with the principal group itself in year one and trained them in a coaching approach. In year two, the principals began coaching other leaders and then these leaders received the same training themselves. In year three, the coaching was extended to all staff, with the training further spread. Full implementation did not really start until year four and continues to this day.

Don't do

These are things that might seem like a good idea, but have no proven impact at all. Sometimes schools respond to poor staff opinion survey outcomes by instituting a program to improve staff morale; commonly involving more social activities, which a number of teachers prefer not to attend. The problem is that improving morale in this way simply cannot be done. Staff morale is an outcome of other things—the quality of student behaviour in the school, the professional learning culture in the school, the impact teachers feel they have, and so on—which need to change first if morale is to improve.

ACTIVITY FOR LEADERSHIP TEAMS: COMPLETING A DIFFICULTY IMPACT GRID

The Difficulty Impact Grid can help the school to monitor the implementation of key strategies as well as helping to devise new ones.

Instructions

1 Consider the range of strategies being implemented now to improve your school and allocate each to the blank Difficulty Impact Grid (Figure 5.8). Use the completed grid to discuss:
   - strategies that are working as intended and need to be maintained
   - strategies that are not working as intended and where implementation needs to be improved
   - strategies that are distracting you from your core improvement task.

2 Are there any missing strategies the school should pursue?

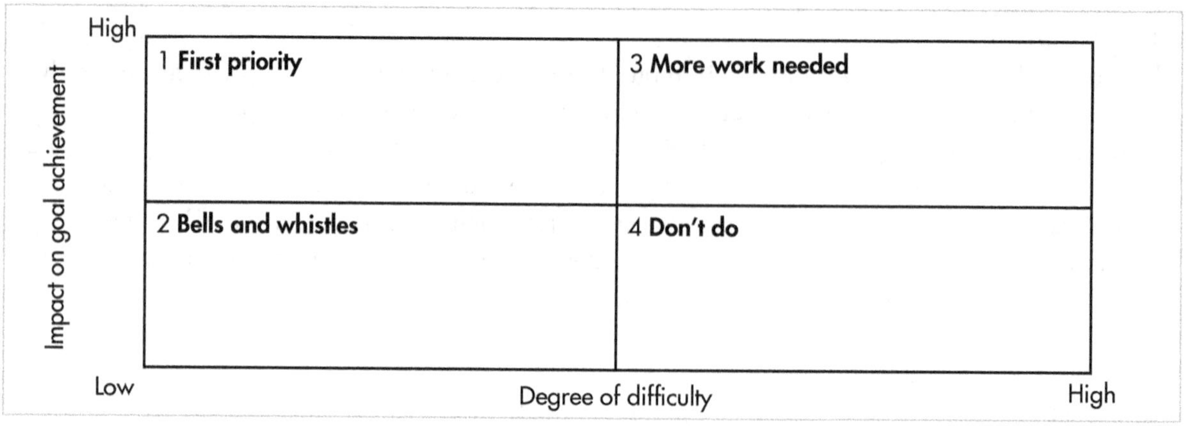

FIGURE 5.8: BLANK DIFFICULTY IMPACT GRID

A 2×2 grid with y-axis "Impact on goal achievement" (Low to High) and x-axis "Degree of difficulty" (Low to High):
- Top-left: 1 First priority
- Bottom-left: 2 Bells and whistles
- Top-right: 3 More work needed
- Bottom-right: 4 Don't do

DETERMINING PRIORITIES

There is an old Russian saying that if you chase two rabbits, you won't catch either. The point of raising it here is to note that having too many priorities is as bad as having none at all. Harking back to our advice in Chapter 2 that we need to avoid taking on too much, schools need to be wary of ensuring that they only set a manageable number of priorities to pursue. In our experience, this suggests only around three or four, especially since there is some evidence to suggest that the average person may only be able to hold three or four things in their mind at once (see, for example, Moskowitz, 2008). And if you can't remember it, you are less likely to do it, with the result that at least one of your priorities will be lost.

This applies as much to the strategies the school adopts and only reinforces the suggestion made in Chapter 2 that schools consider the use of an abandonment audit from time to time to ensure we dispense with those we no longer need, and which ultimately detract from what we are trying to do now.

ACTIVITY FOR PRINCIPAL CLASS TEAMS: CONDUCTING AN ABANDONMENT AUDIT

Note: This is a time-consuming activity that ought to be done only once every three to five years as kind of a 'spring clean' to enable the hard rubbish collection we referred to in Chapter 2.

Instructions

1 Consider the following list of major areas of school activity and extend it as needed to encompass the full range of activities undertaken in the school:
  • Curriculum
  • Teaching and learning
  • Professional learning
  • Reporting
  • Student wellbeing
  • Student discipline
  • Extra-curricular programs and activities
  • Interaction with parents
  • Interaction with other community stakeholders
  • Interaction with other schools
  • Interaction with systemic authorities
  • Liaison with other service providers

- Budget management
- Facilities management
- Occupational health and safety
- Annual reporting

2 For each area identified, list the full range of activities that are expected and undertaken by individuals, teams and/or the whole school. Set aside all activities that must be retained either because they are intrinsic to running a school (for example, developing a timetable or marking rolls) or required by legislation (for example, certain elements of OHS), and then rate each of the remaining, discretionary activities using the following four-point scale:
1 = The activity is using staff time with no discernible impact and/or is detracting from other more important things we should do
2 = The activity has a small-scale positive impact, but at a significant cost in dollars and/or time
3 = The activity has a positive impact in the school and is worth maintaining at this stage
4 = The activity has a significant positive impact on the operations and effectiveness of the school and is essential to our work.

3 Based on the ratings, identify any activities the school undertakes that ought to be dispensed with in order to focus more clearly on the core priorities of the school.

It should be noted that any leadership decision to abandon strategies or expectations of staff is likely to be greeted favourably in a context where teachers generally feel overworked, and is arguably cause for celebration in the school. This can also help to generate a greater level of commitment to those strategies and activities that remain.

CHAPTER 6
STAGE 2: BUILDING TEACHING CAPACITY

The fact that the preconditions can only take you so far is evident in the word, 'preconditions' itself. It implies simply a start on which further work can be built. That said, it is building that can only occur if the foundations—the preconditions—are in place.

Once the preconditions are sustainably established in the school, you can turn your attention to building the teaching capacity of staff; especially given the variability in teacher effectiveness demonstrated in Chapter 1, and the consequent realisation that the greatest source of improvement in any school is the extent to which we can support more teachers to work like the best.

Somewhat ironically in this context, we don't necessarily know what constitutes the 'best'. Often in workshops Vic will show the short 'Anyone, anyone' clip from the film, *Ferris Bueller's day off* (which can be located via searching online video portals). It portrays a teacher talking way over the heads of some incredibly bored and disengaged students in his class, continually asking questions with the request 'anyone, anyone' which, when he receives no response, he answers himself. The students themselves have glazed eyes, chew gum and blow bubbles and in one case, sleep and drool on the desk. Apart from the fact it raises awareness of the extent to which all of us at one time or another have said 'anyone, anyone' in class, subsequent discussions reveal that workshop participants know what is wrong with this approach.

But do they know what is right? When he then poses the question, 'If the challenge we face is to support more teachers to work like the best, how do we know an effective teacher when we see one?', there is not necessarily a ready response.

The point is that teachers do not have an agreed or even codified understanding of what constitutes effective work in their profession, in the way that other professions seem to have.[1] This is a gap that needs to be filled if schools are to support teachers to increase their effectiveness and thereby enable more teachers to work like the best.

---

[1] We acknowledge that the Australian Professional Standards for Teachers (see http://www.aitsl.edu.au/australian-professional-standards-for-teachers/standards/list) set out at a high level the prerequisites for teachers to perform effectively in the classroom. While this falls short of the sort of codified understanding of effective classroom practice that underpins a school's efforts to support more teachers to work like the best, it can inform the sort of discussion envisaged in the following activity for staff and provide a starting point for it. Perhaps then teachers will be able to readily respond to the question Vic asks—How do you know an effective teacher when you see one?—in the way that doctors, lawyers and architects could by describing what an effective practitioner in their profession does.

We have found that simply posing the question, 'How do we know the best when we see it?', stimulates discussion about effective teaching that can underpin the development of a shared view to guide the capacity building strategies the school can then adopt.

ACTIVITY FOR STAFF: DEVELOPING A SHARED VIEW OF EFFECTIVE TEACHING IN THE SCHOOL

Instructions

1 Show the short 'Anyone, anyone' video clip referenced earlier to inform a discussion about what is wrong with this teacher's approach.
2 Having identified the shortcomings of the approach, consider what is needed to make it right. More specifically, ask staff to work in small groups to answer the question, 'How do you know an effective teacher when you see one?' Their responses can then be shared and compared with the outline provided in Box 6.1 to develop a whole-staff view to inform capacity building efforts in the school.

Box 6.1
CHARACTERISTICS OF AN EFFECTIVE TEACHER

Effective teachers:
- have high expectations for all students and focus clearly on the learning progress that each student makes
- contribute to the development of well-rounded students who achieve positive attitudinal and social as well as academic outcomes
- have an in-depth knowledge of the developmental continuum in their subject areas and how to sequence its delivery
- use a range of resources and repertoire of teaching strategies to plan and deliver engaging learning opportunities for students
- monitor student progress during the lesson and adapt their teaching accordingly
- collect and analyse multiple sources of evidence to evaluate student learning
- contribute to the development of classrooms and schools that value diversity and encourage students to see themselves as members of communities, whether they be the classroom, the school or the wider community in which they live
- collaborate with other professionals as needed, as well as parents, to meet the needs of all students, but especially those who are 'at risk'
- reflect on their own practice and collaborate with fellow teachers and school leaders to continually improve.

PLANNING GOOD LESSONS

Good planning can help teachers to be more effective and thereby support more teachers to work like the best. Planning is especially needed to ensure that lessons and units do, in fact, achieve their purposes and enable student learning to occur.

There is an important understanding about time in this context and, in particular, the notion of time on task. Building on Archer and Hughes's (2011) point that the instructional variable of time is a product of both the time spent teaching and the time spent learning, Hattie and Yates (2014) relate a hypothetical, but thoroughly believable, story of a one-hour maths lesson scheduled to start at 9.30 a.m. in one school.

'(S)chool announcements meant that the lesson started at 9.37, so 7 minutes were lost upfront'. Analysing the on-task engagement of students revealed that, on average, 'the students are engaged (time on task) for 36 of the 53 minutes ... (with a) range of engagement across the 23 students ... from 21 to 49 minutes'. Looking more closely still at academic learning time—that is, the time the students are successfully engaged on tasks—they find the figure declines further to 'between 9 and 45 minutes', with the result that 'some students (are) experiencing about one-quarter of the academic learning time experienced by others within the same class' (Hattie & Yates, 2014, pp. 37–38).

This accords with findings that Archer and Hughes (2011) cite to demonstrate that 'increasing instructional time alone does not always lead to an increase in time that students spend learning or in the total amount learned' (p. 5). More specifically, of the six and a half hours generally available in any school day, and the five hours usually devoted to timetabled instruction, there is research which shows that 'students are engaged during less than half of the time allocated for instruction, or approximately two hours per day' and 'the amount of time students are successfully engaged in academic tasks at the appropriate level of difficulty ... occurs, on average, for only a small percentage of the day (i.e. about 20% of allocated time or 50 minutes per day) in many classrooms' (Archer & Hughes, 2011, p. 6).

The challenge that good planning helps to meet is to increase these depressingly low percentages of engaged and successfully engaged student learning time.

Hattie and Yates (2014) provide a helpful approach for thinking about this in the form of a matrix that relates these differing concepts of time to the threats and facilitators that can apply to each. It's an approach we have adapted and used to develop the following activity for staff.

ACTIVITY FOR STAFF: IDENTIFYING OPPORTUNITIES TO INCREASE STUDENT LEARNING TIME

Note: The time concepts we have used derive from Archer and Hughes (2011), as outlined above, rather than the categories that Hattie and Yates (2014) adopt in their book.

Instructions
Work with a partner and use the following table (Table 6.1) to identify:
- the major threats that exist in your school to each of the time categories
- any facilitators that exist or could be developed for increasing the time
- a key action that could be taken to reduce a threat and/or maximise the impact of a facilitator.

We have provided a sample threat and facilitator for each time category listed to get you started in the task.

CHAPTER 6 Stage 2: Building teaching capacity

TABLE 6.1: IDENTIFYING OPPORTUNITIES TO INCREASE STUDENT LEARNING TIME

Time concept	Major threats	Major facilitators[2]	Key action to maximise the value of this time
Available time: From when students arrive to the time they leave school	Time out of the school such as excursions or sports days	Out-of-hours programs that engage students in meaningful ways	
Allocated time: The five hours usually devoted to timetabled instruction	Periodic announcements and inefficient marking of rolls	Reducing or eliminating lateness to class	
Engaged time/ time on task: The time the student is actively engaged in a learning task including listening to the teacher or other students	A lack of clarity about the purpose of the learning and hence the task	Sharing the learning goal with the students and giving clear instructions about how it will be pursued	
Academic learning time: The time the student is successfully engaged in academic tasks at an appropriate level of difficulty	Failing to identify gaps in prior knowledge that need to be remedied before moving on	Promoting the importance of effort for higher levels of academic achievement at school	

© Pamela Macklin and Vic Zbar, *Driving School Improvement*, Australian Council for Educational Research, 2017

---

[2] Hattie and Yates (2014, p. 37) provide a range of examples of major threats and facilitators that can be compared to the ones we have provided as well as those identified by the staff. Bear in mind, however, the slightly different time concepts used in this activity, as noted above.

USING AN INSTRUCTIONAL MODEL FOR CONSISTENTLY MORE EFFECTIVE TEACHING

Developing and implementing a whole-school instructional model can provide a key means of improving planning and thereby building teacher capacity and driving better teaching through the school.

As Hampton Park Primary School in Victoria found, it contributes to greater consistency of good teaching practice by ensuring that there is:
- a common understanding of the structure of a lesson or learning sequence
- consistent language used by teachers across the school
- a clear expectation of the learning that is to take place in each lesson or learning sequence
- an understanding of how students can demonstrate that they have achieved the learning goal
- sufficient guidance provided to students so that they are able to transfer their learning to different situations
- adequate feedback given to students about their learning so that they can continue to demonstrate improvement in learning outcomes.

Developing an instructional model involves answering four critical planning questions that teachers need to address:
- How will the lesson begin?
- What is the nature of your own presentation?
- What form will students' guided and independent practice take?
- How will you conclude the lesson and know if it has achieved its goal?

This almost always takes the form of a model that comprises the following elements:
- *Beginning of the lesson*, including a hook, learning goal and success criteria, and identification of prior knowledge the students have
- *Purposeful learning*, which includes some explicit teaching, guided and independent student practice, and differentiation as required
- *Reflection and review* to reinforce the learning goal and success criteria, and determine the extent to which they have been achieved.

The presence of these elements is readily evident in the instructional models developed by Lyndhurst Secondary College, Darwin Middle School, Sanderson Middle School and Hampton Park Primary School provided in Figure 6.1. The model for Hampton Park Primary School is a revised version of the one published in the first edition of this book. It is equally seen in the three additional models included in Figure 6.2 that we have subsequently gathered from the Queechy Alliance and Central Coast Cluster of schools in Tasmania and Palmerston College[3] in the Northern Territory, which all arguably have something of a more modern, if not even organic look, in part because they have learned from the sort of examples provided in Figure 6.1.

---

[3] Over the last three years or more the Tasmanian Education Department has supported schools to work in clusters through its Middle Years Literacy Project, with the result some strong and effective alliances have been formed.

CHAPTER 6 Stage 2: Building teaching capacity

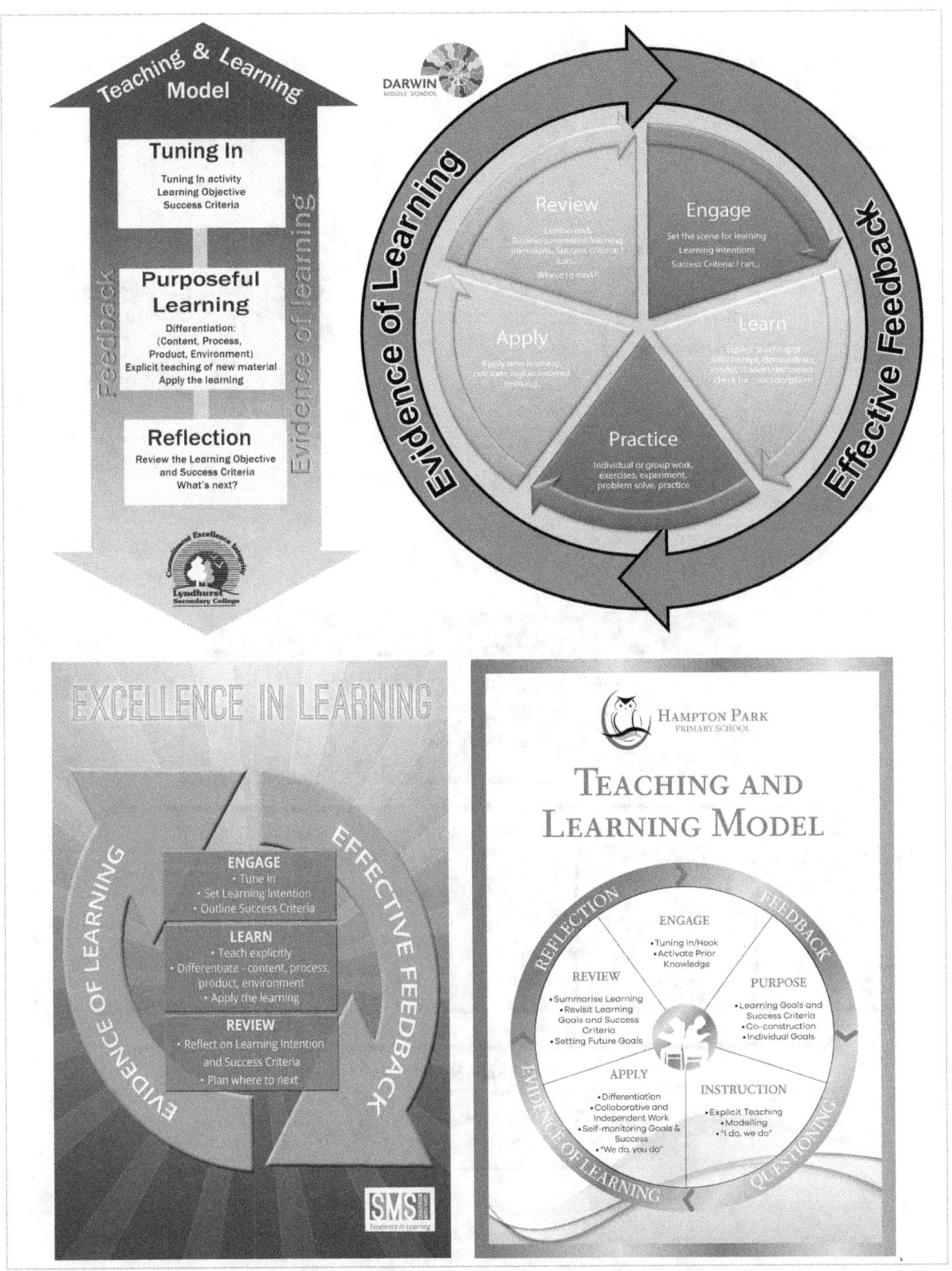

FIGURE 6.1: VICTORIAN AND NORTHERN TERRITORY SCHOOL INSTRUCTIONAL MODELS

Note: The Hampton Park Primary School instructional model has been updated since the first edition of this book.

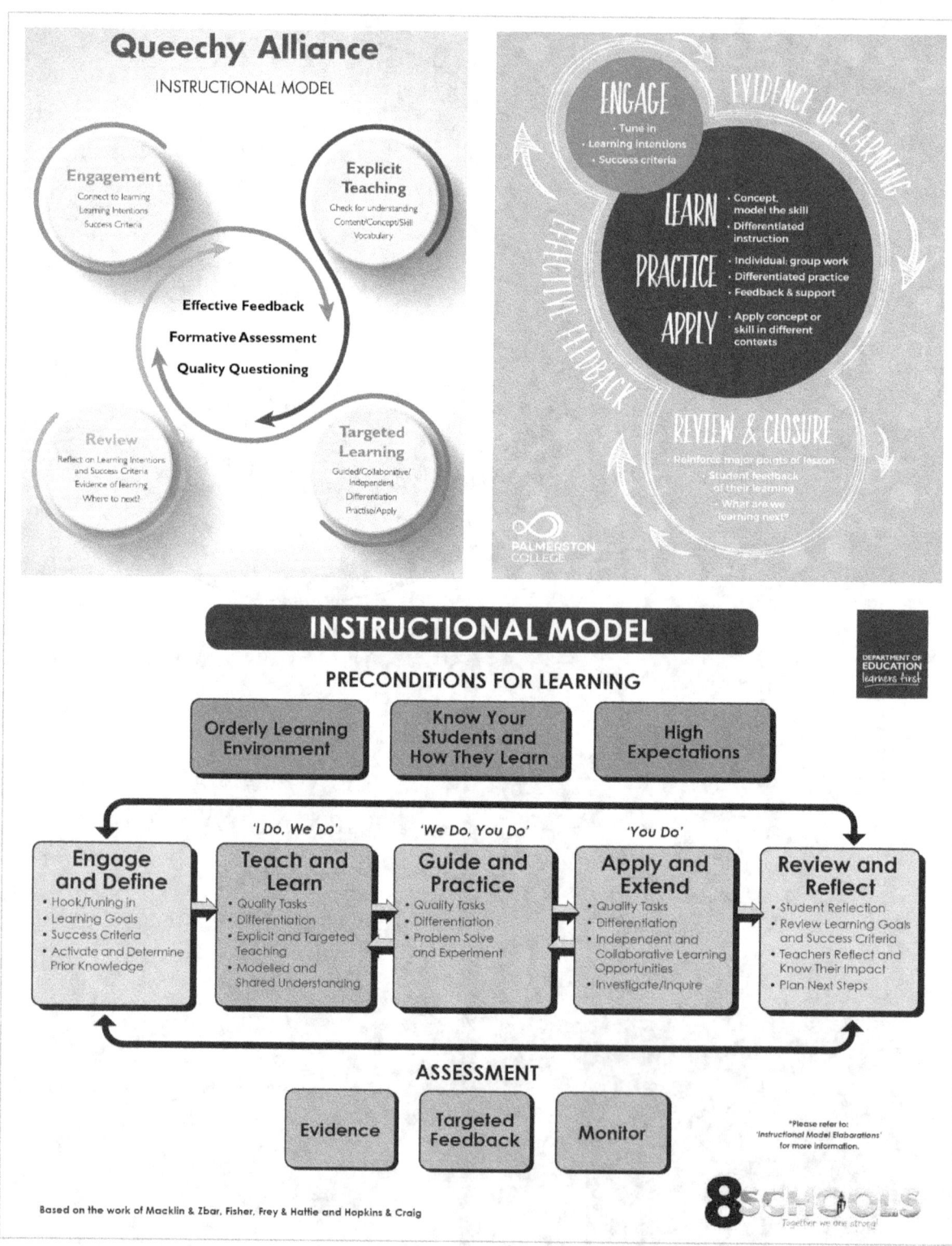

FIGURE 6.2: TASMANIAN AND NORTHERN TERRITORY SCHOOL INSTRUCTIONAL MODELS

Note: We would like to acknowledge the support of the Tasmanian Department of Education throughout this book, specifically with the involvement of the Central Coast Cluster, the muka layna Collaboration and the Queechy Alliance of schools.

This range of examples has been included to illustrate the variety of forms an instructional model can take, albeit all conforming to the common structure outlined, from tuning in to reflection and review, and bounded by evidence of learning and feedback during the lesson itself. What is more, it is a structure that, according to Goodwin (2018), reflects how student learning works. More specifically, he explains that if teachers are to effectively support students to move 'a new bit of knowledge … (to) a home in their long-term memory', then the lessons they design must:

- first capture the students' interest either by stirring their emotions or stimulating their curiosity, which is where the tuning in, or hook comes in
- then help them to commit to learning by relating the new knowledge and skills to a broader purpose and context through the learning goal and associated success criteria that are outlined
- get them to actively think about what they are learning using such strategies as note taking while something is explained, close reading of a text or following a process that is modelled by the teacher through the explicit instruction they provide
- help them to practise using the knowledge so they apply it more than once and begin to store it in their long-term memory
- support the development of multiple connections to the new learning in a variety of contexts through the process of reflection and review.

As Goodwin (2018) has demonstrated, an instructional model provides a mechanism for teachers to support students to cement new knowledge into their long-term memory while avoiding any cognitive overload. Guided (explicit) instruction and work samples can assist in this regard since, as Sweller (as cited in Russell, 2019) explains, the students 'are much less likely to experience an unnecessary overload on their working memory'. Students, he suggests 'should initially be given lots of explicit guidance to reduce their working memory load' and then once they are more knowledgeable, 'that (explicit) guidance is unnecessary and … so should be faded out to be replaced by problem-solving' (para. 9). This, it is noted, is similar to Fisher and Frey's (2013) gradual release model that is being used in many schools.

In all cases, the process for developing the school's instructional model when it does not have one is as important as the model itself, since it engages teachers in discussing the features of effective teaching that need to be represented in the graphic they then devise.

Not surprisingly, it needs to start with where the school currently is at. The following activity helps to identify how systematically you work to improve teaching throughout the school.

ACTIVITY FOR LEADERSHIP TEAMS: HOW SYSTEMATIC IS TEACHING IN OUR SCHOOL?

Instructions

1 Individually rate how effectively your school works to ensure consistently good teaching in all classrooms using a four-point scale where:
   1 = Totally ineffective, 2 = Ineffective, 3 = Effective and 4 = Fully effective.
2 Compare your ratings and discuss ways in which you can work to systematically ensure quality teaching occurs in all classrooms in the school.

DEVELOPING AN INSTRUCTIONAL MODEL

Note: Schools often use the term 'teaching and learning model' (TLM) rather than 'instructional model' (IM) and in the discussion that follows we use whichever terminology the school adopts. Developing an instructional model, as noted earlier, involves answering the four key questions about how any lesson will be planned and then will unfold.

Pamela has worked with a number of schools and networks to implement a developmental process that actively engages teachers at every step along the way and, in the case of the Queechy Alliance of seven schools in Tasmania for instance, spanned virtually an entire year. The process, which is outlined in Box 6.2 with reference to Noble Park Secondary College in Victoria where it was also rigorously applied, takes time, but helps ensure substantially more teacher ownership than otherwise would be the case, and hence contributes to the long-term sustainability of the model throughout the school.

Box 6.2

DEVELOPING AND IMPLEMENTING AN INSTRUCTIONAL MODEL AT NOBLE PARK SECONDARY COLLEGE

Preparing for collaborative professional learning

The process started with a rationale and initial professional learning session as outlined in the following email from the principal to all staff:

Dear colleagues,

To build on the successful teaching and learning practice at our school, we are going to develop a simple instructional model based on staff advice and input. In response to staff feedback, we are aware that the school has a range of curriculum and teaching documents which could be simplified and modified to better suit our needs. We know that staff are already working hard and very busy at this time of the year, so we have constructed a process to seek your input and consult with teachers across the school using existing meeting times, rather than add any further meetings or create any extra work. Three staff meetings this term will be allocated to this collaborative work.

Aim

The aim of the first session ... is for teachers to share and document the components of effective teaching and learning being used in all areas of our school. This will take place in small cross-school groups of teachers, led by a nominated staff member. This consultative process with teachers across the school is to help guide the development of a whole-school approach to what constitutes best teaching and learning practice in our context.

We already have exemplary teaching and learning practices taking place and we would like to support the sharing and strengthening of that in order to develop the NPSC IM [Noble Park Secondary College instructional model]. In order to develop our own instructional model, we need to hear from all staff regarding examples of sound, effective teaching and learning practice.

What you need to think about and bring to the session:
1 Think about the following questions and be ready to answer them in relation to how you construct your lessons.
  • How does the lesson begin?
  • What is the nature of your own presentation?
  • What kind of guided practice and independent practice is there?
  • How do you conclude a lesson and tie it into a coherent whole?

2 Bring along ideas and examples of at least two effective teaching strategies that you currently employ in your classroom. They can be related to any area of teaching—e.g. how to engage students in the lesson, giving feedback to students, differentiation, explicit teaching, reviewing the lesson.

The first session to get people engaged

The learning intention for the first professional learning session was to develop a shared understanding of the research and practice that informs the development of the Noble Park Secondary College (SC) instructional model (IM), including developing a shared language. This was accompanied by the two success criteria: 'I can explain why it is important for us to develop and implement a consistent IM for our school'; and 'I have shared and explained effective teaching strategies I use and key elements of a successful lesson'.

Input for consideration by staff focused on the research behind the use of an instructional model and examples of models from other schools. It made clear that an instructional model would be 'a consistent agreed structure *developed by you* to strengthen teaching and learning', and not 'a straightjacket' to be used in a 'prescriptive way to teach' or 'a fad' that is going away.

Then staff were invited to undertake two activities to commence the process of developing their own model for the school:

- Task 1—to consider the four questions outlined in point 1 above, and provide an example from their own experience of how they currently address each
- Task 2—to provide current quality examples of effective teaching and learning strategies being used in the school.

The session then ended by inviting staff to ask the questions 'you have about the development of our instructional model?' so their concerns could be heard, acknowledged and addressed.

Dealing with the questions

The range of questions identified were considered in depth by the leadership team which collaboratively prioritised them, developed a response and then progressively answered them over ensuing professional learning sessions with one or more questions addressed at the start of each to ensure they were all dealt with over time. Among other things this overall approach, which was mirrored in the other schools and networks with which Pamela worked, made the process more open, collaborative and hence real to the staff involved. It helped overcome the sense that many teachers often have that things are being 'done to' them and that leaders 'don't really know what it's like'.

Typical of the sort of questions that emerged across the schools and networks using the process outlined in this Box were:

- What will be the forum/process for updating and reviewing the model and best practices?
- How do we know it is embedded?
- How will we manage the transition as new school leaders move into our schools from outside?
- Should we have lesson plan pro formas that reflect the instructional model?
- How do you intend to target teachers who don't change the way they teach?
- Is there any suggested time allocations for each phase?
- How do we change the reality of a classroom—e.g. behaviour/trauma—to implement an IM?
- If it is taking 3 to 5 years to embed, is it being funded over this whole time?
- How do we ensure that the model is more than just posters around the school?

Answering these and the many other questions to arise, required leaders to consciously think

Continued...

through both the implementation of the model over time, the logistical issues that need to be taken into account, and the feeling among many staff about issues they felt need to be addressed. It constituted a very important strategy for engaging and hence carrying staff with the new approach.

The second session where the model starts to take shape

The learning intention for the second session was that, 'Staff will have collaboratively constructed the first draft of our Noble Park Secondary College instructional model'. The accompanying success criteria were that, 'By the end of the session, we will have reached a consensus within our groups on: the names of phases of our IM; the most important elements of a lesson; and the "givens" that will apply'.

The group work undertaken yielded broad agreement that the key phases and elements for a whole-school IM were:

Phases	Elements
Connect	Tune in Goals Success criteria
Teach	Modelling Worked examples Guided practice
Learn	Independent practice Applied learning
Reflect	Self-reflection Recap lesson

Underpinning these phases and elements were the 'essentials' of differentiation, evidence of learning, formative assessment and feedback.

The third session where there is consideration of the design

Staff were presented with the agreed phases, elements and essentials decided at the previous session and asked to work in groups to provide input to the IM design. More specifically, each group was provided with sample designs, such as those contained in Figures 6.1 and 6.2, and then divided into two sub-groups. Each sub-group was asked to identify 'preferred design features' and incorporate them on butchers' paper into an initial sub-group design. The sub-groups then shared their designs and created a joint whole-group model to be shared with the staff. All the designs were then collected and posted in the staff room for deeper consideration and any additional feedback that teachers chose to provide.

The school's leaders undertook to meet and develop a design brief for an instructional model based on the input from the staff. The model was then subject to further feedback and finalised so that posters could be printed and posted in every classroom from the commencement of the following school year. Having spent substantial time in 2018 getting to this point, the agreed instructional model in Figure 6.3 was then the focus of the first professional learning day to commence the following year.

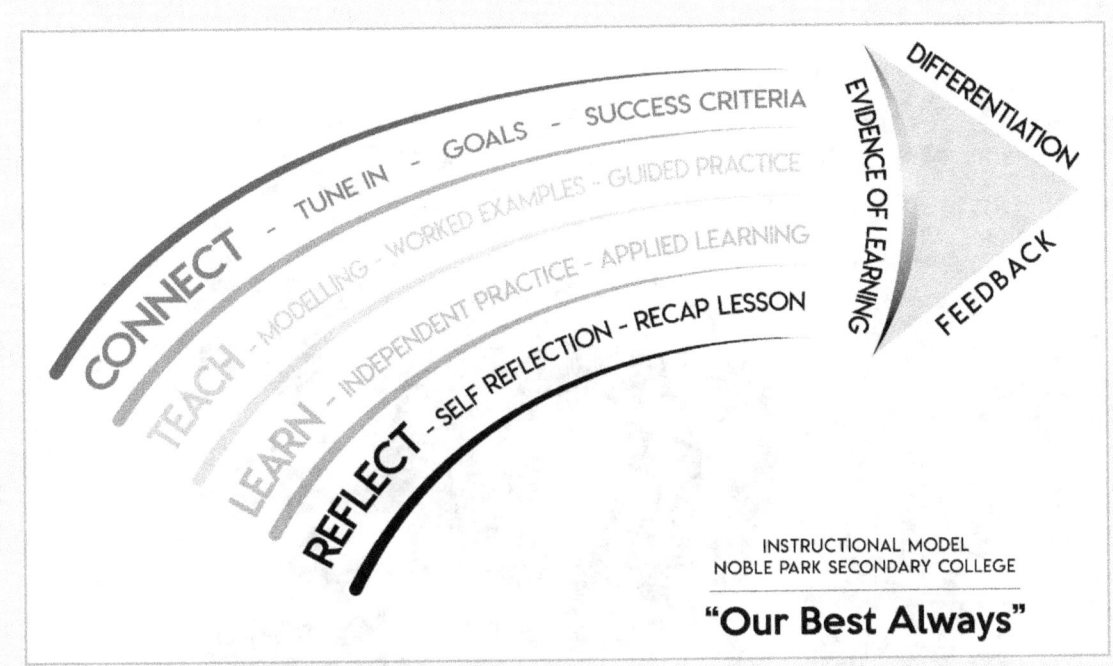

FIGURE 6.3: NOBLE PARK SECONDARY COLLEGE INSTRUCTIONAL MODEL

Preparing for implementation

The professional learning on the professional learning day had the goal of 'learning to apply the NPSC instructional model' and the associated success criteria that, 'I can: describe what teachers and students are doing during each phase of the model; identify the characteristics of effective learning goals; and write effective goals for my classes starting from tomorrow'.

Achieving this involved staff collaboration, sharing of their collective wisdom, a number of short and sharp activities in which they all engaged, recording of any 'burning questions' so they could be parked and then later addressed, and an expectation that there were 'no passengers' on the day.

Without going into the detail of the program material, suffice to say it both focused on, and established the basis for ongoing work about:

- the establishment of agreed effective practice
- embedding of consistent practice in all classrooms
- how long it realistically will take to embed consistent practice which follows the IM
- how teachers will know embedded effective practice when they see it.

This is work that continued well beyond the professional learning day driven by teachers' ratings of their own degree of understanding and confidence in using the IM, and the consequent identification of both their need for further support and what they feel they need to know more about.

The clear message from the Noble Park experience outlined in Box 6.2 is that developing and implementing an instructional model in a consistent, whole-school way cannot be a quick fix. It requires substantial investment of time, engagement of staff and professional learning if it is to work. Hence, it also needs a clear and coherent implementation plan. While each school or network will need to develop its own, some idea of the elements that such a plan might comprise can be gained from the sample plan developed by Oakleigh Grammar School for successfully developing and rolling out the teaching and learning model (TLM) it devised (see Figure 6.4).

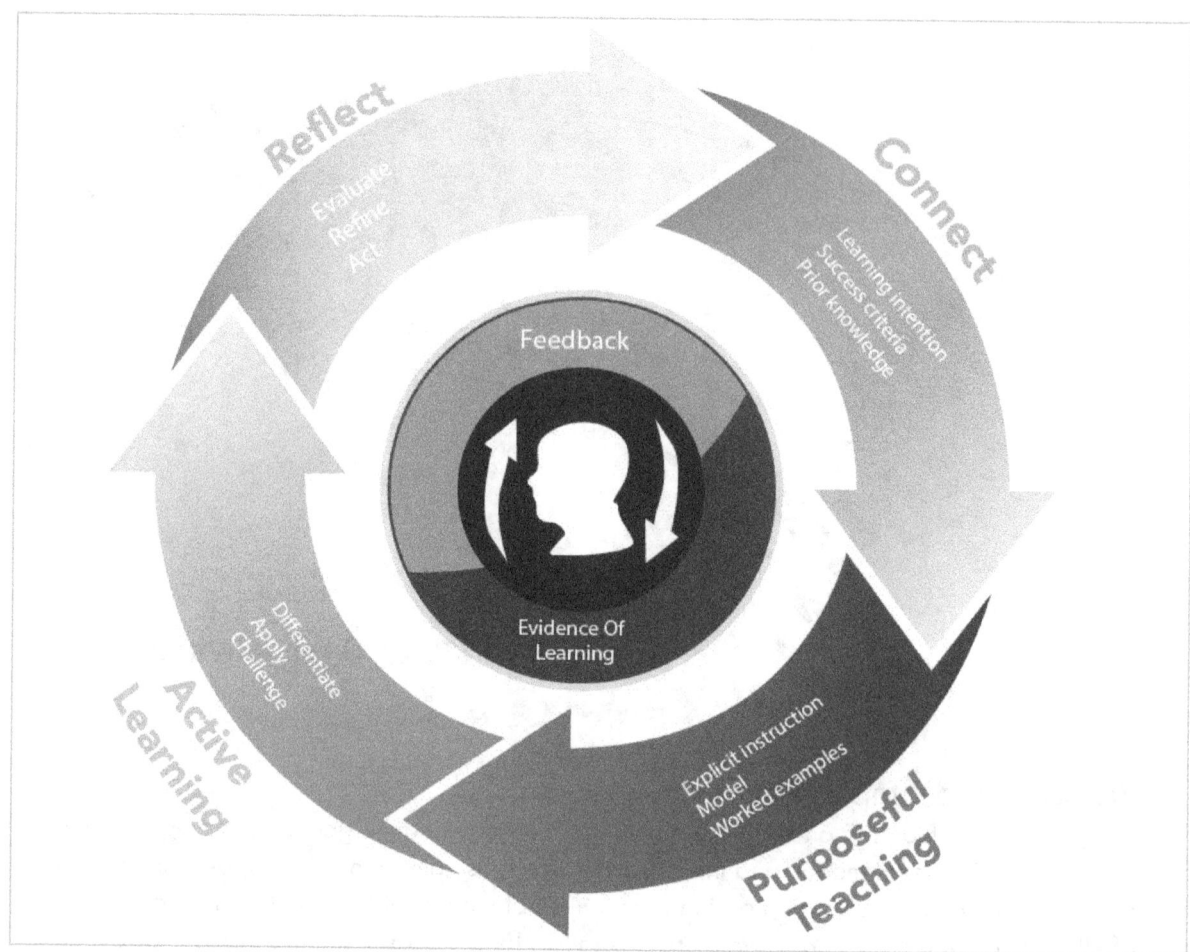

FIGURE 6.4: OAKLEIGH GRAMMAR SCHOOL TLM

The TLM implementation plan (see Table 6.2) contains 40 very specific goals to be achieved as this model is progressively implemented through the school. Each of these goals is accompanied by an outline of the particular tasks to be undertaken, who is responsible, the relevant timeline, success criteria to know when the goal has been reached and evidence of progress, as can be seen in the sample for goals 1 and 2 in Table 6.2.

TABLE 6.2: OAKLEIGH GRAMMAR SCHOOL TLM IMPLEMENTATION ACTION PLAN

Goal	Task	Who	Timeline	Success criteria	Evidence of progress
1. Develop a consistent whole-school Teaching and Learning Model (TLM)	Establish a dedicated team to guide the development and implementation of the TLM	Principal, Deputy Principals, Heads of School, Value Learning Team	March 2018	• TLM Team meets fortnightly to provide input to the action plan and make decisions on implementation • Develop an agreed set of norms and protocols to create a positive, goal-focused expectation • Action Plan is a dynamic document which is regularly reviewed and input sought from the TLM Team and staff groups	• Advise TLM Team members • Place norms and protocols on 18/04 meeting agenda • Update Action Plan and distribute copies
2. Engage staff in contributing to and implementing the TLM	• TLM Team need to meet to decide on key message to staff, how it is delivered and preparation required by all staff for 18 April. All staff need to hear the same messages: Why do we need to have a more consistent structure? (e.g. a need to build on the excellent teaching practice currently occurring, have consistent practice across the school, focus on student learning and growth, collaboration). What messages don't we want? (e.g. it's new, you're not doing a good job, giving up what we already are doing).	[Name deleted] to convene	18 April 2018	• TLM Team members meet with the Education Committee • All TLM Team members need to communicate the main messages about the TLM via meeting structure	• Place key message on 18/04 meeting agenda
	• Put meetings and Professional Learning (PL) sessions on the calendar, which will be dedicated to engaging with staff in the development and implementation of the TLM	[Name deleted]	20 March 2018		• Schedule whole-school staff PL sessions on meeting schedule

Notes: The names of any individuals have been deleted for reasons of anonymity.
While the timelines are specific to the school, they have been included to provide an indication of how much time is needed to develop and begin to implement a TLM for it to be embedded in a school.
The terms in this table have been presented exactly as supplied by the school.

The remaining goals in the plan comprise the following:

3. Identify the top five key components of effective lesson structures (e.g. goals, explicit teaching) currently used by staff
4. Collate and synthesise outcomes of May 7 workshop
5. Develop a range of strategies to ensure the effective implementation of the TLM (June 18 & 19 Executive Coaching sessions)
6. Provide input into the development of the staff professional learning on June 4
7. Collate, review and synthesise the essential components of each phase of the discussion group's TLM (June 4 workshop)
8. Launch the TLM
9. July 23—Brief relevant teams on Phase 4 TLM
10. Plan for Aug 6 and Aug 20, Whole-School Staff Workshops on Phase 1, *Connect*
11. Aug 6—First Whole-School Staff Workshop on Phase 1, *Connect*
12. Aug 20—Second Whole-School Staff Workshop on Phase 1, *Connect*
13. Aug 23—TLM Team Feedback Meeting from Aug 6 and Aug 20 workshops
14. Oct 8 Staff PD Day—further develop teacher skills in writing Learning Intentions (LIs) and Success Criteria (SC)
15. Oct 10—TLM Team Planning Meeting
16. Oct 18—Teacher-led professional learning for the writing of good LIs and SC
17. Nov 29—TLM Team Meeting
18. Confirm 2019 Strategic Plan and preparations for Jan 29 faculty/year level meetings
19. Brief whole-school session on Term 1 TLM professional learning program
20. Begin the consolidation of the Connect phase in faculty/year level groups
21. Determine the Explicit Instruction reading to brief teachers prior to Feb 20 Whole-School Staff Workshop
22. Begin planning Feb 20 Whole-School TLM Workshop on Purposeful Teaching
23. Planning meeting with TLM Team for Feb 20 Whole-School Workshop
24. Whole-School Staff Workshop. Introduce staff to Purposeful Teaching phase
25. Plan Whole-School TLM Workshop on Purposeful Teaching for March 6
26. Development of Purposeful Teaching phase for March 6 workshop
27. Teacher development of Purposeful Teaching phase
28. Review of April 23 Whole-School TLM Workshop
29. Development of Purposeful Teaching phase for June 3 workshop
30. Implement TLM June 3 Whole-School Workshop
31. Development of Aug 12 TLM Workshop
32. Implement TLM Aug 12 Whole-School Workshop
33. Development of Sept 9 TLM Workshop
34. Implement TLM Sept 9 Whole-School Workshop
35. Review, plan and develop, Term 4 TLM professional development
36. Action planning for 2020
37. All teachers, Heads of Faculty, Senior Leadership Team and Executive conduct Learning Walks each term as outlined in agreed Learning Protocols
38. Clearly communicate purpose, process and value of Learning Walks to all staff
39. Gather baseline data from students on presence of and use of LI and SC throughout lessons
40. Work collaboratively with staff to write and implement effective LI and SC.

It is a plan that reinforces the critical message that, if an instructional or teaching and learning model is to be introduced, then staff must be engaged at all stages along the way, albeit with clear leadership on how the model is being developed and implemented over time, and the process cannot be rushed. It will be worth it in the end because of the greater levels of commitment that will flow, and the increased likelihood that the model will be embedded, and hence sustainable, over time.

EXPLICIT INSTRUCTION

Pioneer State High School in Mackay, Queensland is another school that, at the time of the first edition of this book, had unpacked its school-wide pedagogical framework in a handbook for staff. The handbook, which derived from a range of research examined by the school included the explicit instruction lesson sequence in Figure 6.5 that informed the structure of lessons its teachers planned. While the school has subsequently updated its pedagogical model and associated advice for staff, the approach the figure contains reminds us to ensure that lessons do reflect the evidence of learning approaches that work, and a deep understanding of how students learn.

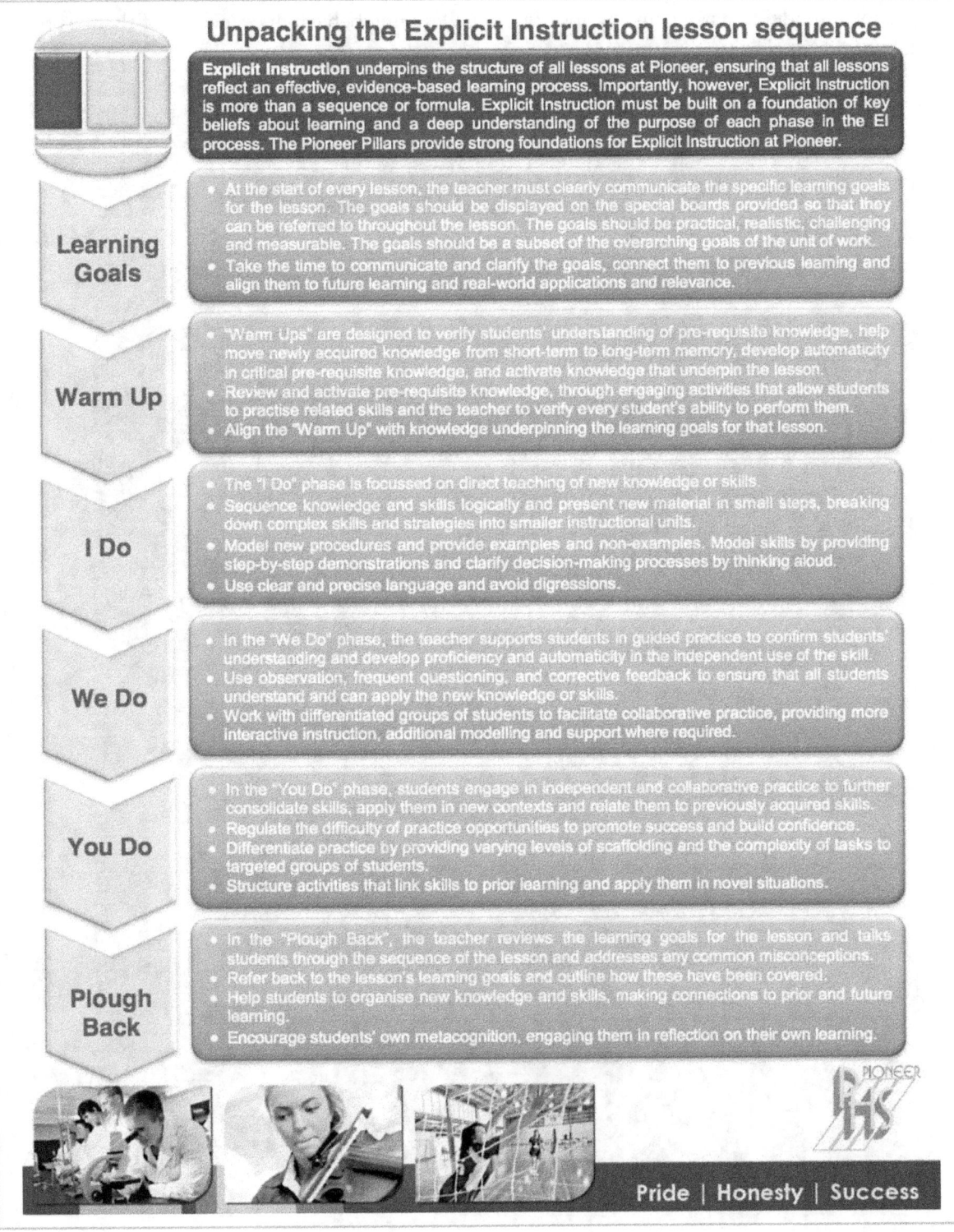

FIGURE 6.5: THE EXPLICIT INSTRUCTION LESSON PROCESS AT PIONEER STATE HIGH

It is important to note at this juncture that it is not sufficient to produce detailed handbooks of this sort to drive an instructional model, and hence consistently better teaching through the school. Such handbooks constitute a very important start, but are only as good as the collaborative planning and professional learning that accompany them in the school's professional learning teams, and the classroom observation that contributes to their consistent implementation across the school. Classroom observation, which is discussed in depth in Chapter 8, is especially needed to ensure that take-up of the model is more than just lip-service in classrooms across the school.

Beyond this, consideration can also be given to how the students can be actively involved. Hampton Park Primary School, for example, has sought to extend the implementation of its instructional model to its students by specifying the learning behaviours expected of them as the model unfolds in class (see Figure 6.6).

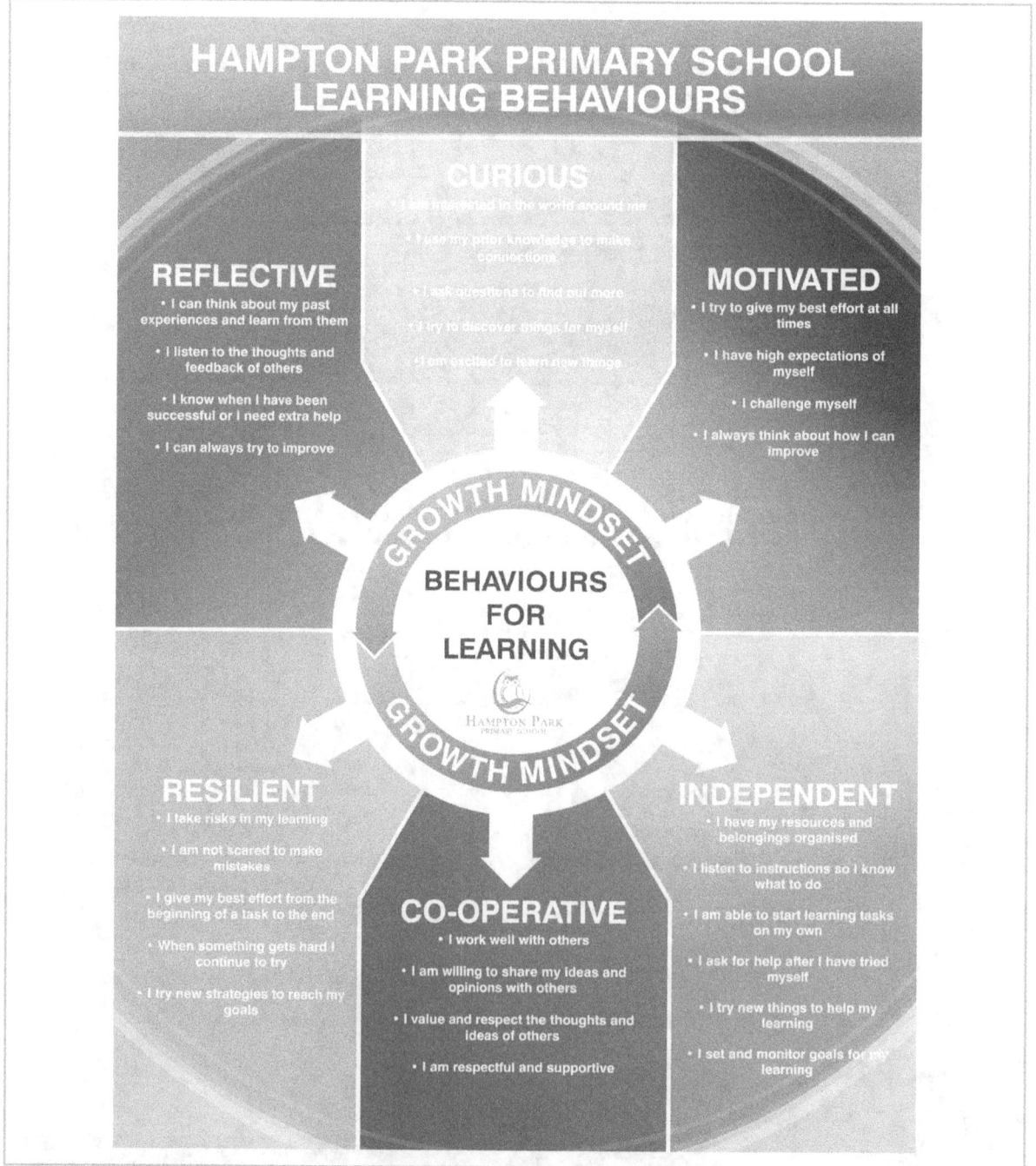

FIGURE 6.6: HAMPTON PARK PRIMARY SCHOOL LEARNING BEHAVIOURS

Note: The development of this model was informed by a set of learning behaviours in use at All Saints' Primary School in the UK that can be retrieved at https://allsaintsprimary.org/children/learning-behaviours/

All of the models included in this chapter, as noted by Pioneer State High, are underpinned by an explicit instruction lesson sequence and a scaffolded approach, so it is worth briefly discussing this in a little more depth.

Explicit instruction, according to Archer and Hughes (2011), is 'an unambiguous and direct approach to teaching that includes both instructional design and delivery procedures … (It) is characterised by a series of supports or scaffolds, whereby students are guided through the learning process with clear statements about the purpose and rationale for learning the new skill, with clear explanations and demonstrations of the instructional target, and supported practice with feedback until independent mastery has been achieved' (p. 1).

They give substance to this definition by outlining 16 elements of explicit instruction that are included in the first chapter of their book, and available as a free download on the explicit instruction website (http://explicitinstruction.org/download/sample-chapter.pdf). In summary form, the 16 elements comprise the following:

1. Focus instruction on critical content
2. Sequence skills logically
3. Break down complex skills and strategies into smaller instructional units
4. Design organised and focused lessons
5. Begin lessons with a clear statement of the lesson's goals and expectations
6. Review prior skills and knowledge before beginning instruction
7. Provide step-by-step demonstrations
8. Use clear and concise language
9. Provide an adequate range of examples and non-examples
10. Provide guided and supported practice
11. Require frequent responses
12. Monitor student performance closely
13. Provide immediate, affirmative and corrective feedback
14. Deliver the lesson at a brisk pace
15. Help students organise knowledge
16. Provide distributed and cumulative practice.

While these are rich in detail and ought to be explored by teachers in depth, they are also arguably difficult for busy teachers to retain and hence implement. The following activity is designed to support teachers to deepen their understanding of the 16 elements enunciated by Archer and Hughes (2011), and package them in a more manageable form. At the very least, asking teachers to distil the elements into a smaller set requires them to think deeply about each element and the linkages between them that can be made.

ACTIVITY FOR STAFF: DEVELOPING UNDERSTANDING OF EXPLICIT INSTRUCTION TO INFORM LESSON PLANNING

Note: When we conduct this activity in schools, we ask participants to read at least pages 1–12 of Archer and Hughes' book (2011) before the session so they have an initial understanding of the 16 elements of explicit instruction that the authors describe.

Instructions

1 Consider the 16 elements of explicit instruction outlined above and work in teams to rationalise them down to five key guiding points for planning more effective lessons in the school.

2 Compare what you develop with our attempt below and amend it as required:
- **Check** the students' grasp of the required knowledge and skills
- **Share** the Learning Goal and Success Criteria with the students, ensure they are tuned in and **present** appropriately scaffolded input
- **Lead guided practice** using challenging, achievable tasks, with timely feedback and support, along with any reteaching that may be required
- **Provide independent practice** to reinforce automaticity
- **Undertake periodic review** to ensure the knowledge and skills are maintained.

3 As an adjunct to this activity, you may like to match either the five points you identified, or ours, to your school's instructional model to see how closely they align. Our experience is that there is often a very close fit, which is reaffirming for the school.

In a somewhat similar vein, Pamela has used an article from Shasta County in California (2009) that distils explicit instruction into a sequence of six supports aligned to the structure of a typical instructional model comprising:
- Setting the stage for learning
- Clear explanation of what to do
- Modelling the process (showing)
- Guided practice
- Independent practice (when the teacher is confident the students will be successful)
- Assessment/Closure (informal or formal).

'Every lesson', it is explained, 'may not have every component, or a lesson may span several days, so not all components would be seen each day' (p. 3).

Used as a pre-reading, the article forms the basis of a professional learning session for staff where, drawing on the example of a day conducted by Oakleigh Grammar School, staff view one or more videos of teachers using explicit instruction[4] and then work collaboratively to answer the following questions:
- Which of the six components of explicit instruction was the teacher using?
- What did you think was effective? Why?
- How was the teacher providing feedback to students?
- What did you see that you could try in your own teaching? What would you do differently?

---

[4] For example, an AITSL video that can be viewed at https://www.aitsl.edu.au/tools-resources/resource/explicit-instruction-illustration-of-practice, or an American example such as https://www.teachingchannel.org/video/improving-teacher-practice

The responses are then used by teachers to each develop a plan of action for the ensuing two weeks that addresses:
- 'the implications for my own teaching as a result of my reading and then viewing the videos'
- 'three explicit instruction strategies I can include in my teaching practice and will commit to include in my lessons this week'
- 'a means of documenting and sharing my explicit teaching practice at our next professional learning session'.

Then at the follow-up session, staff were each provided up to five minutes to present 'evidence of the strategies you have implemented and discuss successes and challenges'. They could choose how to present this, including as 'video, demonstration, student work, planning documents, learning resources or something else'.

MAKING THE INSTRUCTIONAL MODEL HAPPEN IN YOUR SCHOOL

One of the most significant developments we have seen since this book was first published in 2017 is the work that many schools, and in some cases clusters, have done to drive a common instructional model consistently through. We have, as a result, learned much about how this successfully can be achieved, which is worth sharing at this point.

Initially, the schools focused on developing an understanding of why an instructional model matters for improving classroom practice, what the different components of the model mean and some basic strategies that can be used to put the model into effect. Consistent with Knight's (2018) advice cited in Chapter 2, to make things easier for teachers and involve them in the process along the way, they have developed manuals for staff with detailed advice on how the model can best be used in lesson planning and then delivery in class.

Once the model takes hold sufficiently through the school, attention can shift to improving the quality of implementation by focusing on one element of the model at a time, based on staff feedback on where they most need support. Ideally such support should be differentiated via targeted instructional coaching and customised professional learning as outlined in the school experiences that are discussed in the remainder of this chapter and the next.

MANUALS TO SUPPORT IMPLEMENTATION

Glen Waverley Secondary College is a school that has developed a detailed handbook to promote a thorough understanding of its instructional model (Figure 6.7) and to support its consistent implementation through the school.

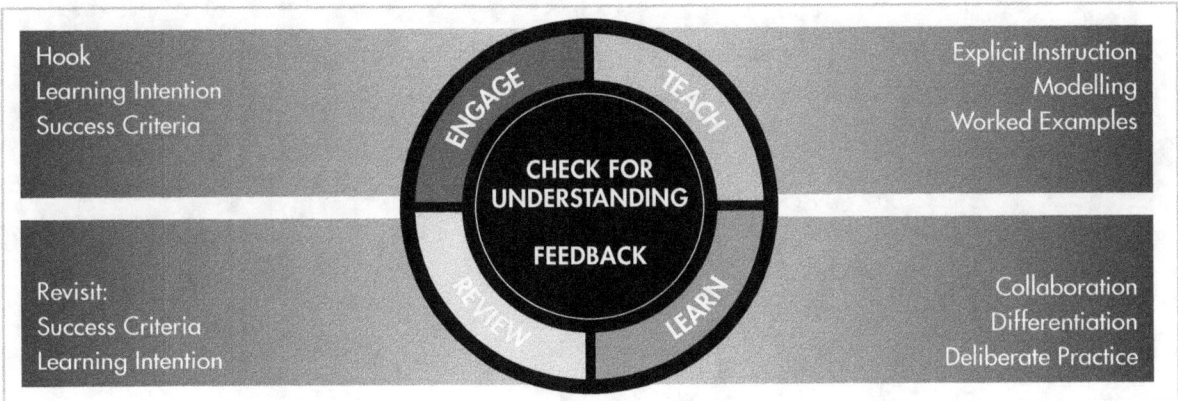

FIGURE 6.7: GLEN WAVERLEY SECONDARY COLLEGE INSTRUCTIONAL MODEL

The handbook starts by outlining what an instructional model is and then proceeds to unpack its components in terms of:
- a description of what the element means
- an outline of why it ought to be used
- an indication of its measured effect size
- a list of examples of how teachers might apply it in class
- some questions for reflection to support ongoing professional learning of the staff.

Some of the flavour of the school's approach can be gained from its outline of the modelling component of the 'Teach' phase (Figure 6.8).

TEACH – MODELLING

What is Modelling?
Modelling is a versatile strategy that is part of explicit instruction. It is a form of 'show and tell' whereby the students and the teacher develop a collective understanding of the process and quality to achieve the task intention. Modelling is a form of scaffolding which supports the student to understand how to achieve by making the process visible to them. This strategy highlights metacognition (thinking). Multiple exposures to modelled tasks allows teachers to embed processes and skills for the learners.

> 'How do students know what is expected of them? Through explicit teacher modelling, the teacher provides students with a clear example of a skill or strategy. The teacher provides a structure to guide students.'
>
> *Intel Teach Program (2012) Designing Effective Projects–Instructional Practices: Modelling.*

Why use it?
'Put simply, telling involves sharing information or knowledge with your students, while showing involves modelling how to do something. Once you are clear about what you want your students to know and be able to do by the end of the lesson, you need to tell them what they need to know and show them how to do the tasks you want them to be able to do.'
Killian (2018) Top 10 Evidence Based Teaching Strategies.

How to use modelling in the classroom
Modelling processes with students involves:
- Establishing clear aims.
- Providing an example.
- Exploring thinking - yours and the students.
- Demonstrating the process.
- Working together through the example.
- Providing prompts (or scaffolds) as appropriate.
- Providing an opportunity for students to work themselves (alone or in pairs).
- Drawing out the key learning.

Oer.educ.cam.ac.uk. (2018) Teaching approaches: Modelling.

Examples of modelling in the classroom
- 'Thinking aloud' as the teacher comments and makes their thinking visible as they read a text.
- Using the 'write around' strategy to show students the thinking process when unpacking a question or task.
- Using a case study or problem-solving scenario related to the learning intention.
- Using samples of high, medium and low examples of a completed task for students to discuss and mark against the assessment criteria, for example model essays.
- Linking learning to a real world task to show application outside the classroom .
- Clearly describing features of the strategy or steps in performing the skill. Breaking the skill into learnable parts.
- A science teacher demonstrating part or all of an experiment.
- An art teacher demonstrating a skill like rendering.
- In Maths, using a worked example and diagrams.

Reflection
Do you draw on a repertoire of strategies when modelling tasks in the classroom?

Have you thought of asking students to model their thinking to the class as a means of nurturing student agency? How do you go about this?

FIGURE 6.8: GLEN WAVERLEY SECONDARY COLLEGE INSTRUCTIONAL MODEL HANDBOOK EXTRACT

The provision of detailed advice of this sort for each element of the model in Figure 6.8 is a crucial first step in supporting teachers to meet the College expectation that they 'follow the structure of the Instructional Model as they plan and deliver the curriculum'. It's an expectation that reflects an understanding that the model, which initially was collaboratively developed by staff in 2015 and then reviewed and refined in 2018 to better reflect the common language of instruction used by teachers at the school, is 'a key driver of improvement for the College'.

Implementation, it is explained, need not necessarily be sequential, though 'it is important that the Engage phase be implemented at the beginning of the lesson and the Review phase be implemented at the end … as well as throughout the lesson', to provide a coherent beginning and ending to the lesson as a whole.

Similarly, Springvale Rise Primary School has developed a detailed handbook for staff to support the implementation of its instructional model in Figure 6.9.

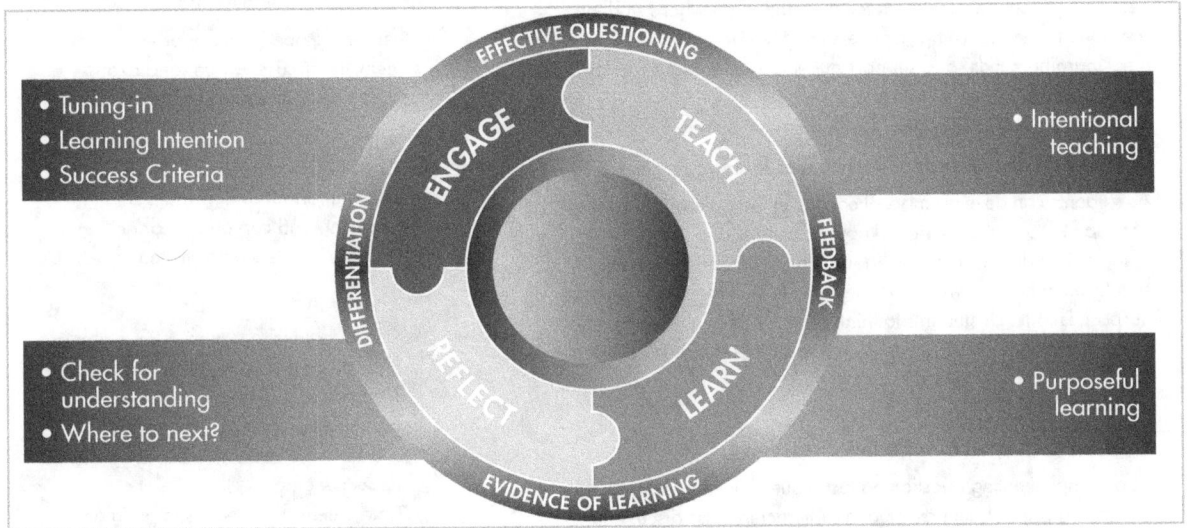

FIGURE 6.9: SPRINGVALE RISE PRIMARY SCHOOL INSTRUCTIONAL MODEL

This model, the handbook explains, 'supports collaboration and consistency of effective practice across the school … and provides a framework that underpins effective instruction'. More specifically it suggests that the model provides:
- a shared language used by all teachers
- a common understanding of the structure of a lesson
- clear expectations of the learning that is to take place in a lesson and what success looks like for the students
- shared understandings about highly effective teaching practices and how they are used to differentiate instruction
- a framework to facilitate collaborative planning and strengthening teacher capacity
- direct links to planning documentation that incorporate the gradual release of responsibility model.[5]

Like Glen Waverley, the Springvale Rise handbook then proceeds to unpack each element of its instructional model in terms of what the element means and how it can be enacted by teachers and students in class. The support for effective questioning provided in Figure 6.10, which is one of the 'through lines which strengthen effective instruction and occur routinely during all phases of the lesson', provides a case in point.

---

[5] The gradual release of responsibility model is a structured method of pedagogy framed around a process devolving responsibility within the learning process from the teacher to the eventual independence of the learner. There is substantial material on the model available on the internet, such as the Association for Supervision and Curriculum Development (ASCD) outline that can be accessed at http://www.ascd.org/publications/books/113006/chapters/Learning,-or-Not-Learning,-in-School.aspx

EFFECTIVE QUESTIONING

Effect size: 0.48

Hattie (December 2017) visiblelearningplus.com

7. QUESTIONING

What is effective questioning?

Questioning is a powerful tool and effective teachers regularly use it for a range of purposes. It engages students, stimulates interest and curiosity in the learning, and makes links to students' lives. Questioning opens up opportunities for students to discuss, argue and express opinions and alternative points of view. Effective questioning yields immediate feedback on student understanding, supports informal and formative assessment, and captures feedback on effectiveness of teaching strategies.

Questioning can be used to prompt students to think about what is being taught and to give teachers information on where students are up to in their learning. Teachers can then adjust instructions to meet learning needs, and support students to progress towards their learning goals.

Why should teachers use effective questioning?

As students can develop misconceptions in their learning, teachers need to find out what students know or believe at a particular point in time during a lesson. The primary purpose of questioning should be to find out what students need to be taught next. Another purpose is to teach students to think critically through questioning requiring deeper analyses rather than a simple yes or no or recall of information.

Practical techniques for effective questioning:

Before implementing questioning techniques it is important to have underlying rules about how students interact in class discussion.

1. Focus on questioning as part of the planning process. Make sure the questions are clear and focused on the task or process at hand to avoid confusion or misunderstanding.
2. Vary the types of questions asked. For example, asking students to recall information, to modify or correct incomplete or incorrect statements, or to 'turn and talk' to a peer.
3. Call on students regardless of whether they have put their hand up. This develops a culture of engaged accountability because all students come to expect and prepare for the possibility that they might be asked to offer an opinion, answer a question or solve a problem at any time.
4. Increase wait time. This provides students with more time to consider and come up with meaningful answers. However, teachers need to be mindful of providing too much wait time as it can slow the pace of a lesson.
5. Listen to the questions that students ask each other. These questions can provide valuable information about what the students know, what they need to know next and the way that they articulate their understanding.

Overview

Questioning is a powerful tool and effctive teachers regularly use it for a range of purposes. It engages students, stimulates interest and curiosity in the learning, and makes links to students' lives.

Questioning opens up opportunities for students to discuss, argue, and express opinions and alternative points of view.

Effective questioning yields immediate feedback on student understanding, supports informal and formative assessment, and captures feedback on the effectiveness of teaching strategies.

Key elements

- Plan questions in advance for probing, extending, revising and reflecting
- Teachers use open questions
- Questions used as an immediate source of feedback to track progress/understanding
- Cold call and strategic sampling are commonly used questioning strategies.

Related effect sizes*

- Questioning – 0.46

FIGURE 6.10: SPRINGVALE RISE PRIMARY SCHOOL INSTRUCTIONAL MODEL HANDBOOK EXTRACT

These and other schools that have developed hard copy handbooks for staff ensure that they are routinely brought to all school-based professional learning sessions since all such sessions are linked to the implementation of the instructional model in some way. In addition, many schools have developed electronic versions of the hard copy handbooks that contain links to practical examples of effective teaching tools and practices, including videos, lesson plans and other teaching resources. Perhaps even more powerful still is the fact that, as teachers gain confidence in their skills and expertise in using the instructional model, they are posting videos of their own practice and sharing resources with colleagues as a matter of course. Generally in this context, a leader is nominated to moderate and support teachers in posting material online to ensure both the quality of what is posted and that it remains a manageable amount.

These are important practices the schools have adopted to help embed and hence ensure the sustainability of the approach.

The extracts from both Glen Waverley and Springvale Rise in Figures 6.8 and 6.10 are examples of how schools can work to make implementation of an instructional model easier, as Knight (2018) recommends, while helping to ensure more consistent implementation through the school.

The following activity can assist leaders to determine the nature and extent of support that teachers will require as they work to implement the instructional model in the school.

ACTIVITY FOR LEADERSHIP TEAMS: SUPPORTING TEACHERS TO IMPLEMENT THE INSTRUCTIONAL MODEL

Instructions

Work together as a team and, taking account of the experience outlined of both Glen Waverley Secondary College and Springvale Rise Primary School, complete Table 6.3 outlining actions that leaders and teachers can take to drive the instructional model through the school. An example has been provided to get you started in each case.

TABLE 6.3: MAKING IT EASIER FOR TEACHERS TO IMPLEMENT THE APPROACH

	Structural support	Professional learning support	Other documentation required
Action leaders can take	Provide sufficient time for PLTs to meet	Model the teaching of lessons planned using the IM	Provide sample lesson plans for teachers to use
Action teachers can take	Ensure you are prepared for each PLT meeting	Observe model lessons and be observed by others	Share lesson plans that have worked well in your class

© Pamela Macklin and Vic Zbar, *Driving School Improvement 2nd Edition*, Australian Council for Educational Research, 2020

EMBEDDING ONE PHASE AT A TIME

Both the Central Coast Cluster of eight schools[6] and the Queechy Alliance of seven schools[7] in Tasmania initially worked to ensure understanding and support for their common instructional models (see Figure 6.2), along the lines of Glen Waverley and Springvale Rise, as the basis for then moving to focus on one element of their model at a time to ensure it is consistently driven through. In each case they started with learning goals and success criteria, since these are the frame for lesson planning as outlined in more detail in Chapter 7. (Note, while the Central Coast Cluster uses the term 'learning goals', the Queechy Alliance uses 'learning intentions' instead, as reflected in the discussion that follows.) In fact, consistent with our advice to use this book in a way that reflects the diagnosis of where your school is at, you may choose to pause at this point and read the section on learning goals in Chapter 7 before continuing to the discussion of Queechy and Central Coast.

Having sufficiently cemented the use of learning goals and associated success criteria, they then each moved directly to the review and reflect phase of their models, based on the clear feedback collected from staff that this is the element where they felt they most needed support.

USING LEARNING GOALS: CENTRAL COAST CLUSTER

Having worked with Vic on the development of their instructional model, the Central Coast Cluster focused its professional learning for staff on supporting the use of learning goals to plan and deliver more effective lessons in class. A series of four after-hours meetings was organised in each school—two on learning goals and then a further two on success criteria—that were contextualised as needed to reflect the stage the school had reached in driving the instructional model through. Each meeting lasted around an hour, and included readings and videos of teacher practice to structure the conversation as illustrated in Tables 6.4 and 6.5 for the two meetings on learning goals.

---

[6] The Central Coast Cluster comprises Ulverstone Secondary College, Penguin District School and East Ulverstone, Forth, Riana, Sprent, Ulverstone and West Ulverstone Primary Schools.

[7] The Queechy Alliance comprises Queechy High School, along with East Launceston, Norwood, Punchbowl, St Leonards, Ravenswood Heights and Waverley Primary Schools.

TABLE 6.4: PROFESSIONAL LEARNING TEAM PLAN FOR MEETING 1

Middle Years Literacy Project (MYLP) Professional Learning Team Meeting Plan 1		
Date: Attendees:	Focus for meeting: Delivery of learning goals	Roles: Facilitator: Note taker: Time keeper:

Review and reflect	**Introduction to the group:** Short introduction about the work of this group—focusing on middle years, consistency of practice.	
Engage and define	**Learning goal:** You will be able to define what makes an effective learning goal and analyse how they are delivered.	
	Success criteria: • Plan in detail how you will deliver a learning goal for one of your future lessons • Provide feedback on other people's elaborations for their learning goals	
	Hook: *(1–5 minutes of tuning in—relevant for meeting focus)* Ninety-eight per cent of staff surveyed said they use learning goals. Out of that 98%, 42% said they used them daily and 11% used them weekly. How can we encourage people to use these every day?	
Teach and learn	**Research/Evidence/Professional learning:** *(Professional reading, video, picture to discuss about the focus)* 'Learning goals as the entry point', Macklin & Zbar (2017), *Driving school improvement* (see pp. 177–83 in this edition) Read this with the viewpoint of where you are at in your own learning so far. **5-3-1** • Everybody decides on the top 5 ideas from the reading. • Pair up and share your ideas, together decide on the top 3 ideas that were shared. • Come back together as a group and share the pairs' ideas, collectively decide on one main idea from the reading and write this as a sentence. Share this sentence with your in-school mentor who will then pass this idea onto [name deleted] for collation.	

Continued…

Table 6.4 (continued)

Guide and practise	**Observation/Discussion:** *(Watch the learning goal described in the video of one of our teachers.)* What was one positive in the video you could identify? What do you do the same and/or differently?
Apply and extend	**Putting it into practice:** Write a learning goal and success criteria for your next literacy lesson. What are two ways you can deliver this learning goal and success criteria? Share with the group for feedback.
Review and reflect	**Actions to complete before the next meeting:** Watch the teaching video again. Pause the video when you find something significant about the learning goal (that hasn't been discussed in this meeting) and write down what you noticed and the time on the video. We will discuss this in the next meeting. Ask students in your class to complete the Google Forms survey that asks them if they know what a learning goal is and what success criteria are. Please ask them to complete the survey at least one week before your next meeting. Deliver your learning goal and be prepared to discuss how it went when we meet again.

TABLE 6.5: PROFESSIONAL LEARNING TEAM PLAN FOR MEETING 2

Middle Years Literacy Project (MYLP) Professional Learning Team Meeting Plan 1			
Date: **Attendees:**		**Focus for meeting:** Delivery of learning goals	**Roles:** Facilitator: Note taker: Time keeper:
Review and reflect	**Follow-up from previous meeting/Reflection:** *(What is working? What challenges are arising?)* What did the student survey tell you about your learning goals? After looking at the delivery of your learning goals last meeting has the way you deliver them changed? If so, how?		
Engage and define	**Hook:** *(1–5 minutes of tuning in — relevant for meeting focus)* Achieving explicit learning goals: https://www.youtube.com/watch?v=0v3iXmT0-oU (4min 36[8])		
Teach and learn	**Research/Evidence/Professional learning:** *(Professional reading, video, picture to discuss about the focus)* After watching the YouTube video and reviewing Figure 7.3 on page 118 of Macklin & Zbar (2017) (Note: Figure 7.3 is on p. 178 of this edition), look at how effective your learning goals were and how well you delivered them: • What would you do the same? • What would you change? • How do you ensure all students are understanding what your learning goals are? • What is another strategy you could use?		

Continued...

---

[8] A videoed illustration of practice developed by AITSL.

Table 6.5 (continued)

Guide and practise	**Observation:** After watching the teacher video again in between sessions, what moments were significant where you needed to stop? What was one positive in the video you could identify? Was the learning goal easy to understand? What went well? What would you do the same/differently?
Apply and extend	**Putting it into practice:** Work with the team on a common learning goal for a priority in your subject that you can trial and bring back as a reflection for our next meeting. (This might mean that your team needs to break into smaller groups.) Discuss how you can deliver the goal to ensure all students are understanding it. Complete the unpacking learning goal sheet as a team to support your goal—focusing on how you deliver the information to your class.
Review and reflect	**Actions to complete before the next meeting:** Trial the learning goal created. Ask students in one of your classes to complete the learning goals survey on Google Forms (from Macklin and Zbar, 2017) (see Figure 7.5, p. 189 in this edition). This survey asks your students if you use learning goals, if learning goals are useful and what makes a good learning goal.

The non-threatening environment created by these interactive sessions across the cluster has helped ensure that the common instructional model has really taken hold, and that learning goals are used to structure the planning and delivery of lessons to students in its schools. This is readily evident in the fact that 79% of students surveyed only one term after implementation commenced indicated that they knew what a learning goal was, while a further 10% said maybe and only 11% did not know. A staggering 92% of students surveyed in the following term felt that having learning goals is useful in order to 'know what I am learning' (61%) and 'know what I am doing' (31%).

Recognising the fact that significant staff turnover tends to occur in cluster schools, a structured induction program was also introduced to prepare and support teachers to understand and be able to use the common instructional model in use, where possible starting before they even arrived in the school.

REVIEW AND REFLECTION: THE QUEECHY ALLIANCE

Prior to focusing on the review and reflect stage of the lesson as indicated above, the Queechy Alliance, like the Central Coast Cluster, worked to ensure that lessons are consistently planned from learning intentions that reflect what teachers expect their students to learn. To help ensure this is the case, the Alliance developed the planning pro forma in Table 6.6 to structure the way in which coherent and effective lessons are devised.

TABLE 6.6: QUEECHY ALLIANCE INSTRUCTIONAL MODEL—LESSON PLAN

	Phase	Elements	What is the teacher saying/doing?	What is the student saying/doing?
Quality questioning, Effective feedback, Formative assessment	Engagement	Connect to learning Learning intentions Success criteria		
	Explicit teaching	Content/concept/skill Vocabulary Check for understanding		
	Targeted learning	Differentiation Practise/apply Guided/collaborative/independent		
	Review	Reflect on learning intentions Evidence of learning Where to next?		

With a strong planning approach in place the Alliance, drawing on Pamela's support, was able to turn its attention to the review and reflection phase of its instructional model, consistent with its teachers' advice that this is where they felt the need for the greatest support.

In doing so, it was able to enlist the commitment of staff across the Alliance schools to trial and then evaluate three review and reflection strategies identified with the support of a targeted reading and professional learning session for the Alliance as a whole.

More specifically, staff in Alliance schools were provided with a common professional reading from the Grandview School District in the US (Sipe, n.d.) that outlines the importance of lesson closure and suggests 40 strategies by which effective closure can be achieved. Recognising that 40 strategies are beyond the capacity of any individual teacher to implement, staff were asked to identify three they would be prepared to trial before a whole of Alliance professional learning day where their experiences could be shared and discussed.

After structured input from school and Alliance leaders on that day, the teachers worked in groups that were all facilitated using a common approach designed both to ensure that everyone has the opportunity to share, and to 'keep things moving and make sure people are on task'. The approach, which was monitored by a time keeper in each group involved teachers responding to the following questions within the time that is outlined:

1 (2 minutes per person—sharing)
Each person shares the most successful strategy they trialled.
What was it?
Why did it work?

2 (1 minute per person—sharing)
What was the least successful strategy that you trialled?
What were the challenges or difficulties you had with this strategy?
What would you do differently next time?

3 (2 minutes per team member to provide feedback to sharing team member)
e.g. Could you try …?
How about …?
Next time …?

4 (2 minutes per person—sharing only)
What evidence of learning did you collect and how did you capture it?
How did you use the evidence of learning to inform your next steps for student learning?

5 (5–7 minutes. Each participant to write their commitment in the box on the compass sheet provided by the facilitator—See Figure 6.11)
What do I commit to do in the review phase to improve my practice and student learning?

The completed compass points sheets were then collected by each group facilitator to support follow-up after the day in each of the Alliance schools.

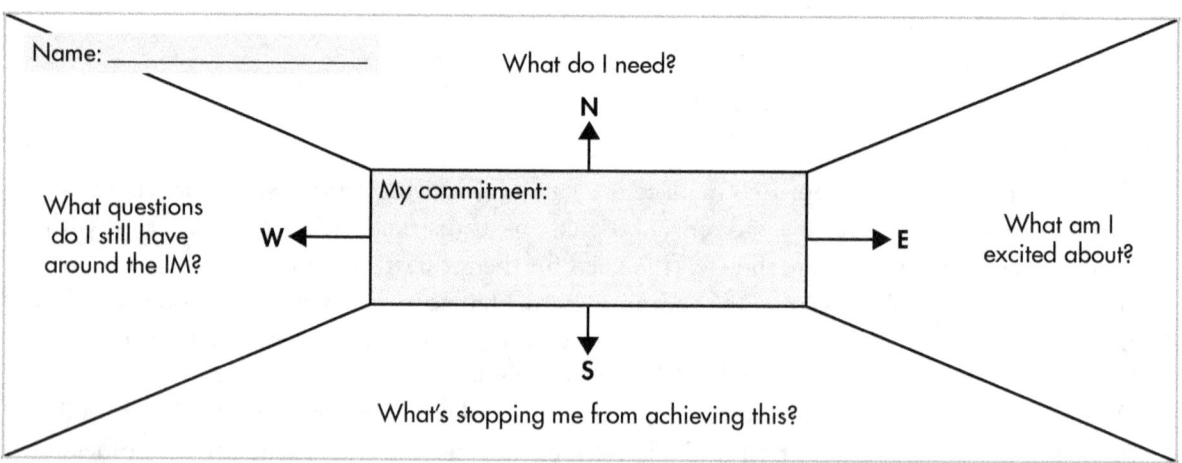

FIGURE 6.11: QUEECHY ALLIANCE COMPASS POINTS TASK

More recently, on the back of this Queechy experience, we have developed the planning tool in Figure 6.12 to support schools we have been working with on the review and reflect phase based on the same article the Alliance used.

Strategy (The strategy identified from the article)	Plan for implementation (How you plan to use it, including an example from something you are teaching)	Evidence I will seek (What I would expect to see as evidence of learning from the students in the review)
Strategy 1		
Strategy 2		
Strategy 3		

FIGURE 6.12: DETERMINING STRATEGIES TO TRIAL

Noble Park Secondary College in Victoria has also developed a protocol for reviewing and extending work on both the beginning and end of lessons, which Pamela subsequently revised after the experience for use with the muka layna Collaboration of schools in Tasmania as outlined in Table 6.7.

TABLE 6.7: REVIEWING AND PROGRESSING THE IMPLEMENTATION OF INSTRUCTIONAL MODEL PHASES AT NOBLE PARK AND THE MUKA LAYNA COLLABORATION[9]

Learning intention for the session:

To identify, select and use strategies which support effective implementation of the review phase in my classroom.

Success criteria—I can:

- self-assess the extent to which I am currently implementing the review phase of the common instructional model
- identify review strategies I am currently using
- share review strategies with colleagues
- select and implement three review strategies in my classroom that I have not used before.

Turn and talk:

How well do you think we are implementing learning intentions (LIs) and success criteria (SC) at the school? What are you doing well? What is challenging? How can you address those challenges?

Reality check:

How are we going with implementing the engage and review phases of the instructional model?

Continued...

---

[9] The table uses the terminology of the muka layna instructional model, since the approach was slightly revised to reflect what was learned from the experience of Noble Park.

Table 6.7 (continued)

Engage phase — reality check
Everyone stand up. Remain standing if for this term you have consistently:
(Note: It is important to pause after each of the following steps to allow sufficient time for people to quickly reflect and then either remain standing or sit down.)
1 Displayed LIs and SC throughout each lesson (e.g. written on the board, on a presentation, on student materials)
2 Read aloud to the students the LI and SC for each lesson.
3 Explained and unpacked the LI and SC for each lesson with students.
4 Co-constructed the LI and SC with students for each lesson? (Note: Anyone still standing at this point should be asked to share their strategies with the group as a whole before proceeding to Step 5.)
5 Is there anything else you have been doing to implement the engage phase of the lesson?
Review phase — reality check
Everyone stand up. Remain standing if for this term you have consistently:
1 Reviewed the LI and SC at the end of the lesson.
2 Asked students to reflect on what they have learned in relation to the LI and SC.
3 Collected evidence of student learning in relation to the LI and SC.
4 Is there anything else you have been doing to implement the review phase of the lesson?
Collegiate group session
Small group activities:
• To what extent are you implementing the review phase?
• What are you doing during the review part of the lesson?
• What is working well?
• Read handout — tick the strategies that you currently use.[10]
• Which strategies do you use that aren't on the list? Share with colleagues.
Mark three strategies that you don't use that you will commit to trialling this term, and/or choose others you have learned about that aren't on the list.
We will meet again on … to share how we have implemented these strategies and assess their effectiveness. Please bring evidence — e.g. student work, teacher resources, planning documents, video.
Effective strategies are then documented and shared on a central portal within and between each school.

Cementing the introduction of an instructional model by phases proved particularly successful at Hampton Park Primary School where, together with a coaching program along the lines discussed in Chapter 3, it has underpinned significant improvement in student results. More specifically, the school implemented and effectively embedded the instructional model in Figure 6.1 by:
• breaking the model down in order to gain collective understanding of the terminology of each

---

[10] The same Grandview District article used with the Queechy Alliance of schools.

phase so it became part of what the school describes as its 'everyday language'
- working with staff from where they were at and developing their individual capabilities, thereby contributing to greater consistency of knowledge and practice through the school
- relentlessly pursuing and promoting the model through the school's coaching program, which in turn fostered an understanding that this simply 'was not going away'
- ensuring that all professional learning was focused on the key priority of driving through the use of the instructional model and linking it to each teacher's performance and development plan
- monitoring implementation through walk throughs, along with coaching and peer observations and associated feedback, along the lines discussed in more detail in Chapter 8.

The school's leadership team reinforced the impact of this approach by regularly unpacking concerns and addressing the consequent problems of practice that emerged, while Principal Liz Davey sought to ensure what she refers to as, the 'right people' were in the 'right leadership roles', and that she worked with each leader to help them to get the best out of their work. Among other things, this involved working collaboratively to set high expectations and goals for each member of the team, having the 'hard conversations' that sometimes were required and celebrating successes as they were achieved.

Regardless of the approach adopted, from guiding manuals to embedding one phase at a time it is worth remembering, as Deb Cottier, the Principal of Springvale Rise Primary School put it, that

> full implementation of the instructional model will not happen overnight. We (the leadership team) have continually had to remind ourselves that change takes time and that we are aiming for a deep understanding of the IM, not a surface-level one.

One thing the school has learned in this context is that 'staff's adoption of new teaching and learning practices moves along in a fairly lock-step way', with the result 'we have to build knowledge (raise awareness), develop shared knowledge/understanding to ensure greater consistency, embed the change into actual day-to-day practice (and put accountability measures in place), then ensure consistency and ultimately quality of the practice across the school'.

At a practical level this also means that the school must 'privilege the time' for this work, both for the leadership team and the staff, factor it into the school's professional learning budget, think creatively about how to find and free up time, and 'be in it for the long haul … for as long as it takes'.

MONITORING IMPLEMENTATION

Just as important as driving through the implementation of an instructional model in the school is the need to monitor that implementation in order to reflect on its progress and adjust the strategies in place to ensure they are having the desired effect. With this in mind, the Queechy Alliance has developed the rubric for implementation, provided as Figure 6.13, that specifies the role of different stakeholders within each school and which can readily be adapted to the context of other schools and the instructional models they use.

Queechy Alliance Instructional Model Implementation Rubric			
	Emergent Visible (Medium)	**Immersing** Practiced (High)	**Embedded** Culture (Outstanding)
Instruction Model (IM)	• The poster is displayed appropriately in the classroom/teaching space.	• The phases of the IM are referred to as part of the lesson structure.	• The IM is part of the teaching and learning practice in the classroom.
Teachers	• The teacher makes reference to the process and refers to components of the IM with students and colleagues.	• The teacher is working with a PLT and planning to reflect the components of the IM.	• The teachers use the IM and planning reflects the components. • Teachers are skilled at using an observation and feedback process on the IM.
Students	• The students are aware of the IM and know about the Learning Intentions and Success Criteria.	• The students are aware of an explicit teaching process, and understand the importance of formative assessment and feedback to bump up learning.	• The students expect the IM will guide their learning in all classes.
Principals	• The Principal works collaboratively with the Queechy Alliance Principals to build teachers' capacity to utilise the IM.	• The Principal works collaboratively to implement the IM and build/support leadership capacity.	• The Leadership Team ensures that all teachers use the IM.
In-school Leaders	• The In-School Leaders and key stakeholders collaborate to provide professional learning to support the implementation of the IM.	• Facilitate building capacity across staff to develop effective classroom practices based upon components of the IM. • The In-School Leader supports the implementation across the Alliance.	• The In-School Leader maintains the integrity and momentum of the project within individual schools and the Alliance.
Literacy Coaches	• The Literacy Coach is building their capacity and knowledge around the IM and coaching practices.	• The Literacy Coach is coaching teams/individuals on components of the IM.	• Coaching is targeted using feedback and data from the PL.
Parents	• The parents are informed of the use of the IM.	• Parents are familiar with the IM and are able to comment on the benefits of/impact on their child's learning.	• Parents expect teachers to teach using the IM.

FIGURE 6.13: QUEECHY ALLIANCE INSTRUCTIONAL MODEL IMPLEMENTATION RUBRIC

STRUCTURES FOR COLLABORATION SO MORE CAN WORK LIKE THE BEST

One of our favourite educational quotes is Rick DuFour's (2011) observation that 'professional doesn't mean autonomous'. There simply is not, as he explains, 'any dictionary definition that defines a professional as someone who can do whatever he or she pleases', nor caveat that collaboration occurs 'only if each person wants to' (pp. 58–60).

This accords with the McKinsey Company's finding that schools in the best school systems in the world focus on providing the 'high-quality, collaborative, job-focused professional development' that generally occurs in professional learning communities where teachers work together to improve individual and collective efficacy and classroom practice (Barber & Mourshed, 2009, p. 30).

In a major study of more than 2500 fourth grade students in 47 schools in the mid-west of the United States, Goddard, Goddard and Tschannen-Moran (2007) found an association between increased student achievement and the degree of teacher collaboration in the school. 'When teachers collaborate', they explained, 'they share experiences and knowledge that can promote learning for instructional improvement … Such learning can help teachers solve educational problems, which in turn has the potential to benefit students academically'. Collaboration, they speculated, 'encourages teachers to move beyond reliance on their own memories and experiences with schooling and toward engagement with others around important questions of teaching and learning', thereby fostering, 'learning that improved instruction' (p. 892).

Of course, merely having professional learning teams (PLTs) does not guarantee that they will collaborate well and work to any great effect.[11] Consider the following vignette from Platt and Tipp (2008).

'Period 3 common planning time at River High School. Five minutes after the last bell, Team 9B teachers are amiably catching up one another's weekends while waiting for the perpetual stragglers to arrive. Maria, the team leader, seems to be the only one with a sense of urgency … "Let's go. We need to spend a few minutes planning April's field trip. Then we have to talk about how we're doing with the interdisciplinary writing prompts" … Instead of a few minutes, the field trip discussion took more than half the meeting. A tangent into a student discipline issue chewed up another 15 minutes. Team 9B got to the main agenda item with 10 minutes left … No-one expressed dismay over how time had been used or the failure to address the one agenda item that would have a direct impact on student performance'. (Platt & Tipp, 2008, pp 18-19)

It's a far from unfamiliar story in schools, and dramatises the fact that, although the existence of PLTs is a prerequisite for professional collaboration and learning to occur, their mere existence will not guarantee that these valued outcomes are achieved. It depends on how effectively they work.

One issue that has arisen from the outset in schools with which we work is how the PLTs should be structured and composed. Should they be based on year level teams, or key learning areas, or some other approach? Put simply, there is no one answer to this question, other than that it depends on the circumstances and strategic analysis of the school. We have seen effective PLTs based on year levels aimed at strengthening the year-level team's focus on delivering improved educational outcomes for students in that year. Similarly, we have seen successful subject-based PLTs aimed at delivering better teaching and learning outcomes within that discipline in the school. In schools where a degree of suspicion exists about the challenge to private practice that PLTs present, we have seen teachers asked to nominate a number of others they would happily work with, so school leaders can then construct functioning teams where all teachers are matched to at least some others with whom they feel comfortable and aligned. It's a case of working out the best approach for the school to enable collaboration to occur, and then focus more on the work of the teams than how they are composed.

One approach used extensively in the Achievement Improvement Zones (AiZ) project in Victoria was to encourage collaborative planning in teams of three, known as triads. Three, the region found, was the best number for ensuring teacher sharing in a context where challenge could also occur. When teachers worked in pairs, the relationship was sometimes so strong that the pair would share effectively, but then avoid the challenge lest the relationship be infringed. In teams of more than three, it was common for one person to drift out of the conversation and effectively leave it to the rest. While there are myriad logistical problems to making a triad system work, it did prove effective in many schools and is worth considering when structuring professional learning teams; if nothing else to at least consciously consider how large or small they should be.

---

[11] The terms 'professional learning team' (PLT) and 'professional learning community' (PLC) are often used interchangeably by schools and we work with whatever terminology the school or network adopts.

ACTIVITY FOR LEADERSHIP TEAMS: STRUCTURING YOUR PLTS

Instructions

1 Consider the range of structural options for PLTs included in Table 6.8 and add any that have been suggested and are under consideration in the school.
2 Identify the pros and cons of each approach and the implications they have for how PLTs are structured in the school.

TABLE 6.8: STRUCTURING YOUR PLTS

Structural option	Pros	Cons	Implications for our PLTs
Year level teams			
Key learning areas (KLAs)			
Mixed experience teams			
Teams structured by leaders based on submission			
Self-constructed teams			

© Pamela Macklin and Vic Zbar, *Driving School Improvement*, Australian Council for Educational Research, 2017

EFFECTIVE PROFESSIONAL LEARNING

It is important in this context to have a clear sense of what effective professional learning is, since it lies at the heart of the work of PLTs. Our colleague Peter Cole, who famously called professional development 'a great way to avoid change' (Cole, 2004), defines effective professional learning as formal and informal learning opportunities, mostly provided within the school, that:
- are shared and supported by one's colleagues
- contribute to a whole-school improvement plan
- cumulatively improve classroom practice
- build the school's collective effectiveness (adapted from Cole, 2016).

Taking it a stage further still, he explains that effective professional learning:
- is guided by the school's theories of action and instructional model
- is school-managed and mostly school-located
- involves all teachers
- is collegiate, continuous and cumulative
- exposes teachers to actual practice, rather than descriptions of practice
- changes instructional behaviours
- is built on explicit 'bite-sized' micro-teaching techniques
- builds school-wide instructional consistency
- achieves school-wide collective effectiveness.

More recently, Jensen (2019), who also observes that 'professional development continually fails to improve teaching and learning in many systems across many countries', has sought to resolve the conundrum whereby, 'on the one hand, professional development expenditure is normally ineffective and on the other hand, it's very difficult to find a system that has improved significantly without professional development being a key driver of improvement'. The answer, he suggests, lies in the need to locate professional development directly in 'student learning of the curriculum' as opposed to the more nebulous student learning per se.

Focusing on student learning of the curriculum, Jensen (2019) argues, provides a much sharper focus for the professional development that occurs, and hence ensures more 'rigour and specificity' as a result. It helps to develop what Loughran (2008) calls the 'language of teaching and learning … (that) allows us to discuss what we know and how we know it in meaningful ways … (and) makes sharing professional knowledge both efficient and helpful for those of us who use that knowledge in their daily practice' (p. 48).

Some confirmation for this view is evident in Fullan's (2019) outline of research with eight middle schools in two districts with similar demographic characteristics that were all seeking to implement professional learning communities in order to improve. 'The findings for the eight schools', he explains, 'were similar in terms of teacher survey responses to such items as "agreement about the need to collaborate" and about "what should be a learning community"'. But when it came to details, there were specific differences—particularly when it involved making specific links to student learning. There were major differences on questions pertaining to whether 'teachers examine and compare student learning results', 'teachers discuss instructional methods used to teach students', and 'seek new teaching methods, testing and reflecting on results'. Without going into the detail of the results, the mean score of District B responses to these items was higher than District A, with evidence of greater levels of student achievement in District B. The difference, according to Fullan (2019), was the implementation of 'specific actions known to affect learning … It is when the group, well led, works through the issues, gets skilled at the particular actions, sees the results and builds on them that the results start to accumulate' (pp. 81–82).

The focus for professional development and, in particular, the work of professional learning teams, is a question we will return to later in this chapter.

Pamela works intensively with PLTs in several schools to flesh out how they will ensure professional learning of the sort that Cole and Jensen describe. It generally starts with defining some key terms based on some shared professional readings she provides, for example, DuFour (2011).

ACTIVITY FOR STAFF: OUR PLC, PLTS AND THEIR WORK

Instructions

1 Work together in your PLTs to determine your definition of:
- a professional learning community (PLC)
- a professional learning team (PLT)
- collaboration.

2 Share the definitions developed by each team and seek agreement on a set of whole-school definitions to adopt.

DEFINITIONS

Here are some definitions to get you started if you are stuck, or to use as points of comparison once you have developed your own in the activity above.

Professional learning community (PLC)

A professional learning community:
- represents a collective effort to enhance student learning
- promotes and sustains the learning of all professionals in the school
- builds knowledge through inquiry
- analyses and uses data for reflection and improvement (Bolan et al. 2005, as cited in Ontario Ministry of Education, 2007, p. 1).

Professional learning teams (PLTs)

PLTs, according to Narre Warren South P–12 College[12], are the structure the school adopts to assist teachers 'to work collaboratively in the pursuit of improved student learning outcomes and high expectations'. It is interesting to note, as an aside at this point, that this school focuses the work of its PLTs on planning assessment tasks that reflect the knowledge and skills being taught, using the planning cycle in Figure 6.14.

---

[12] Narre Warren South P–12 College. (n.d.). Narre Warren South PLTs. Provided to the authors by the school.

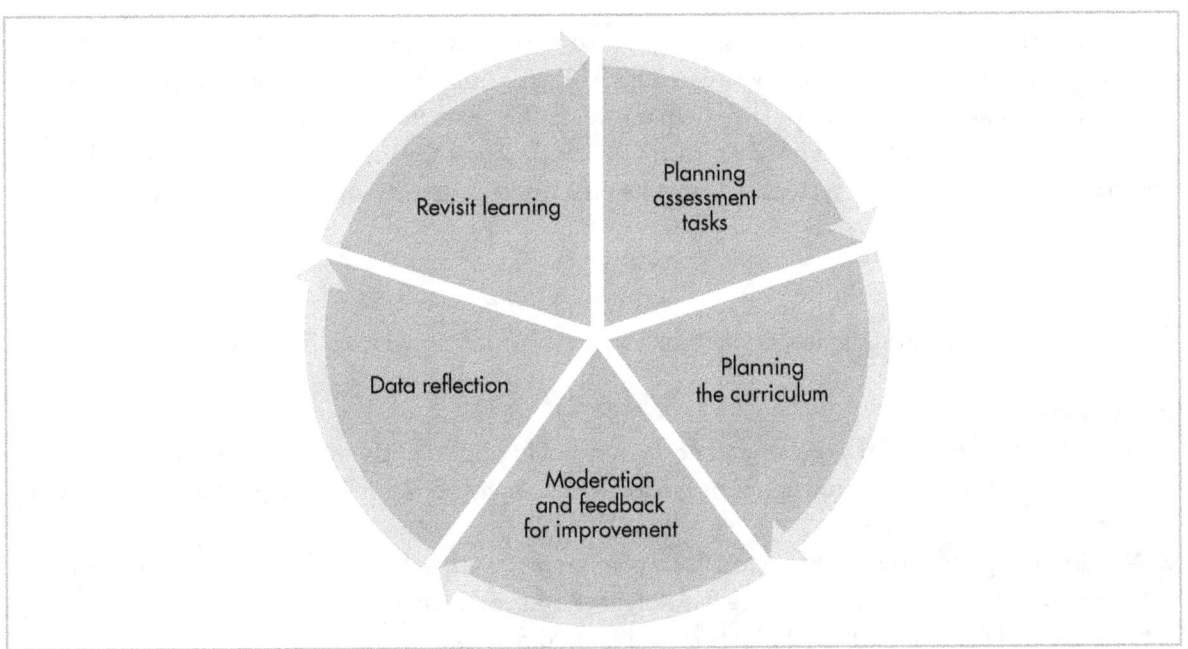

FIGURE 6.14: NARRE WARREN SOUTH P–12 PLANNING CYCLE FOR PLTS

Collaboration

Collaboration, as DuFour and colleagues (n.d.) explain, means to 'co-labor'. It involves a 'systematic process in which we work together, interdependently, to analyze and impact professional practice in order to improve our individual and collective results' (DuFour, DuFour & Eacker, n.d., slide 6). For Melbourne Girls' College, collaboration involves a mindset where 'we can and should learn from one another in a structured environment … (i.e.) our PLTs'.[13] It involves a process of reflection, research, debate, discussion and problem-solving and ultimately, in a nod the Principal Karen Money gave to the work of Cole, 'is about our daily work, not an add on'.

Promoting a professional learning community through the collaborative work of professional learning teams not only contributes to collective efficacy in the school, but also the perceived efficacy of individual staff. The OECD's Teaching and Learning International Survey (TALIS) of 107 000 teachers across 34 countries in 2013, for example, found that teachers who work together on at least a weekly basis had more belief in their ability to execute the skills needed to improve student learning than those who worked together less frequently. It also had the added benefit that they were more satisfied with their jobs (OECD, 2014). More recently, TALIS 2018 confirmed that '(t)eachers who report participating in impactful training tend to display higher levels of self-efficacy and job satisfaction … In addition, teachers participating in training focusing on the implementation of pedagogical practices tend to report a more frequent implementation of effective practices' (OECD, 2018, p. 152).

GUIDING NORMS

Having identified what it understands a professional learning community (PLC), professional learning teams (PLTs) and collaboration to mean, the school can now turn its attention to the guiding norms for the work of its teams.

PLT norms represent protocols and commitments developed to guide members in working together collaboratively to achieve shared goals. For example, we start and finish on time, we actively listen to what others have to say, seeking first to understand and then be understood, and we use

---

[13] Identified by the principal at a whole-school professional learning day in July, 2016.

data to inform decisions whenever possible. Agreed norms that are consistently implemented over time are commonly the difference between a high-functioning PLT and something that is more akin to a low-stakes, social group. They help reinforce the characteristics of effective teams identified in Box 5.1 in Chapter 5. They also provide the basis for inducting newcomers to the team, and hence contribute to the sustainability of its effectiveness despite any changes in personnel.

ACTIVITY FOR STAFF: DEVELOPING SHARED NORMS FOR PLT WORK

This activity is designed to be undertaken by leaders of professional learning teams.

Instructions

1 Consider the following list of operating norms that could apply to PLTs in your school. In developing norms, it is better to ensure fewer norms that are consistently adhered to, than a proverbial laundry list that never fully gets done.

2 Work in small groups to identify the top three norms from the list below that should apply to your team:
- Keep to time for agenda items, meeting start time and conclusion.
- The work of the team will be student centred and data driven.
- All members are to have prepared for the meeting.
- Agreed actions are to be completed by the designated person(s) within the agreed timeline.
- All devices are to be on silent and laptops closed unless otherwise agreed.
- All voices are equally heard, valued and respected.
- Active listening is essential.
- All members will seek shared understandings, consensus and solutions.
- Leadership will be distributed and hence high expectations of self and others are required.

3 Compare the outcomes of the group deliberations and compile a list of up to five agreed norms to guide the way in which your PLTs will work.

Having conducted this activity, the school can compare its norms to the sample we have adapted from Clayton (2015) included in Box 6.3, as well as the norms that are being used in a number of schools to support their adoption of the Data Wise approach that is outlined in Chapter 7 (see Boudett, City, & Murnane (Eds.), 2013).

Box 6.3

SAMPLE PLT NORMS

The norms that underpin effective PLTs are designed to:
- ensure a safe, equitable, and trusting environment where team members can freely ask questions of one another
- ensure meaningful and sustained dialogue
- structure the time and work during meetings
- provide time during the meeting to think and time to listen without the need for team members to continually respond
- promote reflection by individuals and the team
- help members to consider differing perspectives and insights

- focus the team's work on the issue it is seeking to address
- prevent conversations wandering off topic
- prevent individual team members from dominating the conversation.

The Data Wise norms
The six Data Wise norms expect that teachers will:
- take an inquiry stance
- assume positive intentions
- ground statements in evidence
- stick to protocols
- be here now
- start and end on time.

Garmston and Wellman (2016) also advance a set of seven norms for collaboration that, as much as anything else, are collaborative practices that individuals and teams can adopt. More specifically, the 'norms' of:
- pausing—in effect, 'wait' or 'think time' for teachers in the same way as described for students in Chapter 5
- paraphrasing—'the key practice in authentic listening'
- posing questions—questions that can explore or specify thinking and clarify vague assertions and terms
- placing ideas on the table—shifting the ownership of ideas from individuals to the group as a whole
- providing data—because qualitative and quantitative data are at the heart of productive, collaborative work
- paying attention to self and others—being aware of what one is saying and how, along with the way in which it is being received
- presuming positive intentions—to encourage honest conversations and demonstrate respect (pp. 42–51).

With a set of agreed norms in place, the school can provide even further direction to the work of its PLTs by specifying any professional 'non-negotiables' about team participation to which all teachers are expected to adhere.

For example, the expectations that all teachers will:
- belong to a PLT contributing to whole-school improvement
- strive to achieve at least one year's growth for every child
- seek to improve their own learning and effectiveness as part of a process of continuous improvement in teaching and learning in the school
- use evidence, data and relevant research to inform and drive their teaching
- participate in peer classroom observations as part of working in their PLT
- work with colleagues to collaboratively improve the quality of teaching and student achievement in the school.

Taken together with the norms in Box 6.3, it's a set of professional expectations that arguably provides the antidote to DuFour's earlier cited concern that some teachers feel they can virtually do what they please.

The role of the PLT leader is critical in this context, since this person must:
- lead the team by example, modelling the desired behaviours, developing a culture of challenge and questioning and explaining how change occurs
- develop the team's capacity by building its pedagogical knowledge and understanding, its assessment practices and use of data, and its overall goal setting and strategy selection
- support collaboration by ensuring regular, focused meetings where the agreed norms are observed.

The Tucson Unified School District (2016–2017) in the United States provides even more detailed advice on the PLT leader's role, suggesting that effective team leaders:
- establish and support team cohesion and effectiveness
- demonstrate excellent planning and organisation skills
- communicate to the school leadership any questions, needs and concerns of the team
- develop the agenda in consultation with team members and distribute it in advance
- maintain focus on the four key questions that sum up the challenge of improving learning (see ahead)
- ensure that all voices are heard (p. 11, adapted for the Australian context).

Pamela has used the following set of questions to support PLT leaders to examine both their own leadership and the effectiveness of their teams:
- What are your goals and plans for improving your effectiveness as an instructional leader?
- How will you work to spread knowledge and strategies building on your understanding of what makes an effective teacher?
- What is proving most effective about your team? What is proving least effective? Why? How do you know? What action needs to be taken to enable your team to improve its effectiveness?
- How do you proactively develop your capacity as a PLT leader?
- How do you get feedback on your leadership and the effectiveness of the team?

This in turn can support discussion between PLT leaders within the school on such questions as:
- What is happening in the team?
- How are the data conversations going?
- How would you describe the team dynamics?
- Are all groups of students having their learning needs met?
- What is the most important thing for PLT leaders to achieve in this semester?
- What is the PLT role in mentoring?
- How is good practice being shared?

Discussing these together can help spread effective PLT practice through the school and provide support for those who need it in their leadership role.

With a clear set of operating norms in place, the teams can turn their attention to the important challenge of ensuring that all students can learn, and a consequent focus on results. There are four key questions that effectively sum up the challenge of improving learning, which PLTs need to address:
1 What is it that we expect our students to learn?
2 How will we know when they have learned it?
3 How will we respond when they do not learn it?
4 How will we respond when they already know it?

In a somewhat similar vein, Sharratt (2019) has suggested that the five critical questions that leaders should invite staff to consider are:
1 What am I teaching?
2 Why am I teaching it?
3 How will I teach it?
4 How will I know when students have learned it or not?
5 What is next … if this works? If it doesn't work? Where do I go for help? (p. 61).

The Ontario Literacy and Numeracy Secretariat (Ontario Ministry of Education, 2007) has then given both sets of questions more focus still, by suggesting that teams consider:
- How closely is our focus linked to teaching and learning?
- Does research indicate that our focus enhances student learning?
- How closely is our focus connected to the needs of the students?
- How explicit is our focus? Can participants describe what they intend 'to do'?
- Is our focus widely shared as a priority by all?
- How challenging is our focus? Will it foster new thinking and changes in practice? (p. 2).

With such a challenging set of questions in mind, the Secretariat advises that regular team meetings occur (e.g. weekly or even bi-weekly) and include 'processes for reviewing current student information and progress, setting goals, determining whether identified actions and interventions are making a difference, studying and discussing new ideas and strategies, and identifying other professional learning needed to support success' (p. 2).

Griffin (2010) has adopted a similar view and codified it into the flow chart in Figure 6.15 that almost provides an agenda for the work of any PLT.

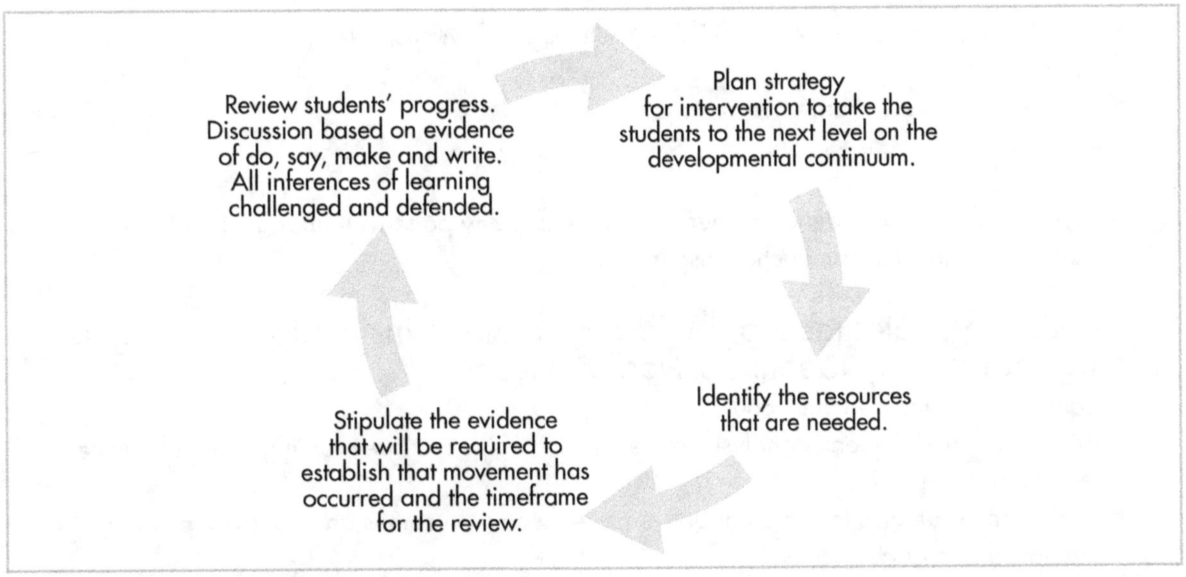

FIGURE 6.15: GRIFFIN'S PLT PROCESS

At possibly an even more expansive level still, the Tucson Unified School District (2016–2017) recommends a cyclical PLT process that involves:
- gathering evidence of current levels of student learning
- identifying strategies that build on teachers' instructional strengths and address any identified weaknesses
- developing common assessments to monitor student learning
- implementing the agreed instructional strategies and assessments
- analysing the impact on student learning to determine which strategies are proving effective
- applying the new knowledge in the next cycle of continuous improvement (p. 13, adapted for the Australian context).

These elements can be described in more detail for implementation by the teams, as illustrated in the sample we have developed in Box 6.4, which is aligned to the Tucson process outlined above.

Box 6.4

STRUCTURE FOR IMPLEMENTING THE CYCLICAL PLT PROCESS

Gathering evidence of current levels of student learning

Focus on data and evidence to inform decisions. Data and evidence considered could include:
- pre-tests and post-tests
- common assessment tasks and work samples
- system-wide testing—e.g. NAPLAN
- school based assessment—e.g. PAT Comprehension or Maths tests[14]
- surveys
- data from peer classroom observations
- student profiles or case studies.

Analyse the data and evidence gathered and identify any patterns that ought to inform the instructional strategies that teachers use in class.

Identifying strategies that build on teachers' instructional strengths and address any identified weaknesses

To complete this step, teachers could:
- use the data and evidence analysis to identify strategies that are working well and hence need to be maintained
- identify any strategies that are not delivering expected outcomes and consider possible alternative approaches to try
- consider whether or not there is a need to seek advice from others in the school and/or to undertake some targeted research.

---

[14] PAT stands for Progressive Achievement Tests, which are a national series of tests designed by the Australian Council for Educational Research (ACER) to provide objective, norm-referenced information to teachers about their students' skills and understandings in a range of key areas. They are widely used in Australian schools.

Always keep in mind the four key questions the team is seeking to address:
- What is it that we expect our students to learn?
- How will we know when they have learned it?
- How will we respond when they do not learn it?
- How will we respond when they already know it?

Developing common assessments to monitor student learning

To complete this step, teachers could:
- specify the consistent assessment tools that will be used to determine where students are at and how to move them to the next stage of learning
- use these assessments to monitor the effectiveness of the instructional strategies the team has chosen to adopt.

Implementing the agreed instructional strategies and assessments

To complete this step, teachers could consistently apply the agreed approach for improving student learning outcomes and monitor its implementation, including through classroom observation and feedback as required. This effectively sets the baseline for PLT practice over the coming year.

Analysing the impact on student learning to determine which strategies are proving effective

To complete this step, teachers could continue gathering data and evidence of student progress to determine which strategies are proving effective and which may need to be tweaked or even replaced to ensure the level of impact on student learning the PLT seeks.

Applying the new knowledge in the next cycle of continuous improvement

To complete this step, teachers could apply the teaching and learning approach the team has developed in the coming cycle and commence the process again to support continuous improvement in the school.

This broad PLT process is made manageable in the meetings the team conducts by using a consistent meeting planner, such as the sample provided in Figure 6.15. Planners of this sort can help overcome the tension to which Garmston and Wellman (2016) point, whereby 'groups have more tasks to accomplish than time in which to accomplish them'. This puts a premium on using the time available for meeting in groups to the best effect and also reflecting on the operations of the group because, as they put it, 'any group that is too busy to reflect on process is too busy to improve' (p. 42). If nothing else, good planners help to ensure that a clear agenda for the meeting exists, and it is then run well.

[NAME OF SCHOOL]
Professional Learning Team Meeting Summary   **Date:**
(Note: The topics identified may require several meetings to address)

Follow up from previous meeting: A brief report on actions taken (be specific)

Data and evidence to be discussed at this meeting
☐ Assessment data   ☐ Classroom observations   ☐ Surveys/Student profiles   ☐ Other

Reflection: What is working? What challenges are we experiencing?

Key question:
What do the data/evidence and our reflections suggest we most need to address?

What should we be doing about this?

What assistance and/or research is needed to inform our approach?

What key action(s) will we implement after this meeting to further improve student learning?
(Be specific and focus on small, achievable actions that all team members will implement in class.)

What support will team members need and receive to help them to implement the agreed action(s)?

What do we need to bring to the next PLT meeting?

FIGURE 6.16: SAMPLE PLT PLANNER AND MEETING SUMMARY

© Pamela Macklin and Vic Zbar, *Driving School Improvement*, Australian Council for Educational Research, 2017

Professional learning teams that work in this way can collaboratively produce high-quality lesson plans that support more teachers to work like the best, as illustrated in the sample extract in Box 6.5 from the plans developed by a team of teachers at Dandenong North Primary School during 2018.

Box 6.5

SAMPLE PLANNER FROM DANDENONG NORTH PRIMARY SCHOOL, 2018 (EXTRACT FOR FOUNDATION LEVEL)

Writing — Language

Victorian Curriculum link	Essential learning	Practice tasks	Differentiation
Understand that some language in written texts is unlike everyday spoken language (VCELA155)[15] • learning that written text in Standard Australian English has conventions about words, spaces between words, layout on the page and consistent spelling because it has to communicate when the speaker/writer is not present Understand that punctuation is a feature of written text different from letters and recognise how capital letters are used for names, and that capital letters and full stops signal the beginning and end of sentences (VCELA156)[16] • pointing to the letters and the punctuation in a text • commenting on punctuation encountered in the everyday texts, for example 'That's the letter that starts my name', 'The name of my family and my town has a capital letter'	The students will continue to develop the following: • using capital letters to start a sentence • writing on the solid line • using full stops at the end of sentences • including spaces between words • drawing illustrations to match text • using capital letters for proper nouns • writing from left to right, top to bottom • learning the difference between letters, words and sentences	• letter, word, sentence sorts (e.g. p, pig, 'Here is a pink pig'.) • think it, say it, write it, read it • match and sequence a sentence • identify capital letters and full stops in teacher model • edit in missing full stops and capital letters in a sentence • big book—identify capital letters and full stops • Kung Fu punctuation—use visual cues to draw attention to different grammar. Specific focus on capital letters, full stops, question marks and exclamation marks • vocabulary development through exploring/labelling pictures • innovate a known story map to create own text (T4W—Bad Tempered Lady Bird)	Support: • continue phonemic awareness activities with single sounds • continue to learn about capital letters and full stops with teacher support • dictate a sentence to a teacher to scribe • trace and copy a sentence Extension: • use phonemic awareness to sound out words, focusing on initial and ending sounds • focus on using capital letter for names • use adjectives when writing • develop use of complex sentences (use words such as: and, because, so etc.)

Learning intentions

- To attempt to use upper and lowercase letters correctly
- To be able to distinguish between letters, words and sentences in written language
- To be able to use a full stop correctly
- To be able to know the Kung Fu actions for capital letters, full stops etc.

'I can' statements

- I can use capital and lowercase letters
- I know the difference between a letter, word and sentence
- I can use a full stop
- I can use my Kung Fu actions when re-reading my story

---

[15] See https://victoriancurriculum.vcaa.vic.edu.au/Curriculum/ContentDescription/VCELA155
[16] See https://victoriancurriculum.vcaa.vic.edu.au/Curriculum/ContentDescription/VCELA156

Sometimes, such as when a school is developing its overall PLT approach and gaining buy-in from the staff, there may be a need for more direction to ensure consistency of communication, and hence focus across disparate teams. For example, Narre Warren South P–12, which is a very big school with myriad teams, developed the checklist in Box 6.6 for PLT leaders to use in their team discussions and thereby help to ensure consistent and effective team meetings across the school.

Box 6.6

CHECKLIST FOR PLT DISCUSSIONS AT NARRE WARREN SOUTH P–12 COLLEGE

1 Inform staff that we want to create a model that is both unique to Narre Warren South P–12 College, and at the same time reflects the work already being done in PLTs.
2 Introduce each component of the model and discuss what each should involve.
3 Gain feedback and comments on each section of the model and record comments/discussion on an A3 sheet.
4 Include feedback for what procedures or actions of a PLT should be included and agreed to, as well as the role of a PLT leader.
5 Make sure everyone has a say. Inform staff that this feedback will be collated and discussed in the Curriculum Committee. (Name deleted) will email out any modifications and provide one more opportunity for feedback. It will then become the modus operandi for PLTs in 2017. It will be a 'live document' and progress as changes to our PLT culture evolve.

More recently, Pamela has worked with a number of schools to examine the clarity, consistency and impact of their PLTs in a session for PLT leaders that can be structured along the following lines.

ACTIVITY FOR STAFF: MAXIMISING THE PERFORMANCE OF PLTS

Note: The following outline merges both the questions asked in advance and the way in which discussion was managed on the day.

Clarity, consistency impact session
The focus of the session will be maximising the performance of PLT teams to improve student learning outcomes. Please come prepared to share your responses to the following questions and bring along any documentation which might help clarify, or exemplify your work as a leader in response to these specific questions:
- How do you ensure that improving student learning is the major focus of your PLT meetings?
  In pairs, share ideas and report back the top two.
- How do you ensure that all team members contribute in meaningful ways to the discussion?
  Group share.
- What evidence does your team regularly share to monitor and improve student learning?
  Move to a new partner to share ideas and then report back the top two.
- What are the key questions all PLT leaders use to support teachers to analyse the data and evidence effectively?
  Group share.

- How do you select the most effective teaching strategies to respond to student learning needs? Move to a new partner to share ideas and then report back on the top two.
- What have you implemented as a team that has had the biggest impact on student learning? How do you know?
  Write, then share.
- As a team of leaders, how do we ensure that there is a consistent approach taken in the work of PLTs?
- As a team of leaders, what could we improve upon? Actions: ...

Finish with two stars and a wish—Write down two things you do well as a PLT leader and one you would like to improve on.

This session can then be followed by a detailed consideration of:

How are we going?—An update on progress: Actions/activities/milestones
- Discuss key actions—What has been implemented/what is the impact/how do we know?
- What are the next logical steps?
- What are the enabling factors promoting success/factors limiting successful implementation?

How do we know?—Evidence of impact
- What changes in behaviour and practice have we seen?
- What is the evidence of impact at this stage?
- What is the evidence you can draw on to inform progress?

Where to now?—Next steps
- What will we prioritise for action next term?
- How will we plan to collect the evidence of impact?
- Are any resource shifts required to succeed?
- When/how will we check on progress?

PHASING THE INTRODUCTION OF PLTS: AN APPROACH TO CONSIDER

Rather than launch into the full-scale introduction of PLTs, Glen Waverley Secondary College spent all of 2019 trialing what it called 'Pre-PLTs' (described in Box 6.7) to ensure the full range of issues outlined were addressed, and that implementation could be tweaked to ensure successful implementation in 2020 when it applies across the school.

Box 6.7
PRE-PLTS AT GLEN WAVERLEY SECONDARY COLLEGE

The aim of the Pre-PLTs was to enable the school to start slowly in introducing PLTs and provide participating teachers with the opportunity to work collaboratively with a focus on student learning, rather than simply planning lessons and resources as was the case in the past. This focus is neatly captured in Figure 6.17 which clarifies the role of PLTs in the school.

Continued...

Figure 6.17 content:

Center: PLTs have an unrelenting focus on achieving student learning growth. Teams collect and analyse data to find out where students are currently at with their learning and work out where to concentrate their efforts to lead to a greater chance of improved learning outcomes. This is achieved in a PLT by …

- Reviewing SACs, CATs and other assessment tasks in response to the evidence collected on student learning.
- Planning activities that challenge and support the different learners.
- Developing and reviewing assessment rubrics to be used for identifying a base line and measuring impact.
- Undertaking moderation of students' work to gain a shared understanding of student achievement.
- Sharing teacher strategies to assist in planning for differentiation that caters for all students.
- Challenging each other and reflecting on teacher practice including what's working and what's not for particular students.
- Upskilling members of the PLT in different areas to improve knowledge and skill where required.
- Reflecting on the College professional learning sessions and thinking about how ideas can be implemented.

FIGURE 6.17: THE ROLE AND WORK OF PLTS IN THE SCHOOL

Teachers involved were encouraged to use data to determine where students currently were at, before determining the appropriate teaching and learning intervention to adopt. Recognising the fact that many teachers are intimidated by data, in concept at least, the school sought to reassure them with examples of the differing forms of data they can use that are included in Figure 6.18. This helped shift thinking beyond the sort of big data that NAPLAN provides, to an understanding that anything that helps teachers to determine where students are at is valuable data to use; from writing pieces, to exit slips, surveys or homework tasks.

CHAPTER 6 Stage 2: Building teaching capacity

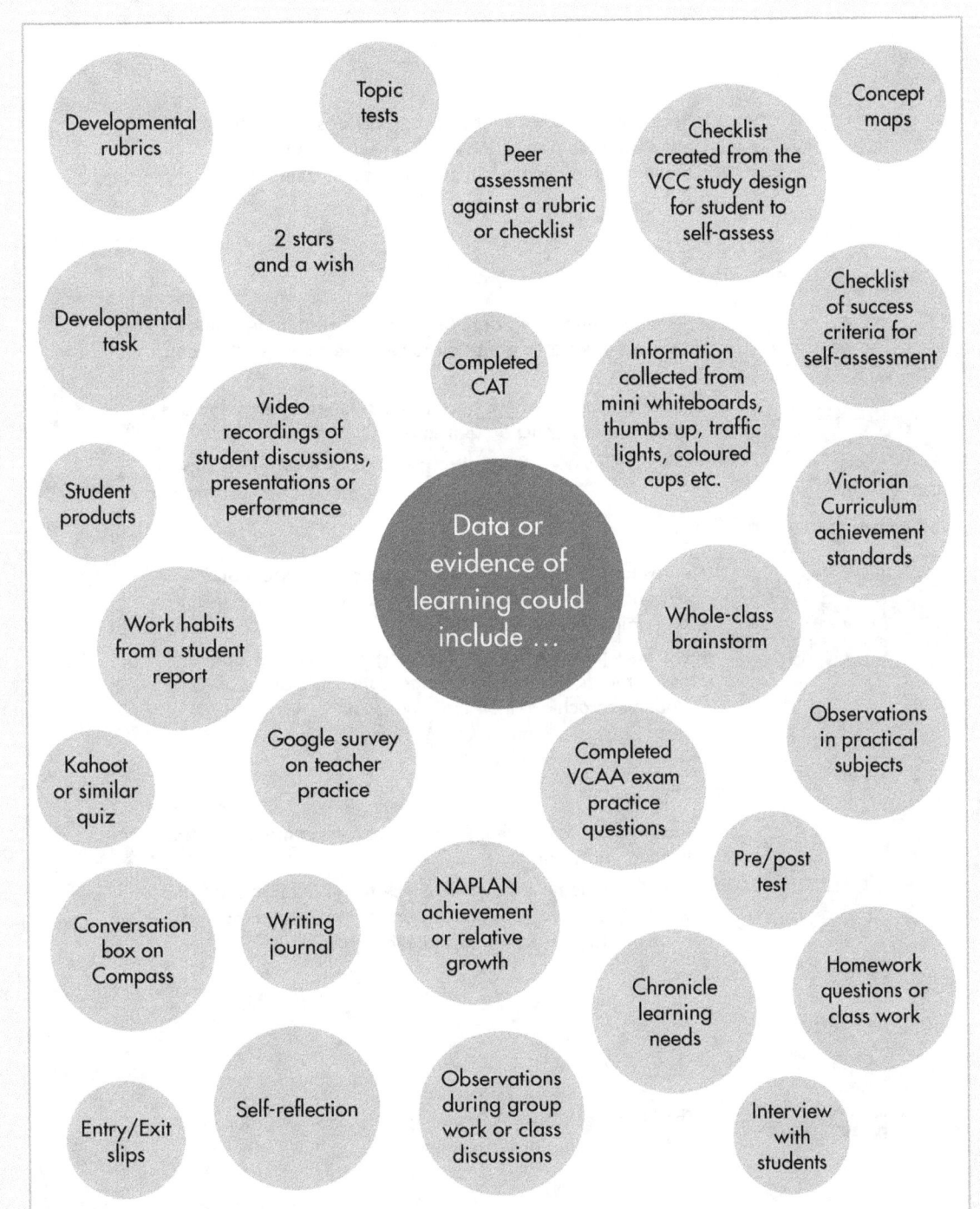

FIGURE 6.18: FORMS THAT USEFUL DATA CAN TAKE

Central to the success of Pre-PLTs in the school was the opportunity for teachers to have an input to the team they wanted to join, and the focus of the team's work. As a result, as one school leader explains, 'teachers felt more invested in what they did and felt like the work was relevant rather than being imposed'.

Prompts were provided about what to discuss for teams that needed them, aligned to the meeting structure in Figure 6.19.

Continued...

Review
- Teachers follow up on the **agreed actions** and **reflect on student learning** and teaching practices that have taken place since the **previous PLT meeting**.

Evaluate and diagnose
- Teachers **share their data/evidence of student learning** to find out **what is going on for their learners** so they can set goals.
- Teachers decide where to **concentrate their energy** to have the greatest **impact on learning**.
- Data is also used to **monitor progress** and **evaluate impact**.

Discuss and plan
- In response to the data/evidence teachers discuss and plan how they will **support and challenge** students using high-impact teaching strategies.
- **Teachers plan curriculum, learning activities, formative assessments and teaching approaches** that allow all students to achieve their learning goals.

Commit
- Teachers agree on what PLT members will **commit to action** between now and the next PLT.
- Could include how they will **'check for understanding'** and what evidence they will collect and bring to **monitor and measure the impact** throughout the cycle.

Review
- The PLT reflects on a PLT meeting norm that was identified at the beginning of the meeting.

Light grey: Sections should be completed in every PLT meeting.
Dark grey: Majority of time in the PLT should be spent in the dark grey section.
PLTs may focus on one or both of these dark grey sections in every PLT.

FIGURE 6.19: THE PLT MEETING STRUCTURE

This was supplemented by guiding questions that teams could use which, in the case of the school's suggested ten minutes for 'Review' at the start of the meeting, included:
- What have we learned and how will this inform our instruction in the future?
- What worked well to improve student learning and what didn't?
- How do we know?

- What formative assessment strategies did you use to help measure your success?
- What have been the successes and challenges this week?

Asking PLTs from different faculties to share their work with the rest of the school through the year then helped to build the constituency for the approach as teachers saw that not all PLTs looked the same, but they all were doing good work. It also helped to reassure those who were more reluctant to embrace the approach, while demonstrating that mistakes will be made, and that's all right because we learn from them. Mistakes also provide the sort of feedback needed to tweak the program as needed before full roll-out through the school.

A mix of Heads of Faculty and teachers were trained as part of a broader Departmental Professional Learning Community initiative, which contributed to a deeper understanding of PLTs in the school that was filtered back to the trial group of Pre-PLTs. In addition, PLT leaders were trained during 2019 in preparation for the following year, so they all knew the processes, inquiry cycle and protocols to make the initiative work. It meant that full implementation could begin with professional learning for all staff led by the team leaders themselves, in a way that ensured broader ownership than if it had been the Executive Team.

There is ongoing support for leaders of PLTs and the school developed a 'frequently asked questions' document for staff that addresses the range of concerns they have expressed.

Asked to describe the key lessons learned from the experience, Assistant Principal Jackie Knight who played a key role in the trial and subsequent implementation work, suggests the need to

> start slow, but make sure you start. It won't be perfect to begin with, but if you wait for perfection it will never happen. Let teachers have a go and mould the process as you go. Don't be afraid to change things as you go along and receive feedback from teachers, but most importantly make sure teachers have input on what they focus on in their teams.
>
> In the first year, provide ideas to support people, but create flexibility so people feel like they have ownership. Don't make the processes too complex. The simpler the better so people do not feel overwhelmed. Celebrate good work and remind people this is hard and challenging work and we won't always have success, which is OK. It's the reflection, discussion and what we do in response that makes a good PLT. Find PLTs to share what they are doing, including their successes and challenges.
>
> Have teachers take basic minutes of meetings so they are recording the main discussion point and ideas, and have these stored in a Google shared file so they can be readily accessed.

In a somewhat similar vein, Springvale Rise Primary School puts the success of its collaborative planning processes down to a combination of:
- formally scheduling two hours of collaborative planning a week for each teaching team and explaining how this links to the prevailing industrial agreement
- working with all staff to establish agreed meeting norms that are regularly revisited and reviewed
- initially working with the leadership team, and subsequently the middle leaders, to develop a shared understanding of what constitutes an effective collaborative planning session, which then was documented and regularly reviewed to preserve and promote its use
- seeking to learn as a leadership team about how to strategically lead their teams, while also being responsive to individual and collective needs.

These actions in turn are reflected in PLT meetings where team leaders ensure a specific focus on both student outcome data ('what our students know and need to know') and individual and team needs ('what our teachers know and need to know'), aligned to the school's overarching strategic and annual implementation plans. It's an approach that is further supported by a number of mantras the school has devised, such as 'what is the most important piece of learning for us right now?'

To help ensure effective preparation for PLT meetings, leaders are provided with the opportunity to 'share or pitch' their planning sessions to the full leadership team, so they can then improve their plans based on the feedback they receive. This also contributes to greater levels of consistency across the school in how its PLTs work.

AN EFFECTIVE PLT

Just as we asked, how do we know an effective teacher when we see one, earlier in this chapter, it is worth asking how we know a functioning and effective PLT?

According to Ciesak, Elliot and Romstedt (2013), the key elements of high functioning professional learning communities and the teams that comprise them are:
- shared and supportive leadership
- shared values and vision
- collective learning and application of learning
- shared personal practices
- supportive conditions.

All of these, it is noted, are highly resonant with the characteristics of effective teams we outlined in Box 5.1 in Chapter 5. At a more detailed level, we suggest that effective PLTs:
- are focused on evidence rather than inference—the evidence, as Griffin (2010) put it in his AiZ presentation cited earlier, of what students say, do, make and write
- challenge as well as share
- accept the sort of group responsibility that shifts its members' thinking from 'my class' to 'our students', and from 'your problem' to 'our solution'
- adopt a developmental rather than deficit approach
- focus on peer accountability rather than system reporting
- focus on the expectations of ALL students in the school.

From time to time it is also worth examining the way in which the team works together by asking the sort of questions leaders at Springvale Rise Primary posed:
- Who is doing the talking?
- Who is 'leading' the planning?
- Who is typing?
- Who writes the learning intentions and success criteria?
- How do we ensure we stay on task?
- Is there pre-meeting work?
- Is there post-meeting work?
- Documentation?
- How is technology used?
- What is the physical layout for the meetings?
- Timing?
- Accountability?

Apart from anything else, it's a set of questions that can help ensure that PLT work is the work of the many and not the few.

ACTIVITY FOR STAFF: EVALUATING THE EFFECTIVENESS OF PLTS

Instructions

Individually complete the following survey about the PLT (Table 6.9) to which you belong, using a four-point rating scale where:

1 = Does not apply to our team, 2 = Weakly applies to our team, 3 = Applies to our team and 4 = Strongly applies to our team.

TABLE 6.9: EVALUATING THE EFFECTIVENESS OF PLTS

Characteristic	Rating (1–4)	Evidence for the rating	Action to improve the rating
There is sufficient time for our PLT to meet to discuss and decide on actions to improve student learning			
The school's leadership see PLTs as central in improving teaching and supporting their work			
Our team operates based on agreed and understood protocols that are adhered to by all members			
Our PLT focuses clearly on teaching and learning and provides a means of building teaching capacity and our effectiveness in class			
Our PLT discussions are informed by evidence of student learning and this is used to set improvement goals			
Our PLT uses research as needed to inform its discussions and improve teaching			
Our PLT monitors the implementation of its strategies for pursuing its goals and adjusts them as required			
The key strategy we can adopt to improve the overall effectiveness of our team is:			

© Pamela Macklin and Vic Zbar, *Driving School Improvement*, Australian Council for Educational Research, 2017

At a more focused level, Figure 6.20 below provides an example of how the English team at Lyndhurst Secondary College evaluated its effectiveness in guaranteeing that sufficient capacity exists to support students to meet the requirements of the English curriculum in the school.

Based on what has been shared in key learning area (KLA) meetings this year ...	INFORMATION I have a general understanding of this	KNOWLEDGE I can work this out with some support/by working with colleagues	KNOW-HOW I feel pretty secure in my knowledge of this	Wisdom I could comfortably and skilfully support other staff with this
Curriculum and content for English in Years 7–10				
Curriculum and content for VCE English				

Personal reflection ...	Strongly disagree	Disagree	Neutral	Agree	Strongly agree
I know more about the Victorian Curriculum and assessment requirements for Years 7–10 English now than I did at the start of the year					
I know more about the curriculum and assessment requirements for VCE English now than I did at the start of the year					
I believe that I have made a valuable contribution to the English KLA this year in terms of curriculum development					
I am more confident in my ability to teach English classes now than I was at the start of the year					
Members of the English KLA are expected to work collegially with one another					
I feel that the English key learning area coordinators (KLACs) are knowledgeable in terms of the requirements for Years 7–12 English					
I am confident that the English KLACs are capable and competent in terms of the work that they are required to do					
I feel that the English KLACs acknowledge the work that I have done in the English KLA this year					
All things considered, I feel well supported by my English KLACs					

Looking to the future ...

I need more assistance with the following areas:
KLA meeting elements that are working well/should continue include:
KLA meeting elements that are not working well/should not continue include:

Any other comments?

FIGURE 6.20: ENGLISH KLA SURVEY: LYNDHURST SECONDARY COLLEGE, JULY 2016

It is through detailed, capacity-building work of this sort that PLTs can ultimately realise the benefits of collaboration that Little (1990) identified in answer to the question, 'Why collaborate in schools?' The reason we collaborate, she effectively responded in her article, is that collaboration results in:
- gains in student achievement
- higher quality solutions to problems
- increased confidence among all staff
- teachers able to support one another's strengths and accommodate weaknesses
- ability to test new ideas
- more support for new teachers
- expanded pool of ideas, materials and methods.

Collaboration also provides the means by which teachers can begin to delve deeper into what actually happens in class; as explored in more detail in the following chapter of this book.

CHAPTER 7
STAGE 3: IMPROVING CLASSROOM PRACTICE

Developing and implementing a whole-school instructional model through professional learning teams will contribute to better lesson planning and increased individual and collective efficacy as a result. However, it will not in itself guarantee that what is planned is sufficiently good. It is, after all, possible to plan less than engaging material that fails to generate learning among the target audience of students in the school; especially when it simply reflects a 'good idea' that has no evidence base.

Because we both work nationally and sometimes even internationally, we fly a lot. Everyone who flies regularly recognises that moment when the head cabin steward takes the PA to announce that 'the captain has asked the cabin crew to prepare the cabin for landing', and then goes through the standard spiel. There is something we definitely do not want to hear at that point. We do not want an announcement to the effect that, 'ordinarily in these circumstances, we ask you to return your tray table, put your seat back upright, turn off large electronic devices and other such things, but today the pilots thought they would try something different and see how it goes'. We suspect we are not alone in that view.

Yet there are plenty of teachers who continue to act in this way—trying things out because they think them a good idea, regardless of whether evidence exists to suggest they can work.

The third stage of school improvement, therefore, is to inject a greater measure of evidence into the planning and delivery of what teachers individually and collectively undertake. In other words, to shift the focus from inference of what teachers think might work to evidence of what actually does, including from successful practice in other schools.

EFFECT SIZES

Before proceeding, however, it is important to make some clarifying points about the notion of evidence, and particularly effect sizes and how they are used.

We noted in Chapter 2 that research is sometimes uncertain, often contested and must be contextualised to the actual circumstances of the school. It is more a guide to strategic thinking and action than a 'prescription' in its own right.

Effect sizes are having a growing influence on the use of research in schools, but they are arguably much misunderstood.

Effect size is simply a way of quantifying the size difference between two groups or the same group over time on a common scale, and hence a means of measuring the effectiveness of different interventions that schools adopt.[1] Hattie found that the average effect size of all the interventions he studied was 0.40, and hence nominated this as the 'hinge point' against which the interventions can be judged. Anything higher than 0.40 is seen as significant, while an effect size lower than that is not significant, though this should not be taken to mean you shouldn't do it, since a positive impact is still worth having provided it doesn't cost much in either money or time.

There are, however, some caveats about the use of effect sizes that need to be considered.

Many schools use the effect sizes from Hattie's (2009) Visible Learning work, which derive, as the title of his book suggests, from 'a synthesis of over 800 meta-analyses relating to achievement'. These studies, as the preface acknowledges, are limited to 'studies that have used basic statistics (means, variances, sample sizes)' (p. ix), and not qualitative studies about what happens in schools. While not a criticism of material we regularly draw on ourselves, this means the effect sizes represent the average of different studies that have been examined and used to calculate the effect. Usually this doesn't matter much, since the studies will tend to coalesce and accord with successful practice in schools. However, there are occasions where averaging can mask different ways in which the intervention has been implemented, and hence different outcomes achieved; such as the example of open versus traditional classrooms we described in Chapter 2. This is not to suggest that effect sizes ought not to be used, but rather the need to look behind the number at times to see if any such masking has occurred.

A further issue with effect sizes, and research generally according to Wiliam (2016), is that it only tells you what was and not what might be. Homework provides a case in point. The effect size for homework is a somewhat lowly 0.29, well below the hinge point of 0.40 (Hattie, 2015). However, this neglects the fact that most of the homework teachers set, and on which the studies were based, is not particularly good nor even followed up. By focusing on what might be, rather than what is, it is possible to envisage homework that could support better learning at school. At the very least, this suggests a need to delve under the surface of simple numeric effect sizes in order to become what Wiliam calls, 'critical consumers of research'.

Finally, as Wiliam (2016) also noted, the focus on effect sizes tells us nothing about the cost. There are, for example, strategies that have limited effect, but may still be worth it when we consider the cost. Sending an SMS to parents about preschool literacy classes, he explained, has an effect size only around 0.1, but since they have a very low cost, it is a strategy that is possibly worth undertaking in the school. Similarly, the effect size for extra-curricular programs is only 0.21, but if led by volunteers, can help build the sense of community and engagement in the school at relatively little expense.

The point is that, valuable as they are, effect sizes constitute only one measure of the progress that students make. They should be supplemented by other assessment data, observations, student feedback and more to provide a comprehensive picture of what makes a difference to learners in the school. This range of information can then be used to raise questions and stimulate conversation, especially around the reasons for the differences that exist.

It's about strategically using research to support improvement, which is where research-based theories of action come in.

THEORIES OF ACTION

All of us operate based on theories of action even though we would never use that term. More specifically, the underlying belief that 'if I do this, then the result will be' determines why each of us does what we do.

---

[1] More specifically, an effect size is the difference between two mean scores over time, divided by the average spread.

Ideally our theories of action (our 'if, then' beliefs) would provide common reference points and shared guides to help identify, design, implement and evaluate teaching practices that are demonstrated to lead to better student learning outcomes. In practice, most of our theories of action are never shared.

Raising some proven and effective theories of action that teachers can consider and adopt not only helps plant their seeds within the school, but also provides the context in which the 'mental models' we all hold can be exposed, examined and addressed.

The business theorist Chris Argyris (1990), who was cited earlier in this book, advanced the concept of the 'ladder of inference' (pp. 88–89) to describe the unconscious thinking process we generally adopt from fact to decision or action, as depicted in Figure 7.1.

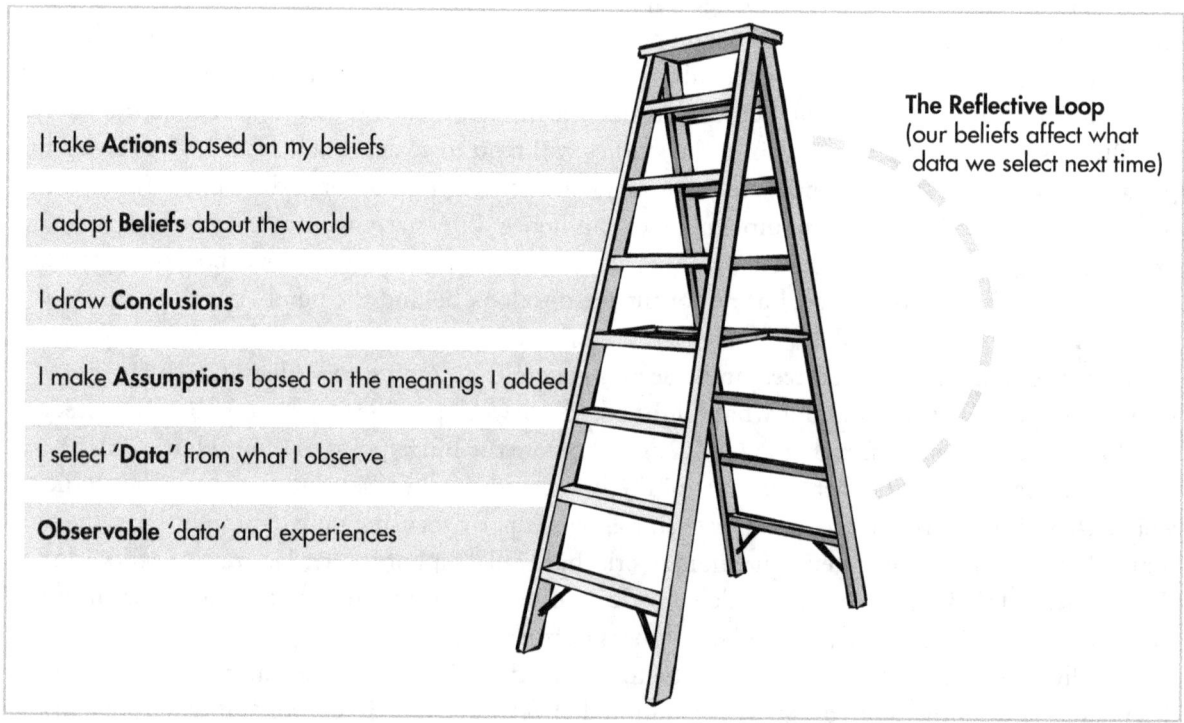

FIGURE 7.1: THE LADDER OF INFERENCE

It may look complex, but is readily understood with reference to an example drawn from everyday life.

During the middle months of the year, we like going to the football to watch the team we follow as a form of release. At many points in the game, along with every other spectator in the stadium, we will observe the awarding of a free kick. We select data from our observation which, in this case, is that the free kick is against our team. Our assumption about this is that it will stop the momentum we were just starting to build. This leads us to the conclusion that this moment could be the difference between winning and losing the game. We adopt the belief we always do, that this umpire hates our team and the action we take is to boo. Thousands of others in the stadium do exactly the same thing. However, thousands of others do not because the data they selected is that the free kick was for their team, which means it could halt their opponents' momentum and get them back into the game. The belief they then adopt is that for once this umpire got it right and so they all cheer.

All of this happens in a nanosecond and only the observable data (the awarding of the free kick) and the action taken (booing or cheering) can be seen. Surfacing the assumptions we make can help us to understand why each of us acts the way we do, and thereby enable the sort of discussion and questioning that can ultimately underpin behavioural change.

Some of the best work we have experienced in this regard was initiated by Hopkins and Craig (2015) through the Achievement Improvement Zones (AiZ) project and subsequently picked up by McRel. They identified six teacher theories of action that can contribute to better teacher practice in

schools. More specifically they suggest that student learning outcomes will be improved if teachers:
- harness learning intentions[2], narrative and pace, so students are more secure about their learning, and more willing to take risks
- ensure that learning tasks are purposeful, clearly defined, differentiated and challenging
- systematically employ higher order questioning
- connect feedback to data about student actions and performance
- commit to peer assessment and assessment for learning
- implement cooperative group structures and techniques to mediate between whole-class instruction and students carrying out tasks.

Consistent with our advice in Chapter 2, that the enemy of effective change is when we take on too much, schools in this stage of the improvement process are urged to focus on just one of these theories and drive it consistently through the school before taking another on board.

In the remainder of this chapter we focus on the two theories of action that schools we work with are using and finding to be particularly effective in supporting more teachers to work like the best—that is, learning goals and associated success criteria, and feedback to students designed to enable them to achieve the learning goals.

A WORD ON DATA

Before proceeding to examine these two theories of action in more depth, however, a word about data is required; since data underpins each of the theories of action outlined.

Ensuring a shift from intuition to evidence requires us to collect data (or information by any other name) that measures the impact we have and helps monitor performance along the way. Evidence and data go hand-in-hand.

Good decisions in any organisation are data-driven and based on the evidence of what does and doesn't work. Our observation is that school leaders and teachers in Australia are much more comfortable using data, than previously was the case, to identify trends and proactively respond to what they find. That said, a challenge always exists to ensure we gather the range of data we need for informed decision-making, as opposed to simply confirming what we thought from the start. At the very least, there is a need to systematically know:
- contextual data such as students' socio-economic circumstances, the linguistic background and other factors that may affect their performance at school
- student achievement data that includes formal assessment results, teachers' observational notes in class, samples of students' work and the like
- other student data relevant to their outcomes such as attendance, behavioural incidents, completion of homework and mobility.

The collection and analysis of such comprehensive data sets enables the school to set appropriate improvement priorities and goals, develop strategies for achieving these and monitor progress along the way. In addition, the use of data to more clearly understand where students are at, can contribute to the better identification of their learning needs and greater differentiation of instruction as a result. The leadership challenge in this context is to ensure that the data is used to inform teachers' practice both individually and in their teams.

The experience of improvement programs in the health sector has some interesting lessons in this regard. Seeking to get better, according to the Scottish National Health Service (NHS Scotland, 2010), requires that we first define what our chosen 'better state' would look like, so we

---

[2] We tend to use the interchangeable term learning goals because of the aspirational connotations associated with the notion of goals as opposed to an intent.

can then measure to see if the things we change deliver the outcomes we seek. The key questions to ask in this context are, 'What does 'better' look like?', 'How will we recognise better when we see it?' and 'How will we know if a change we make constitutes an improvement or not?'

Gathering and analysing data is critical in this regard, since it helps us to plan for improvement, test changes, track implementation, determine outcomes, monitor long-term progress and make improvement visible to all of the stakeholders involved. That is why the systematic gathering of data about the impact the theories of action outlined have is integral to their implementation in any school.

Of course, achieving this is easier said than done. One approach that has proven useful in a number of American schools is the 'Data Wise' Improvement Process first developed by Boudett, City and Murnane in 2006 (see Boudett, City & Murnane, 2013, p. 5). The process depicted in Figure 7.2 was designed to address the problems schools have in managing the sheer amount of data available, finding the time to analyse and use it effectively and identifying where to start, all while building the capacity of teachers in this regard.

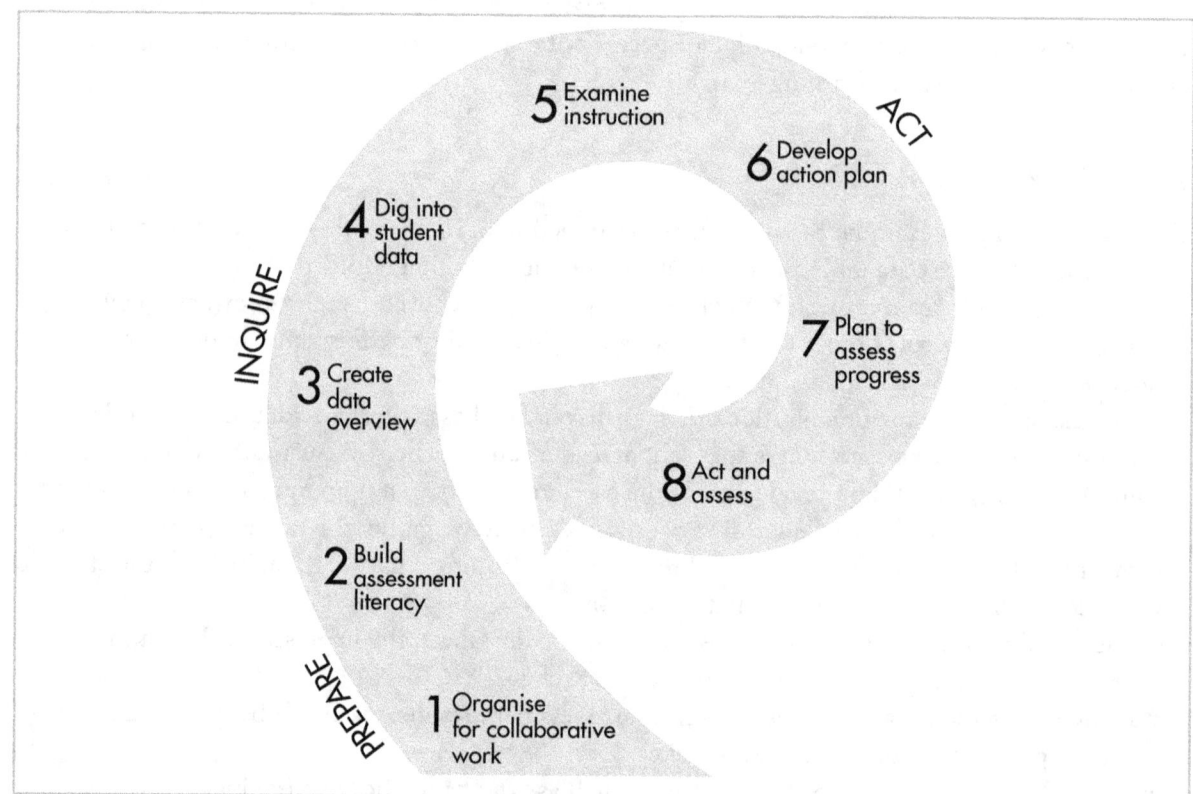

FIGURE 7.2: THE DATA WISE IMPROVEMENT PROCESS
Source: Boudett, City and Murnane (2013). Used with permission.

The process has subsequently been used in schools around the world, including a growing number of Australian schools, with a focus on using it effectively in the meetings that schools conduct. In Table 7.1 we have taken Oberman and Boudett's (2015) outline of how a hypothetical United States school (Highland Academy) might implement the process and adapted it to reflect both the circumstances of Australian schools and our focus in Chapter 6 on the capacity-building role of professional learning teams (PLTs).

TABLE 7.1: APPLYING THE DATA WISE PROCESS THROUGH PLTS

Step	What this step involves
1 Organise for collaborative work	Ensuring that the PLTs are established and functioning effectively in the school.
2 Build assessment literacy	Gathering and discussing agreed data sets in PLTs. Consider appointing a 'data manager' to work with teachers to improve their understanding of key data sets gathered and how they can be used to inform their teaching in class.
3 Create data overview	Consolidating relevant data sets such as an overview of the NAPLAN literacy performance of matched cohorts of students moving from Year 3 to Year 5 in primary, or Year 7 to Year 9 in secondary schools.
4 Dig into student data	Identifying any trends emerging—i.e. above average or below average growth in the matched cohort over the two years.
5 Examine instruction	Delving into the teaching practices that might have contributed to either the above or below average literacy growth identified in Step 4.
6 Develop action plan	Developing a plan for either leveraging the successful teaching practices identified in Step 5 through the rest of the school, or redressing the unsuccessful strategies identified through Step 5.
7 Plan to assess progress	Developing an assessment schedule to monitor the progress of implementation of the action plan.
8 Act and assess	Implementing the action plan, documenting its progress and adjusting as needed in response to the assessments undertaken to ensure success.

We can now turn our attention to the implementation of the two key theories of action being implemented in a significant number of Australian schools.

LEARNING GOALS AS THE ENTRY POINT

We often start working with teachers on learning goals by asking them to define in a single sentence what a learning goal is, only to find that they struggle with the task.

Put simply, a learning goal clearly states what we intend our students to know, understand or be able to do as a result of the teaching. It should make it very clear to the students what they need to attain (in terms of knowledge/skill acquisition) in a period of time (a lesson or series of lessons).

We have found over time that learning goals provide one of the best entry points for enabling more teachers to work like the best.

Learning goals, as we noted in our discussion of change in Chapter 2, have only a moderate effect in their own right.[3] However, this effect is magnified because of the way they connect to other influences with effect sizes of their own. Used appropriately, learning goals frame the planning of lessons that teachers individually and collaboratively undertake. Having decided what students should know, understand or be able to do, the teacher(s) can then determine the teaching and learning activities that will enable them to achieve this, the success criteria that support the students to know the extent to which they have achieved it, and the assessments to determine whether they have or not. The learning goal also provides the anchor for teacher questioning and feedback, and can be used by students to self-assess.

Figure 7.3 depicts the way in which teacher planning flows from the specified learning goal. The figure can be reproduced in the middle of an A3 page and used by teams of teachers as a lesson planning tool.

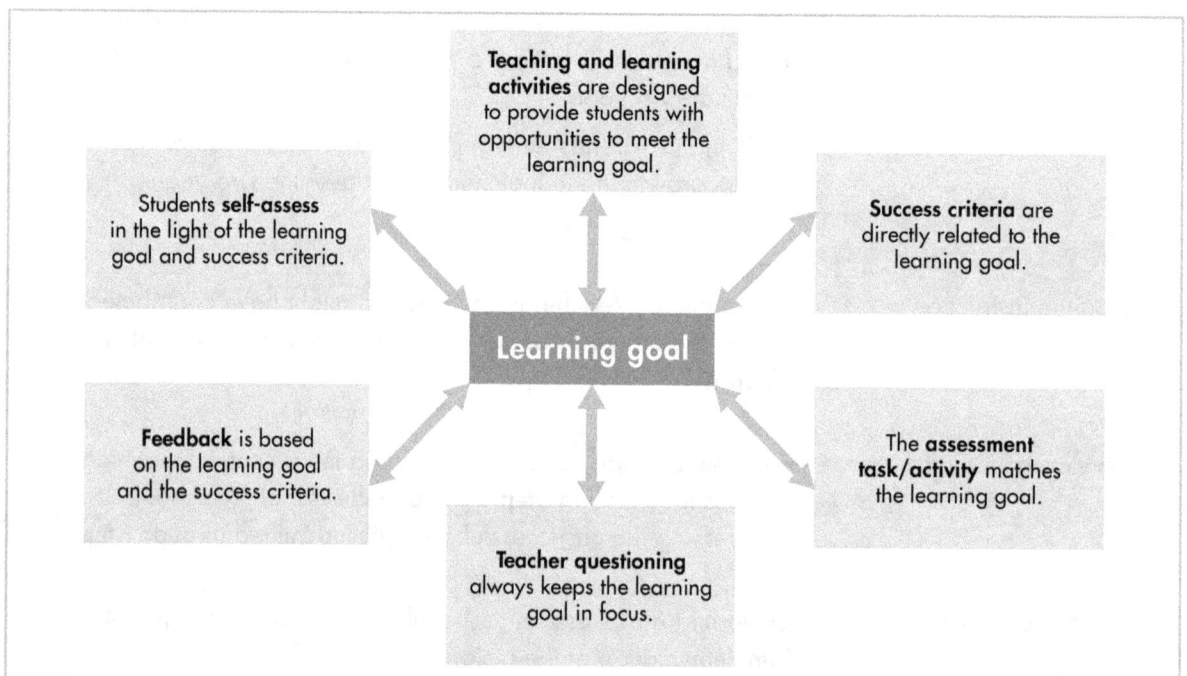

FIGURE 7.3: LEARNING GOALS AS THE FRAME FOR TEACHER PLANNING

Note: The figure is adapted from one included in the (former) Curriculum Corporation Australia's Assessment for Learning, 'Learning Intentions' Professional Learning module.
Source: Curriculum Corporation Australia [now Education Services Australia] (n.d.).

Peter Langham, the then Assistant Principal at Narre Warren South P–12 took this sort of approach and prepared a sample planning guide for teachers in the secondary area for teaching Pythagoras' theorem in maths. The extract from this sample, provided as Figure 7.4, demonstrates the flow from learning intention, which is the term used in this school, through to an organised recap at the end.[4]

---

[3] Slipping from an effect size of 0.56 in Hattie's analysis of 138 influences related to learning outcomes in 2009 (see Hattie, 2009) to 0.40 in the ranking of 195 influences online (see Hattie, 2015) and then rising to 0.68 in the ranking of 252 influences in 2019 (see Hattie, 2019).

[4] The full school sample includes the relevant content description and elaborations from the Victorian Curriculum and Assessment Authority (VCAA) website, additional illustrations from the mathematics glossary and two more assessments.

LEARNING INTENTION

- Open the mandated curriculum document for your study
- Locate the appropriate Level/Unit and Topic/Area of study
- Use the Content Descriptors/Key Knowledge Points as your Learning Intentions
- The full Content Descriptor/Key Knowledge Point will be repeated as the Learning until that content has been covered entirely.

Learning Intention: Investigate Pythagoras' Theorem and its application to solving simple problems involving right angled triangles.

SUBJECT SPECIFIC LITERACY

As the Learning Intention will include language that your students may not be familiar with, you should teach the meanings of those terms when you first introduce the new Learning Intention, as well as Recapping terms students should have learnt in the past and any necessary terms that weren't explicitly mentioned in the Learning Intention. A glossary should be provided by VCAA for your subject.

Victorian F–10 Mathematics Glossary: http://victoriancurriculum.vcaa.vic.edu.au/LearningArea/Load-File?learningArea=mathematics&subject=mathematics&name=Mathematics%20Glossary.docx&storage=Glossary

From the Glossary:
Hypotenuse—The longest side of a right-angled triangle, opposite the right angle.

ASSESSMENT

- In your team, design the way you will assess the learning of the Content Descriptors/Key Knowledge Points, referring to any Elaborations provided by the curriculum document.
- Include Assessment of Subject Specific Literacy as well as Assessment of Skills.
- Where possible, break the skill down to accurately assess the learning of each individual as well as the class—Assessment to be designed and agreed upon before teaching commences.

Continued…

1 Referring to the image below, which label represents the hypotenuse?

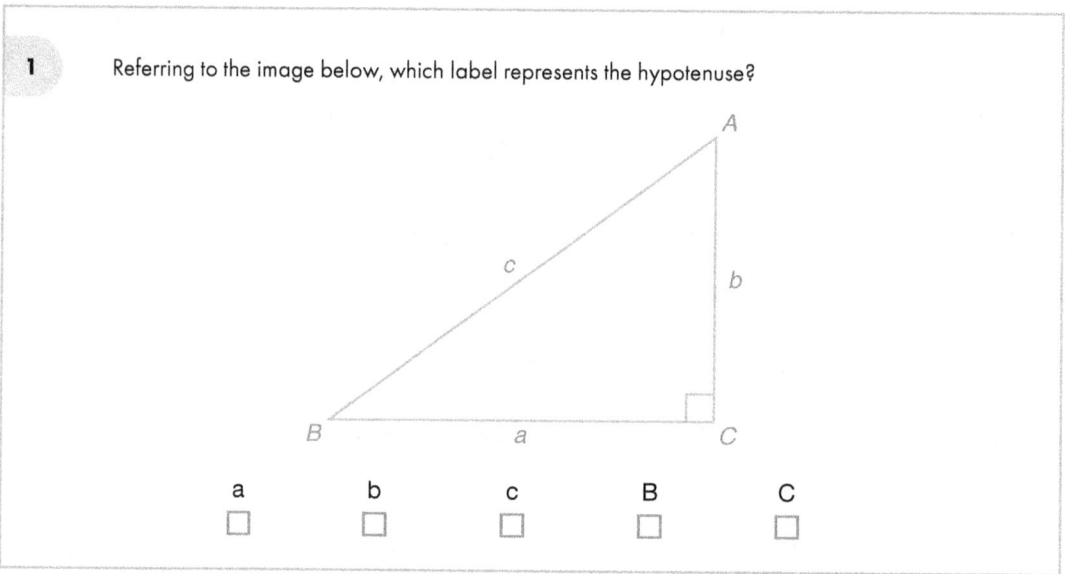

a ☐   b ☐   c ☐   B ☐   C ☐

After assessing the skill breakdown in its simplest form, you can include more advanced questions which combine skills.

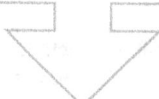

SUCCESS CRITERIA

- Align Success Criteria to each part of the team designed Assessment.
- Success Criteria should reflect the understanding of Subject Specific Literacy as well as the breakdown of skills.

⬇

- I can identify the hypotenuse of a right-angled triangle and explain how I identified it.
- I can recall and use Pythagoras' Theorem to solve right-angled triangles where the length of the hypotenuse is unknown
- I can recall and use Pythagoras' Theorem to solve right-angled triangles where the length of a shorter side is unknown

RECAP

Use targeted questioning in the Recap, choosing different students to recall the meanings of Subject Specific Language from the Learning Intention, and to recall the skills that have been covered in the previous classes—Recap questions to be designed and agreed upon before teaching commences.

⬇

Recap questions and statements linked to Subject Specific Language:
With what type of triangle can you use Pythagoras' theorem to find unknown lengths? What is a right angle? etc.

FIGURE 7.4: PLANNING A LESSON USING PYTHAGORAS' THEOREM, NARRE WARREN SOUTH P–12 (EXTRACT)

Note: The capitalisation of terms throughout Figure 7.4 is that adopted by the school.

More recently, Vic sought to demonstrate that the planning framework in Figure 7.3, when combined with a common instructional model, can support the development of quality lessons by teachers in teams. To do this, he developed two lessons in areas that he essentially knew nothing about.

Vic was a secondary teacher whose background is economics and history. So he determined to plan an infant literacy lesson and a secondary mathematics lesson for which he had no training at all. Since his Year 9 maths lesson, like Langham's Narre Warren South sample, focused on Pythagoras's theorem, it is not reproduced here. However the primary lesson he planned shows that the framework does work. More specifically, having identified a Year 2 outcome from the Australian Curriculum, he then used it to develop the lesson outline provided in Box 7.1.

If the framework can be used to plan acceptable lessons in areas the planner knows nothing about, imagine how good the lessons could be when planned by someone who does.

Box 7.1
PRIMARY LESSON SAMPLE

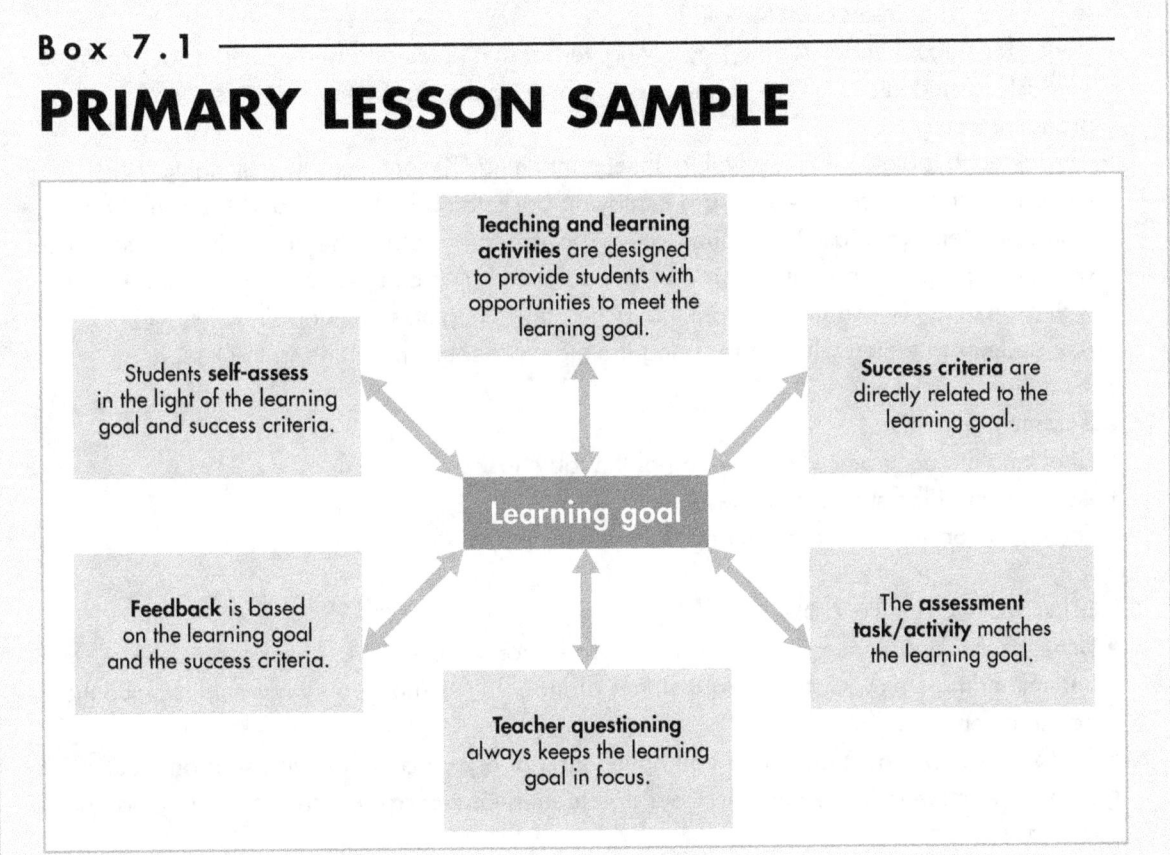

Tuning in
The hook
Provide students with a number of sentences along the following lines:
- 'Rain is playing with Rain's friends. Rain is having a good time. Rain has to go home when it starts to get dark. Rain will have dinner and then a bath after Rain gets home'.

Ask them whether they find the repetition of Rain's name a bit boring, and to think about how they can make it more interesting.

Learning goal (Primary sample)
By the end of the lesson you will be able to use pronouns.[5]

Continued...

---

[5] From the Year 2 English Curriculum, Level Description in the Australian Curriculum for Expressing and Developing Ideas—Understand that nouns represent people, places, concrete objects and abstract concepts; that there are three types of nouns: common, proper and pronouns.

Success criteria
- I can explain what a pronoun is.
- I can list at least eight pronouns.
- I can use these pronouns in a story.

Purposeful learning (i.e. explicit teaching, student practice and differentiation)
Teaching and learning activities
- Explain to your students that a pronoun is a word used instead of a noun. Write the following pronouns on the board: he, she, her, him, I, you, we, and they, and demonstrate how each can be used instead of a proper noun. Have students work in pairs and demonstrate with their partner what these pronouns mean by identifying them in the room (e.g. using 'she' instead of 'the girl').
- Check for student understanding by giving verbal examples and non-examples of pronouns and asking students to give a thumbs up or down on the right and wrong uses of the pronouns you give.
- Provide each table of students with a sheet containing 20 sentences that all contain a person's/persons' names—e.g. Arlo is playing basketball. Binh, Mirò and Lee are doing a maths problem. Then ask the groups to work together to replace the names in each sentence with an appropriate pronoun. This can be conducted as a competition between table teams with a prize at the end for the team that accurately completes the worksheet first.
- Ask students to write a short story using the eight pronouns provided in the lesson.

Assessment activities
- Checking the accuracy of completion of the table task.
- Assessment of the students' stories.
- The check for understanding during the lesson.

Reflection and review
- Use targeted questioning (including questions to non-volunteers) to check for understanding—e.g. 'Can you name three pronouns?', 'What pronoun would replace the boy in a sentence?' etc.
- Think-Pair-Share about one thing you have learned today about how to use pronouns.
- Relate the answers to the learning goal and identify any areas where re-teaching may be required.

A thought-provoking question[6]
Consider asking a thought-provoking question, if appropriate to the level of understanding achieved in the class, such as, 'Why do you think pronouns help us to write a better story?'

Good learning goals, as evident in Figure 7.4 and Box 7.1, contribute to students' learning because they help the student to focus on the purpose of what they are doing, rather than simply seeking to get it done. The learning goal tells the student where to focus their efforts and supports them to take more responsibility for their own learning at school.

---

[6] While not part of any instructional model as outlined in Chapter 6, a thought-provoking question has been added to the planning framework to cater for the needs of higher performing students who we have observed commonly have to wait having finished work earlier than their peers.

This is the theory at least. In practice, the quality of learning goals is variable in schools and many are activities rather than goals. For example, it is not uncommon to see a learning goal posted in class along the lines, 'You will give a speech for or against smoking as part of a debate'. This is an activity and not a learning goal, and reflects a mistake that teachers sometimes make. It is possible to find a series of dot points for or against smoking on the internet, repeat them in the debate and satisfy the requirement of the 'goal' without gaining any capacity to make a persuasive argument when smoking is not involved. The appropriate goal in this example would be for the student to be able to present a point of view in a persuasive way, and then one of the ways they might demonstrate this is through the activity of giving a speech for or against smoking in class.

The challenge that teachers face is to ensure they design good learning goals.

ACTIVITY FOR STAFF: DEVELOPING GOOD LEARNING GOALS

Instructions
1 Ask staff to consider the question, 'How do we know a good learning goal when we see one?' More specifically, ask them to work in groups to identify the characteristics of a good learning goal to then use as criteria to underpin their lesson planning in teams.
2 The outcome of their discussions can be compared to the criteria developed by teachers to support the implementation of assessment for learning in Ontario schools (see Table 7.2).

TABLE 7.2: DEVELOPING GOOD LEARNING GOALS

Criteria	
Content	• Identifies what is to be learned
	• Linked to the overall and specific expectations to be addressed
	• Connected to a big idea
	• Identifies incremental steps to build student knowledge and skills
Language	• Uses clear, concise language
	• Uses language that is student friendly and grade-appropriate
	• Uses verbs that describe specific and observable actions
	• Stated from a students' perspective (e.g. 'We are learning to …')

Source: Ontario Ministry of Education (2010, p. 45). The criteria are part of a larger checklist included in the resource.

WRITING GOOD LEARNING GOALS

Sometimes in education we overcomplicate things and fail to notice the simpler solutions that are hiding in plain sight. Writing good learning goals is a case in point. In fact, it's a case where a three-step process will do. Teachers can write good learning goals by:
1 Creating a stem, generally along the lines 'We are learning to …'
2 Having created the stem, adding a verb—for example, analyse, recognise, compare, provide, solve and so on.
3 Having the stem and verb in place, determining the actual product, process or outcome that is sought.

This process is readily evident in the following examples from a primary and a secondary school in Table 7.3.

TABLE 7.3: SAMPLE LEARNING GOALS

Primary		
Stem	Verb	Product/process outcome
We are learning	to write	compound sentences

Secondary		
Stem	Verb	Product/process outcome
We are learning	to explain	how different materials conduct electricity

It's a process that also lends itself to a good professional learning session for staff.

There is an important caution that needs to be sounded at this point. The caution, identified by Wiliam and Leahy (2015), is the need to avoid the temptation to include context in the learning goal. Learning goals, they observe, 'are far less useful if they specifically include the context of the learning'. Shirley Clarke (2003) provides a good example related to teaching a unit on food production in the developing world to illustrate the point. While the goal the teacher set was 'to understand the effects of banana production on banana producers' (p. 23), it is unlikely she was really interested in students specifically learning about the difficulties banana producers face. The better learning goal would be 'to understand the impact of production on producers' (p. 23) with banana production as the vehicle through which it is learned.

This example, which Wiliam and Leahy (2015) cite, illustrates what they describe as

> a rather important principle at the heart of teaching, which is that when we teach our students how to do something, we are rarely interested in their ability to do the things we have taught them ... If we teach our students to add two numbers, such as 278 and 345, we are no longer interested in those two numbers ... We are interested in whether they can use what they learned to add two different numbers. (p. 31)

Having taken out context in this way, the verb becomes critical to the quality of the learning goal. This is because the task verb, such as list or compare, defines the nature of the teacher's input and the students' assessment task. For example, the difference between asking students to compile a list, and to compare two things that have similarities and differences that need to be identified and described.

Some schools have sought to address this by providing teachers with a list of verbs to consider when designing learning goals that are aligned to the taxonomy developed by Benjamin Bloom (1956).[7] It is an approach that informs the following activity for staff aimed at improving the quality of learning goals and the associated activities that teachers devise.

ACTIVITY FOR STAFF: CHOOSING THE RIGHT VERB FOR YOUR LEARNING GOAL

The following activity is best completed in professional learning teams.

Instructions

1 Expand the range of verbs and possible activities in the following table (Table 7.4) based on learning goals you have used. The outcomes can then be shared to develop a whole-school guide to formulating quality learning goals.

---

[7] Bloom's Taxonomy was developed by Benjamin Bloom and colleagues in the middle of the 20th century as a classification system for intellectual skills and behaviour important for student learning. It has been revised since and is still used widely in schools around the world.

2 Teachers' capacity to develop good learning goals can be further cemented by examining a range of goals, both good and bad, against the criteria identified through the earlier activity for staff ('Developing good learning goals').

TABLE 7.4: CHOOSING THE RIGHT VERB FOR YOUR LEARNING GOAL

	Bloom's Taxonomy	The what—sample verbs[8]	The how—possible activities
Lower order thinking skills	Knowledge—remember previously learned information	• Name • Identify • List • Repeat • • • • •	• Text reading • Using a dictionary • Completing a worksheet • • • • • •
	Comprehension—demonstrate an understanding of the facts and ideas	• Explain • Paraphrase • Classify • Calculate • • • •	• Debate • Prepare a summary • Do a role play • • • • •
	Application—apply the knowledge in a different or new way	• Experiment • Interpret • Apply • Construct • • • •	• Develop a poster • Conduct an experiment • Keep a journal • • • • •

Continued...

---

[8] There are many verb lists available through a Google search. A good one for teachers to consider, having completed this activity, is *Bloom's Taxonomy*, developed by Northern Illinois University (n.d.).

Table 7.4 (continued)

Higher order thinking skills	Analysis—break down objects or ideas into simpler parts, make inferences and find evidence to support generalisations	• Categorise • Differentiate • Compare • Question • • • • • • •	• Develop a survey • Draw a conclusion • Prepare a spreadsheet • • • • • • •
	Synthesis—compile information together into a new whole or propose alternative solutions	• Design • Plan • Forecast • Compose • • • • • • •	• Write an article • Solve a problem • Prepare a report on • • • • • • •
	Evaluation—present and defend opinions by making judgments about information, based on internal evidence or external criteria	• Critique • Defend • Assess • Prioritise • • • • • • •	• Identify a recommendation • Make a judgment • Prepare an editorial • • • • • • •

© Pamela Macklin and Vic Zbar, *Driving School Improvement*, Australian Council for Educational Research, 2017

ACTIVITY FOR STAFF: ANALYSING LEARNING GOALS

Instructions

1 Individually consider the list of 24 learning goals provided below that we gathered from New South Wales primary and Victorian secondary schools. Take a copy of these goals, then find three that meet your criteria for a good learning goal and mark them with a tick (√). If you cannot find any, then mark three you think are getting close to good quality goals with a question mark (?).
2 Then find three learning goals that do not meet your criteria. Write them down on a separate sheet of paper with space in between each. Underneath each one, rewrite the goal so that it does meet your criteria for a good learning goal.
3 Share your deliberations with a colleague and seek agreement on three good goals and three that you can rewrite to make into good learning goals.

Learning goals

1 By the end of this lesson you will have learned to represent data on a compound column graph.
2 We are learning to convince our audience about whether or not stingrays make good pets.
3 Understand how characters are important to create good narratives.
4 Use questioning to comprehend text.
5 Data—how to collect data using surveys.
6 Pick your topic, get in groups and brainstorm ideas for the topic and your project.
7 To experience Indonesian Jump Rope.
8 To learn how light energy works, especially luminous versus non-luminous.
9 Continue working on your Water Wise assignments in your learning groups.
10 Recognise literary elements—genre, plot, character, settings, problem/resolution.
11 We are learning about the purpose and structure of a news article.
12 Looking at how ideas change and grow as we read.
13 Analyse and express data using charts and graphs.
14 Explore the life of Ned Kelly and his family.
15 I am learning to edit my work to improve the meaning of my writing.
16 Complete your Japanese language proficiency test
17 Read for a particular purpose.
18 We use our PL books to improve our writing.
19 We are learning how to divide numbers using long division.
20 Spell, define and use words in sentences.
21 Think about how persuasive language is used in ads.
22 We are learning how to write compound sentences about an animal using a conjunction and best adjectives.
23 We are learning to understand simple scales on maps and plans.
24 We are learning to form predictions about a text.

Glen Waverley Secondary College adopted a similar approach by collating examples of learning intentions and success criteria to inform a professional development session where leaders and mixed groups of teachers not only worked together to identify good examples from the list, but also wrote samples of their own, individually and as a team. The session proved particularly successful according to those involved because the leaders had run the session for themselves in the previous week to prepare effectively for the day. Then at the session itself, leaders participated as co-learners, rather than introducers of the approach, working together to improve their collective capacity to write quality learning intentions and success criteria to inform the lessons they all teach.

It is then, of course, a matter of driving the use of learning goals through the school, which in part can be monitored through the students themselves. Narre Warren South P–12 College has sought direct feedback from students on the use of learning intentions by staff, through the short survey included as Table 7.5.

TABLE 7.5: NARRE WARREN SOUTH P–12 COLLEGE LEARNING INTENTIONS SURVEY

Are you seeing learning intentions in most classes?	Never	Sometimes, maybe two of my teachers used them	Most of the time. Most teachers and most lessons	Every lesson. All teachers and all classes
Which subject/s regularly provide clear and useful learning intentions?	English	Maths	Science elective	PE elective
	Humanities elective	Art elective	Technology elective	Food electives
Are the learning intentions you're seeing in classes useful to you? Choose one of these options:	No—They don't help at all	Sort of—They let me know what I'm learning that lesson	Yes—It gives me a clear idea of what I'm going to be learning and why	Definitely—Knowing what's going on keeps me on track and helps keep me motivated

The school then gained further qualitative feedback on the use of learning intentions through the survey for small groups provided as a pro forma which we have adapted slightly in Figure 7.5. The outcomes of the survey were then shared with staff both to highlight progress since the adoption of the school's instructional model with learning intentions at its heart, and to set the challenge of ensuring consistent implementation of the model, and good learning intentions through the school. The survey was then readministered during Term 4 to inform leaders' strategic planning for the following year.

Question 1—Learning intentions should be being used in most of your classes. What do you think is the purpose of these learning intentions?
Responses:

Question 2—Do you think having learning intentions given to you each lesson helps your learning? Why/Why not?
Responses:

Question 3—What makes a good or useful learning intention for you? What are the characteristics that make it either good or bad?
Responses:

Question 4—What makes a bad or ineffectual learning intention? What are the characteristics that make it either good or bad?
Responses:

Question 5—The survey results from the term two survey suggest that you're seeing the learning intentions, but the effectiveness could be improved. Do you have any hints or tips for teachers to make them more useful?
Responses:

FIGURE 7.5: LEARNING INTENTIONS SURVEY: SMALL GROUP QUESTIONS

Somewhat similarly and perhaps even more expansively, Glen Waverley Secondary College has collected data over time using a set of questions where students are asked to rate on a four-point-scale from 'never' to 'always' the extent to which their teacher:
- at the end of the lesson talks about what I should have learned
- explains how to know if I have met the learning goals of the lesson
- knows whether I have met the goals of lessons
- does not look at my work during the lessons
- checks on our understanding at the end of lessons
- is revisiting the learning intentions and success criteria at the end of the lesson
- knows whether a student has met the success criteria at the end of the lesson.

The students are also asked to use the same four-point-scale to reflect on the extent to which 'I':
- am still working on the main activity for the lesson when the bell goes at the end of the period
- know whether I have met the goals of the lessons
- don't think about the learning goals of lessons
- check to see if I have been successful at the end of lessons
- am aware of whether I have met the success criteria at the end of the lesson.

Student feedback need not be limited to students in the secondary years. Oakleigh Grammar School, for example, has asked three simple questions of students as young as Grades 1 through to 3:
- How do you know what you need to learn in your lesson?
- How do you know if you have achieved this/learned this?
- What do you do when you 'get stuck' or don't understand?

That the students can think meaningfully about these questions in light of their experiences is evident in such responses as:
- I know what I need to learn—because 'the words in the learning intention are always talked about so we know what they mean', 'first we see what work might look like then we make up a learning intention to learn what we need to', and 'we write the learning intention in our books so we know what we have to learn'.
- I know I have achieved/learned it—because 'you can tell if you have achieved it if you check the success criteria', 'the steps are on the board to show the success criteria to get it right', and 'we highlight what we have done in the success criteria and have to work on the other parts'.
- When I get stuck or don't understand I—'check the success criteria, these are our steps', 'talk to my learning partner' and 'ask three before me'.

These approaches provide an effective means of checking the level of implementation across the school as a whole, and hence the degree of variability that exists which, according to Robinson (2018), 'is the biggest obstacle to educational improvement' in any school. To the extent that variability is, as Robinson suggests, generally more 'a matter of skill than will' (p. 66), it is something that can be assessed through the evaluation of teacher confidence embodied in the self-assessment in Table 7.6 later in this chapter, to then inform the nature of support to teachers that the school provides.

ADDING SUCCESS CRITERIA TO THE MIX

Success criteria go hand-in-hand with learning goals since they describe in specific terms, and in language meaningful to students, what successful attainment of the learning goal will look like for them.

The specification of success criteria is central to ensuring that the learning goal is understood by the learner, and that the classroom activities are designed by the teacher to comprehensively address this goal. Put simply, both teachers and students benefit from a clear understanding of what constitutes success. It becomes even more powerful still when combined with work samples that illustrate what quality work looks like when the success criteria are met.

Hattie and Timperley (2007) suggest that the three questions that guide student learning are: 'Where am I going?' (What are the goals?), 'How am I going?' (What progress is being made toward the goal?) and 'Where to next?' (What activities need to be undertaken to make better progress?) (p. 86). Learning goals help students to answer the first, success criteria the second and then feedback, which is explored in more detail below, the third.

ACTIVITY FOR STAFF: DEVELOPING GOOD SUCCESS CRITERIA

Instructions
- Just as we earlier suggested asking staff to consider the question, 'How do we know a good learning goal when we see one?', we could ask what constitutes good success criteria reflecting the goal. More specifically, ask staff to work in groups to identify the characteristics of good success criteria to support their lesson planning in teams.
- The outcome of their discussions can be shared and compared to the criteria identified below as part of developing a whole-school guide on writing quality success criteria in professional learning teams (PLTs). Such agreed criteria can in turn be used by PLTs to examine, and if necessary revise, success criteria already being used in classrooms in the school.

QUALITY SUCCESS CRITERIA

Quality success criteria[9]:
- are linked to, and reflect the learning goal
- focus on learning and not on aspects of student behaviour, such as paying attention or meeting deadlines
- clearly show students how to successfully demonstrate learning at the end of an instructional period
- are written in clear language that students understand
- provide a scaffold and focus for learners while engaging in the learning activity
- are limited in number so students are not overwhelmed by the scope of the task
- allow for differentiation in process and product based on student needs
- are used as the basis for teacher feedback as well as peer feedback and self-assessment when appropriate.

Quality success criteria, as foreshadowed earlier, are also strengthened by the provision of work samples and exemplars to illustrate what, in practice, they mean, as evident in the sample for Year 3, Term 1 from Auburn North Public School in Box 7.2.

---

[9] The following list is informed by the elements of effective success criteria identified by the Victorian Department of Education and Training for teachers in government schools, which has subsequently been absorbed and modified in the Department's High Impact Teaching Strategies (HITS) which can be accessed at https://www.education.vic.gov.au/school/teachers/teachingresources/practice/improve/Pages/hits.aspx (Department of Education and Training, 2017).

Box 7.2
AUBURN NORTH WORK SAMPLE

Learning goal: We are learning to write a well-structured exposition

Plan	I can plan my writing using a mind map
Write	I can write a statement of position with a sneak peak
	I can use connectives (e.g. firstly, furthermore, additionally, finally)
	I can write a paragraph with a topic sentence and extra information
	I can write three reason paragraphs
	I can write an example to match my reason
	I can write a rhetorical question to match my reason
	I can write a conclusion
Explicit grammar	Week 2 — capitals, proper nouns
	Week 3 — connectives
	Week 4 — simple model verbs (e.g. must, need to, have to)
	Week 5 — verbs
	Week 6 — adverbs (e.g. definitely, absolutely, certainly)
	Week 7 — commas in a list
	Week 8 — subject-verb agreement
	Week 9 — possessive apostrophe
	Week 10 — quotation marks
Review	I can add words, change words or remove words so my writing makes sense
Edit	I can spell special adverbs correctly
	I can spell connectives correctly
	I can use a comma to separate my reasons
	I can use a comma after a connective
Publish	I can write neatly and quickly

CHAPTER 7 Stage 3: Improving classroom practice

Annotated work sample

Plastic bags must be banned — *Statement of position*

I strongly believe that plastic bags must be banned right now. This is because it is dangerous to animals, it pollutes the environment and you can use something else instead of plastic. — *Sneak peak*

Reason paragraph one

Firstly, plastic bags have to be banned because it is dangerous for the animals. Animals can get caught in plastic bags or they can eat it and die. For example, they might not get enough room to breath in the plastic bag. Can you believe that people are puting bags everywhere and killing the animals? — *Topic sentence* / *Connectives and comma*

Reason paragraph two

In addition, plastic bags need to be banned because it's polluting the planet. It's making, can make lots of poisonous gas, that is bad to breath in and the plastic also can take over the garbage tip's room. For example, if there was a huge pile of plastic bags, then it would just fly through cities and towns. How would you feel if you could see plastic bags through your window? — *Example to match reason* / *Rhetorical question*

Reason paragraph three

Finally, plastic bags certainly need to be banned because you can just use something else. You can probably use paper bags or boxes, for example, you can use those reuseable bags. How would you feel if your plastic bag broke when there were things in it? — *Simple modal verbs*

Conclusion

In conclusion, every person in the world must stop using plastic bags. This can effect our world like how it's dangerous for animals, it can pollute our lovely envirment and you can use something instead of plastic bags. I urge everyone in this planet to use reuseable bags or boxes or else this whole world will be polluted. — *Comma to separate reasons*

It is also common for schools we have worked with including, as can be seen in Box 7.2 Auburn North, to write their success criteria as a series of 'I can' statements, to indicate to students that this is what they will know, understand or be able to do once the learning goal is achieved.

EXAMPLES OF QUALITY SUCCESS CRITERIA

Some of the flavour of what quality success criteria look like can be gained from the following examples drawn from a primary and secondary school.

Learning goal:
We are learning to write compound sentences.

Success criteria:
I can write a compound sentence using:
- two related facts
- two independent clauses
- an appropriate conjunction (e.g. and, so, but).

Learning goal:
By the end of the lesson we will be able to explain how different materials conduct electricity.

Success criteria:
- I can define 'conductors' and 'insulators'.
- I can identify the characteristics of materials that are conductors and insulators.
- I can explain how materials allow static charge to build up or be discharged.

Glen Waverley Secondary College (SC) has developed the helpful reflection and planning tool in Figure 7.6 to support teachers in using learning goals and success criteria to plan and deliver better lessons in class.

Learning goals: describe what the teacher wants the students to learn.
Reflect: Think about a lesson you have taught recently • Were you clear about what you wanted your students to learn? • Did you tell the students what they were going to learn? If so, how? (verbally, visually) • Did you tell them why you wanted them to learn these things? • What activities did you plan in order to find out whether or not the students learnt what you wanted them to? • Do you know whether or not they did in fact learn these things? Why/Why not?
Plan: Think about a lesson you will teach in the near future • What do you want your students to learn? • What skills, knowledge and understanding do you want your students to gain?
Write this as a learning goal: Students will be able to …
Learning goals need *success criteria* to work effectively. • Success criteria are used by students and teachers to decide whether a student has been **successful in achieving the learning goal**. • They spell out the **skills, knowledge and understanding** that students are expected to demonstrate in a particular activity or task in order to meet the learning goal.
Plan: How will you and your students know when they have achieved the learning goal?
Write success criteria for the learning goal above: By the end of the lesson I will be able to …
Meaningful task or busy work? Think about the learning goal you have planned for your upcoming lesson. • What learning activities will you be planning for the lesson to assist students in reaching the learning goal? • Do they specifically focus on a skill/s that will help your students meet the learning intention? If so, what are they? • Is there scope in them for students to demonstrate different levels of understanding? That is, can weaker students still complete the activity and show some understanding/can strong students be challenged and show the depth of their understanding?

FIGURE 7.6: GLEN WAVERLEY SECONDARY COLLEGE REFLECTION AND PLANNING TOOL

Note: The emphasis throughout Figure 7.6 is that adopted by the school.

As mentioned in Chapter 4, a Years 5 to 6 project team at Dandenong North Primary School in Victoria took the use of success criteria a stage further still and converted the expected standards for different levels in the AusVELS for Mathematics into a series of 'I can' success criteria statements to inform their teaching in these years.[10] While the original intention was simply to build their own understanding of Maths, they found they had created both a means of developing quality learning goals aligned to the standards and a self-assessment tool for students to use.

A sample of the Dandenong North team's work can be seen in the Level 4 Maths statements in Figure 7.7.[11]

Level 4		
Number and place value	**Fractions and decimals**	**Money and financial matters**
• I can check the accuracy of calculations using my knowledge of odd and even numbers when using the four processes. (odd + odd = even)	■ I can use a fraction wall to explain equivalent fractions (halves, quarters and eighths/thirds and sixths)	★ I can solve problems involving purchases and the calculation of change to the nearest five cents
† I can recognise, represent and order numbers to at least tens of thousands	■ I can convert mixed numbers to improper fractions	
† I can recognise that the place value system uses a base 10 approach (multiply by 10 = move decimal place to the right and divide by 10 = move decimal place one spot to the left)	■ I can convert improper fractions to mixed numbers	**Patterns and algebra**
	■ I can count by quarters, halves and thirds	◆ I can identify examples of number patterns in everyday life
	■ I can count by quarters, halves and thirds using mixed numerals	◆ I can describe multiplication number patterns
• I can investigate number sequences involving multiples of 3, 4, 6, 7, 8, and 9	■ I can locate and represent fractions on a number line	◆ I can represent a word problem as a number sentence using the four processes
• I can recall multiplication facts up to 10 × 10 and related division facts (3 × 7 = 21 or 21÷3 = 7)	× I can divide by 10 to understand that the place value system goes from tenths, hundredths, thousandths etc.	◆ I can write a worded problem using a given number sentence which uses the four processes
• I can use known facts and strategies, such as commutativity (7+3 = 10 or 3+7=10), doubling and halving for multiplication, and connecting division to multiplication when there is no remainder	× I can recognise the equivalence between fractions and decimals. E.g. 0.5 = ½	◆ I can use equivalent number sentences involving addition and subtraction to find missing numbers

Key: • Number facts   † Place value   ■ Fractions   × Decimals   ★ Ratio   ◆ Other

FIGURE 7.7: DANDENONG NORTH PRIMARY SCHOOL MATHS STATEMENTS, LEVEL 4

---

[10] AusVELS is the Victorian Curriculum framework. In the learning area of Mathematics, it incorporates the Australian Curriculum.
[11] Level 4 in Victoria covers Years 5 and 6. The team also produced statements for Levels 5 (Years 7 and 8) and 6 (Years 9 and 10).

In a somewhat similar vein, Narre Warren South P–12 has supported its staff to develop rubrics to convey success criteria for a lesson or unit of work using the input and professional learning approach outlined in Box 7.3.

Box 7.3
DEVELOPING SUCCESS CRITERIA RUBRICS AT NARRE WARREN SOUTH

Rubrics can help clearly convey success criteria for a unit of work or lesson. The size and complexity of the rubric will of course vary accordingly.

Step 1
The first step in designing a rubric is to identify the skills, knowledge, understanding, etc. that the teacher wishes the students to demonstrate. These are then specified in terms of the success criteria. For example:
- An ability to …
- Knowledge of …
- Understanding of how/why/the ways in which …

Step 2
The next step is to decide how many levels are to be described and then to write the performance descriptors for each of those criteria. (Note: Not every criterion needs to have the same number of category descriptors.) A good place to start is with the middle or medium level (which should represent a satisfactory level of performance or the 'at level' performance), and proceed from there to write the higher and lower level descriptors. The performance descriptors describe the relative differences between performances at each level.

There are several ways that difference can be presented. For example:
- By referring to specific cognitive aspects of the performance, which will be different at different levels—e.g. lists the effects of … ; interprets the effects of … ; analyses the effects of … ; evaluates the effects of …
- By using adjectives, adjectival phrases, adverbs and adverbial phrases. These extra words are used where the aspects of a performance stay the same across the levels, but there is a qualitative difference to the performance—e.g. explains with limited accuracy/explains with some accuracy/explains with great accuracy; provides a limited explanation/provides a detailed explanation/provides a complex explanation; shows a basic knowledge/shows a sound knowledge/shows a comprehensive knowledge. These descriptions need to be supported by work samples or exemplars in order to make the differences clear to students.
- By using numeric references. Numbers identify quantitative differences between levels—e.g. provides an example/provides two examples/provides three examples; uses few or no strategies/uses some strategies/uses several strategies. However, a word of warning—numeric references on their own can be misleading and they are best teamed with a qualitative reference (e.g. three appropriate and relevant examples) to avoid ignoring quality at the expense of quantity. This kind of description also needs to be supported by work samples or exemplars in order to demonstrate exactly what is meant by 'several', etc.
- By referring to the degree of assistance needed by the student to complete the task. This kind of performance descriptor is explicit about the degree of independence shown by the student while undertaking the task—e.g. with teacher guidance attempts to use/with occasional peer or teacher assistance uses/correctly and independently uses.

Continued…

- By referring to the degree of assistance needed by the student to complete the task. This kind of performance descriptor is explicit about the degree of independence shown by the student while undertaking the task—e.g. with teacher guidance attempts to use/with occasional peer or teacher assistance uses/correctly and independently uses.

The rubric activity

1. In pairs, choose one of your sample learning intentions and success criteria and turn your success criteria into criteria of a marking rubric.
2. Write a performance descriptor that would represent a satisfactory level of performance for the first criterion in your rubric.
3. Now write one or more performance descriptors at a 'below satisfactory' level and one or more at an 'above satisfactory' level.
4. Repeat steps 2 and 3 above for each of your criteria.

A sample rubric: Analysis of a work of art

Criteria	Performance Descriptors				
	0	1	2	3	4
Description	No description.	Attempts to describe the work but the description lacks any detail.	Makes a detailed description of some of the subject matter and/or elements seen in a work.	Makes a detailed description of all of the subject matter and/or elements seen in a work.	
Interpretation	No interpretation.	Relates how the work makes him/her feel personally.	Identifies the literal meaning of the work.	Forms a reasonable hypothesis about the metaphorical or symbolic meaning but is unable to support this with evidence from the work.	Forms a reasonable hypothesis about the metaphorical or symbolic meaning and is able to support this with evidence from the work.
Analysis	No analysis	Attempts some analysis but misses the dominant elements.	Describes some dominant elements and principles used by the artist, but has difficulty describing how these relate to the meaning or feeling of the artwork.	Describes some dominant elements and principles used by the artist and accurately relates how these are used by the artist to reinforce the meaning, mood, or feeling of the artwork.	Describes many dominant elements and principles used by the artist and accurately relates how these are used by the artist to reinforce the meaning, mood, or feeling of the artwork.
Evaluation	No evaluation.	Evaluates work as good or bad based on personal taste.	Tries to use aesthetic criteria to judge artwork, but does not apply the criteria accurately.	Uses 1–2 criteria to judge the artwork, such as composition, expression, creativity, design, communication of ideas.	Uses multiple criteria to judge the artwork, such as composition, expression, creativity, design, communication of ideas.

Given our experience that collaboratively developing quality learning goals and associated success criteria provides a particularly effective means of supporting more teachers to work like the best, it is appropriate that any work to cement these in the school be accompanied by an assessment of how well this is being achieved. Such assessment can also underpin teachers' efforts, both individually and in their professional learning teams to further improve in this regard.

ACTIVITY FOR STAFF: ASSESSING OUR USE OF LEARNING GOALS AND SUCCESS CRITERIA

Instructions

1 Rate each of the statements in Table 7.6 below on a four-point-scale where:
   1 = Strongly disagree, 2 = Disagree, 3 = Agree and 4 = Strongly agree.
2 Based on your ratings, complete the following two sentences:
   - The one thing I can do to improve my use of learning goals is to …
   - The one thing I can do to improve my use of success criteria is to …
3 The completed sentences can be shared in professional learning teams to identify any common areas for improvement that need to collaboratively be addressed.

TABLE 7.6: ASSESSING OUR USE OF LEARNING GOALS AND SUCCESS CRITERIA

Learning goals—I feel confident in my ability to:	Rating (1–4)
Develop learning goals based on the overall curriculum expectations for the year level	
Write specific learning goals in clear language the students understand	
Develop learning goals that identify a progression of incremental, scaffolded knowledge and skills	
Share the learning goal at the start of the lesson and refer to it at appropriate times as the lesson unfolds	
Clarify learning goals with students to ensure they understand what is to be learned	
Support students to monitor their progress in relation to the learning goal	
Provide students the opportunity to reflect on their progress towards the learning goal at the end of the instructional period	
Success criteria—I feel confident in my ability to:	
Identify the criteria for successfully achieving the learning goal	
Develop appropriate assessment tasks aligned to the success criteria	
Share and clarify success criteria with students at the beginning of the lesson and at appropriate times as the lesson unfolds	
Describe the success criteria in clear, understandable language and observable behaviours	
Use samples and exemplars to help further clarify success criteria	
Demonstrate how the success criteria apply to concrete examples of strong and weak work	
Use success criteria as the basis for teacher feedback and, where appropriate, peer- and self-assessment	

© Pamela Macklin and Vic Zbar, *Driving School Improvement*, Australian Council for Educational Research, 2017

FEEDBACK TO STUDENTS

Feedback to students is the third element of the holy trinity of student learning to which Hattie and Timperley (2007) referred—that is: 'Where am I going?' (learning goals), 'How am I going?' (success criteria) and 'Where to next?' (feedback).

While we tend to think of feedback to students in somewhat formal terms, it is really any response from a teacher to a student's performance or behaviour at all. It can be verbal, written, or even gestural, such as giving a thumbs up for the effort made, which will give a strong message to the student involved.

The purpose of feedback to students should always be to reduce the discrepancies between current understanding or performance, and the desired learning goal. It is designed to improve student performance and not put a damper on it. Effective feedback, as foreshadowed earlier, helps identify 'Where to next?' and encourages an attitude of 'I can do this'.

Although the effect size for feedback is relatively high[12] (see Hattie, 2015), the not so good news is that the variability of effectiveness is marked, so we need to specify the forms it should take. In addition, any good strategy can lose its effect from overuse. On occasions, when we have talked with teachers about the value and effect size of feedback, they have gone overboard with it in class to the point where the feedback they give is trivial and students get drowned in feedback and request that it stop.

Teachers generally know more about good feedback than they think, and the following activity can help surface what they know.

ACTIVITY FOR STAFF: IDENTIFYING THE CHARACTERISTICS OF EFFECTIVE FEEDBACK

Most teachers have, at one time or another, sought to learn something new as an adult. Commonly we find when we discuss this with staff teams, it is either a sport (golf and tennis being the most popular), a craft, a language or, in the age of *MasterChef* and *My kitchen rules*, cooking of some sort.

Instructions

1 Ask individuals to think of their own experience learning something new and identify what was the most useful feedback they received.
2 Then share the outcomes in small groups and try to codify it into some characteristics of effective feedback, which can be compared with the following list.

WHAT IS EFFECTIVE FEEDBACK?

Effective feedback to students is:
- *Timely*. This means that you:
  - ensure there is minimal delay. As Marzano, Pickering and Pollock (2001) note, '(t)he more delay that occurs in giving feedback, the less improvement there is in achievement' (p. 97).
  - give feedback as often as possible for all major pieces of work.

- *Constructive/corrective*. This means that you:
  - ask yourself, what are students doing that is correct/not correct?
  - choose areas of feedback that relate to major learning goals and essential elements of the assessment.
  - ensure it is encouraging and helps students to realise that effort leads to learning.

---

[12] 0.73, which is almost double the typical teacher effect of 0.4.

- *Specific to a criterion.* This means that you:
  - ensure it contains precise language on what to do to improve.
  - make sure it references to progress towards the learning goal.
  - ensure it is based on observations.

- *Focused on the product/behaviour, not the student.* This means that you:
  - communicate with the individual student on their performance.
  - give whole-class feedback when a common issue needs to be addressed.

- *Appropriate in amount.* This means that you:
  - provide sufficient feedback to know what to do next, but not so much that they either get overwhelmed with it, or effectively have the work done for them.

- *Delivered in a form appropriate to the circumstances and that ensures it is 'heard'.* This means that you:
  - ensure written feedback is supplied where students need to reflect on the comments and refer to them in future.
  - provide on-the-spot oral feedback to correct errors during the class.
  - demonstrate what meeting the expectation looks like.

- *Verified.* This means that you:
  - ask yourself, did the student understand the feedback?
  - ask yourself, what is my plan to monitor and support the student in this area?

Put simply, effective feedback, to use Moss and Brookhart's (2012) words, is:

> non-judgmental, positive and descriptive. It arrives *while* students are learning so that they can use it to improve their work ... Feedback that feeds forward shares five characteristics:
> 1 It focuses on success criteria from the learning target for today's lesson.
> 2 It describes exactly where the student is in relationship to the criteria.
> 3 It provides a next-step strategy that the student should use to improve or learn more.
> 4 It arrives when the student has the opportunity to use it.
> 5 It is delivered in just the right amount—not so much that it overwhelms, but not so little that it stops short of a useful explanation or suggestion.
> (p. 64)

ACTIVITY FOR STAFF: IDENTIFYING EXAMPLES OF GOOD FEEDBACK TO STUDENTS

This activity is designed to help teachers to become more conscious of the nature of the feedback they give to students in class, so they can ensure it positively supports students to progress towards the learning goal. The activity is best completed in professional learning teams.

Instructions
1 Ask teams to consider the criteria for effective feedback, outlined earlier and summarised in Table 7.7, along with a sample for each criterion to get them started in the task.
2 They then work together to identify at least two additional samples for each criterion, with a view to developing a whole-school list to inform the provision of feedback to students to help them improve at school.

TABLE 7.7: IDENTIFYING EXAMPLES OF GOOD FEEDBACK TO STUDENTS

Effective feedback to students is:

Criterion	Examples of feedback that meet this criterion
Timely	Returning a test and going over it with students the day after it was administered
Constructive/corrective	Immediately correcting a misconception a student expresses in class
Specific to a criterion	Comparing the students' work to an annotated work sample that meets the success criteria
Focused on product/behaviour and not the student	Commenting on the strategies the student adopted to complete the project and the amount of effort they put into it
Appropriate in amount	Giving feedback on two or three key aspects of the student's work as opposed to correcting every error they made
Delivered in appropriate form	Demonstrating a process to one or more students who failed to fully grasp it
Verified	Asking the student to reflect back to you the key feedback points made

THE FOCUS OF FEEDBACK

Whether the feedback to students is effective or not then depends, as Brookhart (2008) explained, on whether it:
- enables the students to learn, as evidenced by the fact their work improves
- makes them more motivated and encourages not only their belief they can learn, but also their desire to learn and take more control over their learning
- contributes to classrooms where feedback is valued and seen as a productive contributor to the work of the class (paraphrased from Chapter 2).

Looking more closely at the content of feedback that teachers provide, Hattie and Timperley (2007) suggest four forms, or 'levels' it can take. More specifically, feedback about:
- the task the student is undertaking, such as feedback about whether answers were right or wrong, or directions to get more information to complete the task
- the processing of the task, such as feedback on the strategies used or strategies that could be used
- self-regulation (i.e. how students monitor and control their own learning), such as feedback about student self-evaluation or self-confidence
- the student as a person, such as pronouncements that the student is 'good' or 'smart'.

Their research strongly suggests that feedback about the qualities of the work and the process or strategies used are the most helpful for students.

Feedback that draws attention to the student's self-regulation strategies or their abilities as learners can be effective if the student hears it in a way that makes them realise they will get the results they want if they expend effort and attention on it. We need to be wary in this context of conveying messages that undermine effort or, subconsciously tell the student they are no good in a particular field. For example, telling a student how 'clever' they are in response to a good outcome on a maths test, may lead them to conclude they are no good at English if they then get a poor result for an essay they wrote. Far better in this context is to comment on the strategies the student used and the amount of effort they must have put into preparing for the test.

Personal comments, such as 'good girl' or 'clever boy' do not draw students' attention to their learning at all.

What is more, feedback, as Hattie and Clarke (2019) have explained, must 'be aligned to where the student is in the learning cycle …' (p. 76). In summary these are:

1. when the student is working at the 'idea' or **surface knowledge phase**, then feedback directed to correct or incorrectness of the task is very valuable
2. when the student is working at **relating or linking ideas** or,
3. **extending the ideas**, then feedback directed to the process strategies and self-regulation (making own improvements), and not so much to the task, is very valuable' (p. 76, emphasis in the original).

So, in giving feedback to students, teachers should aim to describe both the work and the process and the relationship between the two, taking account of where the student is at. They should comment on the student's self-regulation if the comment will foster self-efficacy, and avoid personal comments since they do not help in moving the student towards the learning goal.

ACTIVITY FOR STAFF: DETERMINING THE TYPE OF FEEDBACK TO PROVIDE

Instructions

Read the following vignettes of students responding to the same question from the Australian Science Curriculum for Year 3.[13] Which level of feedback would you provide each of the students: task, process, or regulation feedback?

Teacher: How do shadows change across the day?

Student 1
When the sun rises the shadow gets smaller. Next when it comes down it gets bigger and it goes over and over again. And the Earth rotates around the sun.
Type of feedback provided _____

Student 2
The Earth rotates around the Sun and as it rotates one side of the Earth is getting further and further away. So the Earth rotates while the Sun stays still. This makes the shadows move.
Type of feedback provided _____

Student 3
the Earth rowtates around the sun = Days
Type of feedback provided _____

---

[13] Samples to inform the development of examples in other subjects and/or year levels can be found at https://www.australiancurriculum.edu.au/resources/work-samples/

There may also be value in this context in considering the use of simple feedback techniques from the students themselves to help teachers monitor the extent to which they have grasped the essential content being taught, and thereby inform the nature of the teaching they will then pursue. A range of strategies can help teachers to quickly assess the extent to which students understand what they are being taught and which, if any, students might need additional teaching or other support.

For example, many teachers use what is known as the 'fist-to-five' technique that asks students to indicate using one hand the extent to which they understand what has been taught. A closed fist indicates they do not understand at all, while a display of all five fingers means it's completely understood. A single finger can mean 'I need help', two fingers that 'I could use more practice', three that 'I understand pretty well' and four that 'I mostly understand'. In a similar vein, teachers sometimes use a simple thumbs up for 'I get it', thumbs down for 'I don't' and a sideways thumb to indicate 'I somewhat understand' or 'I'm not sure'. Regardless of the technique employed, it not only supports the monitoring of student learning as the teaching unfolds, but also conveys that feedback is a two-way street.

ACTIVITY FOR STAFF: EVALUATING THE EFFECTIVENESS OF MY FEEDBACK TO STUDENTS

This activity is designed to support teachers to individually assess the quality of feedback they provide to their students and then collectively address how feedback across the school can be improved.

Instructions

1 In the first part of Table 7.8, rate each of the following statements about how you provide feedback to your students on a four-point scale where:

1 = I don't do this, 2 = I sometimes do this, 3 = I often do this and 4 = This is a routine part of my teaching.

2 Then, taking account of your responses to the first part of the pro forma, fill in the second part of the table.

3 When you have completed the pro forma, share it with the colleagues in your professional learning team and see what, if any, common strengths and weaknesses exist that can be worked on together.

TABLE 7.8: EVALUATING THE EFFECTIVENESS OF MY FEEDBACK TO STUDENTS

My feedback to students is:	Rating (1–4)
Educative in nature—i.e. it gives students an explanation of what they are doing correctly and incorrectly	
Designed to 'feed forward' and indicate what the student needs to think about to bring their task performance closer to the goals	
Given in a timely manner	
Sensitive to the individual needs of the student	
Referenced to a skill or specific knowledge rather than seeking to correct everything	
Designed to keep students on target for achievement	
Expressed in a way that encourages positive motivational beliefs and self-esteem	
Given verbally, non-verbally or in written form as appropriate	
Supportive of students giving feedback to each other	
Used to inform and shape my teaching	

The major strength in giving feedback on which I can build:	The evidence for this strength: ● ● ●
A key aspect of giving feedback to students that I really need to develop:	The evidence for identifying this area: ● ● ●

© Pamela Macklin and Vic Zbar, *Driving School Improvement*, Australian Council for Educational Research, 2017

A NOTE ON DIFFERENTIATING YOUR DELIVERY

Differentiation is the subject of many good books as evident in the substantial contributions of people such as Carol-Ann Tomlinson in the United States (see, for example, Tomlinson, 2014), and hence is not a major focus in this book. That said, it does need to be briefly discussed here since it has implications for the learning goals and success criteria that teachers plan, and hence the subsequent feedback they give.

Differentiation is a general term used to describe the range of strategies used to ensure students' needs are met. More specifically, it's a process used to maximise student learning by improving the match between a student's individual needs and the curriculum. It refers to the need to tailor teaching environments and practices to create appropriately different learning experiences for different students. As Tomlinson has observed, 'whenever a teacher reaches out to an individual or small group to vary their teaching in order to create the best learning experience possible, that teacher is differentiating instruction' (Tomlinson, 2000, p. 1).

It is important to state at this juncture that teachers ought not to differentiate the learning goal for students, but rather the success criteria they devise. Differentiated goals run the risk of dumbing down our expectations for some students and locking them into lesser learning work. By contrast, differentiating success criteria can allow for different ways in which the learning goal might be demonstrated and achieved. For example, in learning to apply a particular mathematical formula, higher performing students could be challenged to complete a number of difficult problems without support, while the weaker students in the class could work on problems supported by a scaffolded guide to how the formula is applied. Alternatively, students in English could be asked to write essays on differing topics and/or of different lengths.

Table 7.9 reinforces the point and takes it further by specifying what differentiation is, and is not.

TABLE 7.9: WHAT DIFFERENTIATION IS, AND IS NOT

Differentiated instruction means	Differentiated instruction does not mean
Teachers provide several learning options, or different paths to learning which help students take in information and make sense of concepts and skills	Teachers develop a separate lesson plan for each student in a classroom
Teachers provide appropriate levels of challenge for all students	Teachers 'water down' the curriculum for some students
Flexible, short-term groupings that allow students to work with a variety of peers with the same or different strengths and interests	Labelling students or locking them into ability groupings
Engaging and interesting tasks (that address the same skills) for all student levels of readiness and interest	Confining some students to low level, rote tasks while others engage in higher order thinking
A reasonable number of well-constructed choices that address identified learning needs	Unlimited freedom for a student to choose whatever they want to do on any day
Routines, procedures and classroom agreements are in place	A chaotic or unstructured classroom environment

Source: The table is adapted from one included in Edugains (2016, p. 8).

Fundamental to effective differentiation, and often neglected in our quest to determine the best strategies for differentiation to pursue, is the need for teachers to know their students really well. As Tomlinson (2008) simply observes, '(t)he teacher needs to know what each student knows and can do at a given moment. How else could we plan instruction to increase the likelihood that students stay on course toward the destination' (pp. 1–2).

Achieving this, she goes on to advise, requires teachers to:
- build trust so that 'students believe the teacher is on their side'
- ensure fit by setting student work that is appropriately challenging (i.e. neither too easy nor too hard for the level the student is at) and connected to the things that matter to them
- strengthen the opportunities for student voice to be both expressed and heard
- support the development of student awareness so they can develop their own metacognitive skills (pp. 2–5).

When teachers do know their students well, the four elements of classroom practice that they can differentiate are:
- Content—what topic the students learn about and where they enter the learning.
- Process—the way in which the students learn and the activities they undertake to gain an understanding of the content.
- Product—how they demonstrate their learning.
- Learning environment—the way in which the classroom works and feels.

ACTIVITY FOR STAFF: OPTIONS FOR DIFFERENTIATION IN CLASS

This activity is designed to encourage staff to think about ways in which they can differentiate their teaching to cater for all students in the class.

Instructions
1 Work in small teams to identify successful strategies you have used to differentiate content, process, product and the learning environment to meet a broader range of student learning needs.
2 Share the ideas as a whole-staff team and compare them to the following examples in order to compile a guide for differentiating in your school.

EXAMPLES OF DIFFERENTIATION IN PRACTICE[14]

Differentiating content
- Use pre-tests to assess where individual students need to begin study of a given topic or unit.
- Use reading material of varying difficulty.
- Break assignments into smaller, more manageable parts that include structured direction for each part.
- Use spelling or vocabulary lists at a range of ability levels for students.
- Provide opportunities for students to explore aspects of the class topic that particularly interest them.
- Work with small groups to re-teach an idea or skill for struggling learners, or to extend the thinking or skills of advanced learners.

Differentiating process
- Structure activities so all students work through the same important content and skills, but with differing levels of support, challenge and/or complexity.
- Offer manipulatives (e.g. graphic organisers, puzzles, etc.) or other hands-on supports for students who need them.

---

[14] The following list of ideas has been informed by the New South Wales Department of Education and Communities (2015) advice for teachers on differentiating content, process, product, learning environment.

- Provide access to a variety of materials that target differing levels of readiness and/or reading ability.
- Use reading buddies.
- Use flexible grouping at appropriate times during the class.
- Present ideas through a range of media—text, audio and visual means.

Differentiating product
- Give students more than one option for how they can demonstrate the required learning (e.g. creating a role play, developing a mural with labels, writing a letter or making an oral presentation).
- Use rubrics that match and extend students' varied skill levels.
- Allow students to work in small groups as well as on their own to complete their products.
- Encourage students to create their own product assignments, provided they contain required elements so the learning goal is met.

Differentiating the learning environment
- Make sure there are places in the room for uninterrupted, quiet work as well as places where students can work collaboratively.
- Ensure the location for student learning reflects the nature of the task, such as laboratory learning for science or working outside at appropriate times.
- Develop routines that enable students to get help from others when teachers are busy and cannot immediately respond to their concern.
- Help students to recognise when it is OK to move around the room to learn and when it is necessary to sit quietly and work.

The Queechy Alliance of Schools has taken these sorts of examples a stage further still by developing such illustrations in practice for staff as:

1 In the Prep–1 class, students have been exploring changes that occur in the seasons. There are a number of prep students who are still unable to write independently, so the teacher gets them to record themselves talking about the changes on the iPads. The other students are asked to record on a prepared template. One child has broken their arm and is unable to write so a teacher assistant (TA) is acting as a scribe.
2 The teacher has explicitly taught students about the daily rituals of Samurai Warriors. Students are given a choice of four independent tasks to do based on Samurai Warriors.
3 The teacher has just completed an interactive read aloud where he modelled making text to self connections and how this supports him to read and understand the text. In the targeted teaching phase, he has a reading response pro forma and each student is required to independently read a 'just right' text and to independently record their text to self connections. At the end of this activity, the teacher is intending to ask each student to share a text to self connection.
4 A primary class is learning about the structural and language features of a narrative. A small group of students is unpacking an A standard exemplar assessing against a co-constructed rubric, another group is working with the teacher to do the same and two students are practising writing sentences supported by a TA.
5 A Grade 5/6 classroom is working on a HASS (Humanities and Social Sciences) unit and to differentiate the teacher expects a written response from all students. The requirements for length and presentation are as follows: A–B students, 2–3 pages, size 12 font; C students, 1–2 pages, size 12 font; and D students, ½–1 page, size 12 font or hand written. Referencing is required for all students.
6 A primary class is working on an inquiry of student choice within a specific topic. The students are encouraged to present their final work in a way that they feel demonstrates their understanding of their investigation. Students are able to work individually or with a partner.
7 The Grade 6 teacher groups their students carefully according to their reading ability and creates information texts on earthquakes of varying difficulty.

EFFECTIVE CLASSROOM ROUTINES

Differentiation in the classroom can be supported by using consistent routines that, for the most part, vary little during the year. Establishing classroom routines right from the start of the school year is an investment that provides teachers with more time to teach, and students with a greater opportunity to learn.

Classrooms typically require many routines to operate efficiently and effectively. Common routines apply to how students enter and leave the room, how the roll is marked, transitions between different instructional activities, forming groups for different purposes, and movement around the room.

Research suggests that effective teachers use routines for daily tasks more than their ineffective counterparts (see, for example, Stronge, Ward, Tucker & Hindman, 2007). They invest time at the start of the school year to teach the routines. By establishing and practising routines that require little monitoring they ensure that the focus of the classroom is more clearly on instruction and ensuring that all students' learning needs can be met.

ACTIVITY FOR STAFF: ESTABLISHING EFFECTIVE CLASSROOM ROUTINES

This activity is designed to support teachers to identify and establish effective routines to apply in their classrooms. It is best undertaken collaboratively in teams, such as year level teams.

Instructions

1 Identify the range of predictable, regularly recurring events that occur in each and every class—for example, administrative procedures such as marking the roll, behavioural procedures such as entering and leaving the room, instructional tasks such as paying attention to the teacher, and interactive practices such as taking turns in a classroom discussion.
2 Having identified these events, determine the precise procedures for handling them that students can readily understand and the way in which they will be taught at the start of the school year.

When it comes to actually teaching a routine, it is important to ensure that students understand why it is being introduced, and see it modelled in practice so they are clear about how it works. It may then be necessary to revisit and reinforce the practice through the year.

CHAPTER 8
CLASSROOM OBSERVATION TO SUPPORT THE SHIFT

Sometimes in workshops, Vic will ask participants whether, when asked to judge some aspect of their performance, they judge themselves too harshly or too leniently compared to the view others might have. Invariably they come down on the side of too harsh. He will then ask them to raise their hands if they consider themselves an above average driver, only to be met by a sea of hands. Despite the fact, that statistically half of all drivers must be below average, studies find that most respondents do not think this the case. Svenson (1981), for example, found that 88% of a United States sample and 77% of a Swedish sample of respondents rated themselves as being 'safer than the median driver' or, in effect, above average.

This sort of cognitive bias reflects what Dunning (2006) refers to as 'the frequently tenuous association between the perception and reality of self' (p. 600). Despite what many of us think, it is often the case that others have a better sense of our competence, performance and prospects than we have ourselves. What is more, our self-perception, according to Dunning, tends towards overconfidence, as reflected in the driving example cited above.

'On average', he explains, 'people think of themselves as anything but average. The average person claims to be more disciplined, idealistic, socially skilled, a better driver, good at leadership, and healthier than the average person. Mathematically, this cannot be right—the average person cannot be above average. But many surveys … have shown that people believe they excel among their contemporaries. Ironically, people also claim to be better than most other people at producing unbiased and realistic self-estimates' (Dunning, 2006, p. 601).

This arguably reflects the fact identified by Hattie and Yates (2014) that people generally 'have great difficulty in benchmarking the notion of "average",' though regardless of what it is, 'we all know that we are a great deal better' (p. 229).

Recognising and addressing this in large part comes through working with others who, as Dunning demonstrates, may have a more accurate perception of the quality of performance of our work.

This is where classroom observation comes in. It is not possible for others to reflect on an individual teacher's performance, let alone how to support them to improve it, without viewing that performance.

In addition, to the extent that it provides evidence of the implementation of strategies the school has decided to adopt, classroom observation can help to drive change and improvement through the school, regardless of the stage of improvement the school is in.

Put simply, classroom observation is central to helping each other improve in a school, since it informs feedback and broader collaborative work. When teachers open the classroom door, they invite feedback on their teaching that can enable them to improve. They also gain the opportunity to see others teach, provide them with feedback as well, and learn from their approach. Thus, it also provides a means by which good teaching practice can be spread through the entire school.

THE PURPOSES OF CLASSROOM OBSERVATION

There is a tendency to assume that classroom observation is solely about a focus on teaching and learning in class, and hence does not apply to the first stage of school improvement where the focus is getting the preconditions in place. However, there is evidence to suggest that classroom observation can help to identify support that teachers need to ensure that an orderly learning environment exists, which is commonly the starting point for whole-school improvement as outlined in Chapter 5.

For example, during 2013 to 2014 the then principal and leadership team at William Ruthven Secondary College (WRSC) in Melbourne's north were seeking to ensure that 'every teacher … has highly effective behaviour management skills'. A whole-school Developmental Behaviour Management (DBM) coaching model was introduced to support teachers in achieving this goal, which included classroom observation as part of the process of gaining evidence and feedback on the behaviours that were required. The rubric in Table 8.1 was used to gain 'three points of view' about teachers' DBM skills—that is, the teacher's own evaluation, the evaluation of a peer and the evaluation of their DBM coach—including through observation of their work in class.

TABLE 8.1: THE WRSC DEVELOPMENTAL BEHAVIOUR MANAGEMENT MODEL STUDENT MANAGEMENT RUBRIC, 2014

Baseline DBM Behaviour	VERY HIGH This behaviour is exhibited 95% of the time	HIGH This behaviour is exhibited 90% of the time	MEDIUM This behaviour is exhibited but needs to have an increased focus	LOW This behaviour is not currently exhibited to an acceptable level
Follow each step of the DBM Process				
Invest the time to set up your expectations of student behaviour				
Follow up any exited student with a re-entry discussion 1:1 promptly				
Consistently contact parents with concerns and praise for their child				
Inform year level leader of any severe or 3 x repeat behaviours				
Provide a consequence to students who do not follow your instruction promptly and without arguing				
Arrive to class before students and as punctually as possible				

Continued…

Table 8.1 (continued)

Teacher's personal mobile phone is turned off				
Teacher does not enter the room with food and drink				
Students line up showing they have materials before entering class				
Provide a consequence to late students				
Mark Compass and ensure any adjustments notified to attendance officer				
Students are seated in an orderly manner				
Always use the diary if student needs to leave the room				
Students wear ear phones or use phones for educational purposes only and with your express permission				
Students are not permitted to chew gum or eat				
Check diaries including that homework is written in each day by each student				
Voice is not raised loudly a significant amount of time				
Do not dismiss the class until the bell is sounded				
Students listen attentively when teacher is speaking				
Follow up homework tasks and assessments promptly				

This rubric was supplemented by the Relationship Diagnostic Rubric in Table 8.2 aimed at ensuring that the orderly learning environment was one where students are also well known by the staff. Together, the use of these rubrics provides an example where classroom observation is part of a broader program of support to build teacher capacity and drive an orderly learning environment through the school.

TABLE 8.2: THE WRSC RELATIONSHIP DIAGNOSTIC RUBRIC, 2014

Relationship-based DBM Behaviour	VERY HIGH This behaviour is exhibited 95% of the time	HIGH This behaviour is exhibited 90% of the time	MEDIUM This behaviour is exhibited but needs to have an increased focus	LOW This behaviour is not currently exhibited to an acceptable level
Develops personalised positive relationships with students that make students feel respected and want to succeed				
Creates work focused environment where students and teachers show respect by listening politely to each other				
Deals quietly and effectively with student misbehaviour without letting it interfere with the work. A negatively phrased way of putting this might be: Consistently resorts to shouting to gain students' attention				
Cultivates an atmosphere of positivity where good behaviours are recognised				
Employs seating plans where appropriate				
Maintains awareness and control of what is happening in the class at all times				
Employs teaching activities that suit the needs of the students				

More commonly, though, classroom observation is introduced in Stages 2 and 3 of the school improvement process outlined in this book, primarily to monitor the implementation of the school's instructional model and/or the adoption and impact of identified strategies for improving the quality of teaching and learning in class.

Its purpose in this context is to examine observable classroom processes, including specific teacher practices, aspects of instruction and interactions between teachers and students in order to provide constructive and supportive feedback to the teacher to help them to improve. This is as much about identifying strengths the teacher exhibits which should be reinforced as any shortcomings they may need to address.

OPTIONS FOR CLASSROOM OBSERVATION

Classroom observation can be introduced in a range of ways, depending on which works best for the school. In all cases, it is predicated on a set of agreed principles for ensuring it genuinely supports the improvement of teaching throughout the school. The following activity is designed to ensure staff are involved in determining how classroom observation will be undertaken, thereby contributing to buy-in for the processes the school subsequently adopts.

ACTIVITY FOR STAFF: GOVERNING PRINCIPLES FOR CLASSROOM OBSERVATION IN THE SCHOOL

Instructions

1 In small groups, consider the following draft set of principles for classroom observation and identify:
- any principle that is unclear and needs to be further discussed and explained
- any principle with which you disagree
- any additional principle that needs to be included in the list.

2 Your answers will inform a whole-staff discussion about the ground rules for any classroom observation process that is introduced in the school.

DRAFT SET OF PRINCIPLES FOR CONSIDERATION

It is proposed that any process of classroom observation introduced in the school should be:
- supportive and developmental with no judgment involved
- an opportunity for teachers to receive constructive feedback from colleagues on their strengths and ways in which they can improve
- the basis for further professional reflection, professional development and other support
- planned and agreed in advance so there are no surprises involved, with a clear focus linked to improving teaching, and hence student learning outcomes
- based on clear, simple, sustainable processes that are known, understood and agreed by the staff
- a means of collaboratively developing and sharing good practice throughout school classrooms.

LEARNING WALKS

In many schools, classroom observation has started with learning walks that teams of teachers conduct. Learning walks, according to the Australian Institute of Teaching and School Leadership, involve 'a group of teachers visiting multiple classrooms at their own school' (AITSL, 2014). The walks specifically focus on the walkers' own goals or needs aligned to the priorities of the school or team, such as monitoring the implementation of learning goals. They are designed to 'foster conversation about teaching and learning in order to develop a shared vision of high-quality teaching that impacts on student learning'.

At Kambrya College, for example, learning walks, as described in the first edition of this book, were conducted by all teachers, on a scheduled basis, in teams of three as part of a broader focus on better instruction that includes peer observation and targeted coaching for teachers who are likely to benefit most from it. The walks particularly focused on implementation of the school's instructional model and were promoted as a benefit to walkers as much as their hosts. They were part of the process of sharing good practice across the school, so more teachers can work like the best. The walkers took notes on three areas of practice—differentiation in the lesson, learning goals and success criteria, and student workbooks—and then provided both generic feedback on the range of classes observed, and individual feedback in the form of a thankyou note, which outlined both positive things seen and 'wonderings' that might cause the teacher to think.

A sample of teachers we spoke to, as part of co-authoring an article about the school in the wake of its involvement in the documentary *Revolution school* (see Zbar, Macklin, Muscat, Naidu & Wastle, 2016), talked of how they felt the walks informed their own teaching practice and helped them to reflect on what they do well and how they can continue to improve.

Middle schools in the Northern Territory were supported by the Department of Education to conduct learning walks as part of implementing the Middle Years Teaching and Learning Strategy in that jurisdiction (Northern Territory Government, 2019). Box 8.1 outlines the broad advice for schools on conducting learning walks from the former Loddon Mallee Region in Victoria that the Department provided to schools.

Box 8.1
Advice to schools—Implementation of the Learning Walk[1]

Pre-walk discussion—15 minutes
This should take place just prior to the classroom visits. All walkers involved should have a clear understanding of the:
- protocols and purpose
- timetable
- focus of the walk
- names of the walkers
- classrooms to be visited
- date and time of whole-school reflection.

All walkers are given a Learning Walk Handbook with appropriate templates for gathering evidence during the walk.

Classroom visits—1 hour
The walkers visit each classroom for 10 minutes. They 'look and listen' to the learning and take notes on any evidence that links to the focus. Walkers may speak to students and teachers only if the learning allows for such interactions. Any discussion should be brief and unobtrusive. When walkers leave each classroom, they meet for 5 minutes outside the classroom to share observations. The evidence that is cited must be specific to the focus. This is not a time for open discussion or judgment.

Post-walk discussion—30 minutes
At the end of the classroom visits, all walkers convene for a debriefing session. They share the observations collected and identify any patterns that may have emerged. Wonderings may then be formulated based on the evidence. Conclusions are not formed. All evidence and wonderings are collated by the Lead Walker.

Visited teachers' reflection—optional
Feedback may be shared with classroom teachers visited prior to whole-staff reflection. These teachers are asked to read and discuss feedback as a team and identify trends to direct future development. Our own experience is that feedback to the teachers visited is not only valuable to them, but generally is sought and appreciated.

Whole-staff reflection
Within one week of the Learning Walk, the collated evidence and wonderings are shared with the whole staff to identify trends and direct future development.

Note: The advice provided to middle schools in the Northern Territory includes a pro forma for walkers to use in taking notes that focuses on the use of an instructional model and feedback to students. It includes suggested questions that up to three students can be asked—that is, What are you learning?, Why might you be learning this?, How are you going with this learning? and What do you need to learn next?

---

[1] The complete advice developed by the region can be retrieved from http://doereforms.weebly.com/uploads/5/3/5/2/53522887/learning_walks.pdf

Glen Waverley Secondary College has sought to bridge the divide between learning walks and a more generalised process of peer observation by introducing what it calls 'Learning Talks' based on 'the power of 2s'. More specifically the approach, which is designed to develop instructional leadership and collegial professional practice in the school, involves two staff visiting two classes for two minutes, and asking two students two questions: 'What are you learning today?' and 'How will you know if you've been successful?'

It's a simple, effective and non-threatening means of building an openness to learning within the college, both from colleagues and the students themselves, and hence an important contributor to the collective efficacy of the staff.

OBSERVATION AND FEEDBACK SKILLS

While learning walks are primarily about the observer and identifying whole-staff trends, as evident in Box 8.1, peer observations are more concerned with the observed, and, in particular, the focused, constructive feedback that can help them to improve.

Teachers get better by working together to build on existing strengths and collectively tackling any major problems of practice they face. A willingness to reflect on one's own practice is critical in this regard, but reflection on its own is not enough. Reflection is limited to what we already know and believe, and to a self-assessment of one's work. Reflection needs feedback from others if significant improvements are to be made. Mutual classroom observation by peers provides the context in which such feedback can be given and received.

Peer observation, as the Victorian Department of Education (2018) explains, is something that benefits observed and observer alike because it can:
- provide opportunities to discuss challenges and successes with trusted colleagues
- support the sharing of ideas and expertise among teachers
- build a community of trust through opening classroom practice to a wider audience
- support a focus on improving the impact of learning
- contribute to the collective efficacy of the whole school (p. 9).

There is, of course, a range of logistical issues associated with making classroom observation work in a school, not least of which is the timetabling issues involved. One option several schools have adopted in response has been to video lessons that teachers can then view together either in full or in part. It's an approach that not only solves the timetabling problems the school might face, but also can be undertaken in groups of any size. In addition, a video can be stopped and reviewed, and avoids differing recollections of what might have occurred.

Viewing videos of classroom practice in teams can help build teachers' overall observational and feedback skills.

Videoing lessons is particularly helpful for overcoming the five 'Common Perceptual Errors' of observation that Knight (2018) identified of:
- confirmation bias, whereby we tend to filter information that fits what we already believe in a way that has become prevalent in the political sphere driven by social media posts and bots
- habituation, which sees us think and act in ways that we always have and hence always will do
- primacy effect, whereby first impressions can disproportionately determine the views of people we then adopt
- recency effect, which, somewhat similarly, sees us sometimes disproportionately influenced by what happened or who we spoke to last
- stereotypes, whereby we prejudge people on the basis of the group to which they belong rather than the individuals that they are (p. 29).

Videos can help 'cut through' these perceptual errors because what we see is less ambiguous and hence contestable than what we might say after the event, less reliant on the deficiencies of memory or note taking at the time, and able to be revisited to inform discussion and subsequent development of a supportive coaching plan.

However video will not work to good effect if, as Knight cautions, it is 'carelessly introduced' (2018, p. 31). If the use of video lesson observation is to succeed, then we must first ensure:
- the requisite level of trust between observer and observed
- choice for the teacher to participate or not, since there is no value in someone being forced
- ownership that enables the teacher who is observed to control how the video is used.

It is something that Auburn North Public School has explored in depth, using approaches determined by teachers in each stage. For example, Stage 2 teachers[2] collaboratively plan a lesson that the team leader teaches and videos for the team. The leader watches the video, reflecting on a mutually agreed area of focus (e.g. modelled instruction). The leader then shares the video with the team, pausing it to share their own reflections first, and then invites feedback and feedforward from other members of the team. Any necessary modifications are then made to the lesson and the next team member continues the process until all teachers have taught and filmed the lesson so they can reflect on their practice and receive feedback from their peers.

In a variation on this theme, the Stage 3 team at the school has adopted an approach that involves:
- Define the problem—what do we need to focus on?
- Plan the lesson—one teacher plans the lesson in consultation with others
- Teach the lesson—one person teaches the lesson, which is filmed to enable everyone to view it
- Evaluate and reflect on the lesson—questions related to the focus area
- Revise the lesson—revisions based on previous discussion, done by the next person teaching the lesson
- Teach the revised lesson to a different class, run by a different teacher
- Evaluate and reflect again.

Beyond this, it is worth noting that the process of videoing lessons is something that becomes more accepted as successful implementation proceeds. At Dandenong North Primary School for instance, where the principal, Kevin Mackay, videos classroom experiences as a matter of course, students and teachers have become so inured to it, that it has become part of the fabric of what happens at this school. In fact, they would start to notice if it did not occur.

ACTIVITY FOR STAFF: DEVELOPING CLASSROOM OBSERVATION SKILLS

Note: The AITSL website contains numerous illustrations of practice aligned to different stages in a teacher's career that include classroom footage and can be analysed and discussed by staff.[3] It is suggested that leaders identify two or three relevant video clips to use in the following activity for staff.

Instructions
1. Individually watch the video clips that have been gathered and think about the feedback you might provide to the teacher involved. In particular, consider what you think went well in the lesson and the evidence you would provide for this, and what could have been done better and why.
2. Then, as a whole staff, share your thoughts and identify one strength observed on which the teacher can build, and one piece of advice you could give to the teacher that would help them to improve the quality of lessons they teach.

---

[2] Stage 2 in NSW covers Years 3 and 4, while Stage 3 covers Years 5 and 6.
[3] See http://www.aitsl.edu.au/australian-professional-standards-for-teachers/illustrations-of-practice/find-by-career-stage

PROCESSES AND PRO FORMAS FOR EFFECTIVE CLASSROOM OBSERVATION

Regardless of the form it takes, the effectiveness of classroom observation depends on the quality of processes surrounding it and the use of pro formas to make these work. Quality processes and pro formas also help to ensure that classroom observation is understood and supported by staff, and not seen as an imposition from 'the top'.

More specifically, effective classroom observation depends on good processes for each step along the way, and pro formas that help implement these processes effectively and consistently across the school. There is a need in this context to be clear not only about what happens during the classroom observation, but before and after as well.

BEFORE THE LESSON

There is a range of practicalities that need to be agreed in advance of any observation that occurs in order to ensure its success. In particular:
- Which lesson?
- What will be the focus of the observation and how long will it last?
- What will the students be told since, initially at least, it will be a new experience for them as well?
- Where will the observer(s) sit?

The lesson needs to be viewed in context since it is not a stand-alone event. The observer(s) should understand the intended learning outcomes, where the lesson fits in the broader teaching program, what preceded this lesson and what will come next. The observer(s) and observed should also agree when the feedback discussion will occur and the form it will take.

We have used the pre-observation pro forma in Figure 8.1 in a number of schools to help teachers to effectively prepare for the classroom observations they undertake. It can be shared with staff as the basis for developing an approach that is appropriate to your school.

PREPARING FOR THE OBSERVATION
Key questions for participants to consider

Date for the observation: _____

Class to be observed: _____

Staff member observed: _____

Staff member(s) observing: _____

Background to the observation—The teacher being observed to brief the observer(s) on the intended learning outcomes, how the lesson fits in the broader teaching program and any other relevant factors.

Specific focus of the observation—Identify an agreed teaching focus to be observed and how long it will last (e.g. Is my learning goal clear to the students?; Am I using wait time effectively? etc.)

Anything the observer(s) should look for in particular—Any other teaching and/or student behaviours the teacher may want the observers to look for.

Message to the students—Since classroom observation is only at an early stage, identify what the students will be told.

Logistics—Clarify an agreed approach to any logistical issues that need to be planned in advance, including ones that may arise in the lesson itself (e.g. where the observer(s) will sit; whether or not they will interact with students; what will occur if a student seriously misbehaves; etc.)

Time and date for the feedback discussion _____

FIGURE 8.1: SAMPLE PRO FORMA TO HELP PREPARE FOR A CLASSROOM OBSERVATION

© Pamela Macklin and Vic Zbar, *Driving School Improvement*, Australian Council for Educational Research, 2017

DURING THE LESSON

Observers should arrive before the start of the lesson so it can begin on time. Notes can be kept on a classroom observation pro forma, such as the one provided in Figure 8.2, with specific examples relevant to the previously agreed observation focus.

Observers may talk to students if this was agreed in the pre-observation discussion, but only when this can be done without interrupting the lesson. This also provides an opportunity to view the students' work, which may aid in the feedback.

In the event that the lesson is not going well, or something unexpected happens, the teacher may choose to ask the observer(s) to leave and arrange another time to be observed.

As a matter of courtesy, and since a collaborative and open culture is being built, it is suggested that the observer(s) should thank the teacher at the end of the lesson.

The pro forma in Figure 8.2, which also has been used in several schools, is designed to help observers to keep notes in accordance with the background information they were provided and the agreed focus for the observation. It is strongly recommended that after the feedback conversation has occurred, the completed pro forma(s) be provided to the teacher who was observed to inform their ongoing reflection and professional learning to improve. This helps emphasise that the whole activity exists to support teacher improvement, so more teachers can work like the best, and is not judgmental in any way.

CLASSROOM OBSERVATION PRO FORMA
The completed form is to be provided to the teacher after the feedback discussion

Date: _____ Class: _____

Staff member observed: _____ Staff member(s) observing: _____

Lesson date: _____ Room: _____ Time _____

Observer interaction with students during lesson? ☐ Yes ☐ No ☐ No preference

Specific focus of observation (This is the teaching focus identified by the teacher being observed in the pre-observation discussion):

Background briefing (Relevant information from the pre-observation discussion to keep in mind):

Observer notes to inform the feedback discussion:

What did you see or hear your colleague doing in relation to the chosen focus?
and/or What did you see or hear the students doing in relation to the chosen focus?

What went well in relation to the focus of the observation? (Provide concrete examples.) Was there anything that could be done differently if the lesson was taught again? (Provide reasons for your view.)

Observer feedback:

Do you have any questions to help your colleague think more about what they are trying to achieve in relation to the chosen focus? Any other comments about the chosen focus?

FIGURE 8.2: SAMPLE CLASSROOM OBSERVATION PRO FORMA

© Pamela Macklin and Vic Zbar, *Driving School Improvement*, Australian Council for Educational Research, 2017

AFTER THE LESSON

The feedback discussion should occur as soon as possible after the observation, preferably on the same day, but not immediately since all involved do need time to collect their thoughts.

An effective feedback conversation is descriptive, not evaluative, so no judgment on the quality or style of teaching should be made. The focus is the agreed teaching practices observed and not the teacher as a person. It is important in this context that the teacher observed goes first, describing what they think went well, with specific examples, before describing how they might do things differently if they were to teach the lesson again.

Teachers have not been trained on giving feedback to each other and tend to struggle with the task. That said, it is ultimately a matter of practice and getting better as you go. Figure 8.3 provides a sample script we have used in some schools to help teachers to conduct the feedback conversation in a constructive and non-threatening way.

POST OBSERVATION PRO FORMA SCRIPT
To inform discussion—adapt it as you think is required

Set the scene:
Remind yourselves of the agreed focus of the observation and hence the feedback to be given and received.

Focus on strengths:
Ask the teacher to describe the elements of the lesson they felt went particularly well in relation to the agreed focus, and to give specific examples.

The observer(s) can confirm these examples and add any further aspects of the lesson they observed to have been successful, again with specific examples.

Areas for improvement:
Ask the teacher to describe how, if they were to teach the lesson again, they could do things differently and why.

The observer(s) can add suggestions, if appropriate, of how this aspect of the lesson could be improved in future, based on their own experience and/or other teachers they have observed.

A plan for moving forward:
Summarise any agreed actions for follow up improvement and support.

Conclusion:
Has this been a useful feedback discussion from your point of view?
How can we improve these discussions in future?

FIGURE 8.3: A SAMPLE SCRIPT TO INFORM FEEDBACK CONVERSATIONS

© Pamela Macklin and Vic Zbar, *Driving School Improvement*, Australian Council for Educational Research, 2017

ACTIVITY FOR STAFF: DEVELOPING PRO FORMAS TO SUPPORT CLASSROOM OBSERVATION

Instructions

1 Work in professional learning teams to examine the sample pro formas provided as Figures 8.1 to 8.3 above and note any changes that may be needed for them to work successfully in your school.
2 Share the outcomes of team deliberations to design an agreed set of pre-, during and post-observation pro formas to support the implementation of classroom observation in the school.

QUALITY OF FEEDBACK

Once the school has developed some guiding pro formas to ensure a consistent, supportive and non-threatening approach, the quality of feedback conversation that happens determines the effectiveness of the approach.

Things to keep in mind so the discussion goes well for all involved include that:
- the emphasis is more on sharing information than giving advice
- it is ensured that all agree on what has been said
- a clear plan for follow-up is agreed.

Interestingly enough, the 'rules' for effective feedback conversations between adults are not fundamentally different from the characteristics of effective feedback to students outlined in Chapter 7.

More specifically, good feedback conversations are:
- focused on the teaching and not the teacher
- descriptive and not evaluative
- specific, clear and backed up with evidence of what was observed
- designed to build on strengths and identify opportunities for development.

In addition, as with students, feedback should come in amounts the teacher can use, rather than everything that could possibly be said.

Above all, though, it is important to remember that the more teachers engage in feedback conversations after lesson observations, the better at these they will get. It's a process that will only be enhanced by a willingness to examine how effectively it currently is done.

In the Queechy Alliance, for example, the schools involved have sought to formally consider the following set of questions about classroom observations to help improve their overall approach:

1 Are there regular informal observations and feedback for classroom teachers at your school?
2 What is the purpose of classroom observations and feedback at your school?
3 Who observes and provides feedback?
4 How have observers been trained to conduct quality observations and provide effective feedback?
5 Who is observed and why?
6 How much time is dedicated to observations and feedback?
7 What structures, approaches and documents are used in the observation and feedback process?
8 How is the observation and feedback work regularly reviewed and monitored?
9 How is the impact of observations and feedback known and improved as needed?

ACTIVITY FOR CLASSROOM OBSERVERS: ASSESSING THE QUALITY OF FEEDBACK I GIVE

Instructions
1 Rate each of the statements, in the first part of Table 8.3, about how you provide feedback to colleagues after an observation on a four-point scale where:
   1 = I don't do this, 2 = I sometimes do this, 3 = I often do this and 4 = This is a routine part of the feedback I provide.
2 Taking account of your responses to the preceding pro forma, fill in the second part of the table.
3 Consider sharing your responses with one or more of the colleagues you have observed to see if they would corroborate your ratings and/or identify other aspects of giving feedback you may need to address.

TABLE 8.3: ASSESSING THE QUALITY OF FEEDBACK I GIVE

My feedback to colleagues I have observed is:	Rating (1–4)
Designed to reinforce strengths the teacher exhibits in class	
Limited to one or two main areas for reinforcement and/or improvement	
Focused on strategies that make a significant difference to the quality of teaching and student outcomes	
Appropriate to the experience and expertise of the teacher	
Backed up by evidence and examples of what was observed	
Designed to engender reflection on how the teacher can improve	
Inclusive of strategies or other support the teacher can use in class	
Designed to be within the capacity of the teacher to implement	
Supportive in tone	
Provided as soon as possible after the observation	

The major strength in giving feedback on which I can build:	The evidence for this strength: • • •
A key aspect of giving feedback to colleagues that I really need to develop:	The evidence for identifying this area: • • •

© Pamela Macklin and Vic Zbar, *Driving School Improvement*, Australian Council for Educational Research, 2017

FEEDBACK FROM STUDENTS

It increasingly is being recognised in schools and through research that student feedback can be as informative and useful as feedback from school leaders and one's peers. Student voice, according to Knight (2018), 'is a powerful tool for professional growth that has been sorely underutilized'. After all, as he cogently observes, 'students are the only people with firsthand knowledge of how learning is proceeding' (p. 40). Finding out what students think is an important means of shifting the focus from the experience teachers think they provide, to the one the students actually receive. It constitutes a further reality check on the quality and impact of teaching from the perspective of those it affects the most.

'(S)tudents' insights, creativity, energy and confidence', according to Quaglia and Corso (2014), 'offer important perspectives that can help schools improve' (p. 3). 'The bottom line', they explain, 'is that, in order to truly teach our students, we must be willing to learn from them. Only they can tell us where they would like their journey to take them beyond school, and that is essential information if we are to do the important work of successfully inspiring and equipping them for what lies ahead' (Quaglia & Corso, 2014, p. 7).

Student feedback on teaching can be obtained in a variety of ways, such as informal conversations, interviews, writing prompts and exit tickets which are discussed in some depth by Knight (2018, see Chapter 2), including even some suggested questions to use. It also requires close listening to students in and beyond class and observation of what they do.

Keen to capture some student feedback, while also encouraging them to have and express a stronger voice, leaders at Hampton Park Primary School started with the evidence of students' responses to the annual survey of student attitudes that is conducted in Victorian Government schools. The data was unpacked, initially in the leadership team and then with the staff to determine what it was telling the school. This was supplemented by student focus groups and time for designated teacher leaders to unpack it with the students themselves in their grades, including by seeking to co-construct learning goals and success criteria and modelling and teaching of learning behaviours that help students to achieve success.

However, this only worked because, as the school explains, it has an orderly learning environment in place that ensures what its principal Liz Davey describes as 'the familiarity and security for students to be comfortable'. The school needs to have invested the time to ensure that teachers know their students well and sufficient rapport has been built. In addition, the school was sufficiently committed to capturing and promoting student voice that it designated a leader to ensure it occurred, and adopted a four-year plan to make it work with challenging yet achievable goals and processes for involving staff and supporting them with professional learning they needed along the way.

Perhaps even more expansively still, in relation to student feedback on teaching and learning in the school, is the approach of Dandenong North Primary School described in Box 8.2, which has trained and involved students in the process of classroom observation itself.

Box 8.2

Student observers at Dandenong North Primary School

Having started with a pilot program in 2015 where two students were selected to go 'unannounced' into teaching sessions with a camera and a pro forma to document eight 'things they thought were important about what the teacher was teaching', by 2020 the program involved more than 40 students who, over the course of the year, observe all teachers in the school.

The school applies a rigorous process for selecting students for the observer role. Applicants must first write a 'persuasive text' of at least 100 words. Having received a pass grade for the text, they then sit a test specifically designed to assess their readiness for the role, which must be passed with a mark of 80% or more; although students can resit the test, provided at least two weeks has elapsed. Students who meet the criteria are placed on probation as 'trainee observers' until they have completed two signed-off cycles and hence qualified as observers in their own right.

Student observers are provided with basic training and a structured pro forma comprising eight spaces, which initially were just for photographs and then, as the program developed, for seven photographs and a one minute video of an important part of the lesson they observed. These spaces are accompanied by two columns for 'observation' written during the lesson and 'clarification' arising from the debriefing discussion afterwards.

Further training is provided as required to 'update' the context of their observations. For example, observers have received extensive input on a range of high-impact teaching strategies they could identify in class, as well as a number of vocabulary and teaching strategies used in the Talk 4 Writing program the school employs.[4]

Initially, the students randomly selected teachers to observe, with or without notice, and attended the class with a camera and clipboard with the pro forma attached. They were specifically advised to record 'what had been seen—not anything that might be inferred'. Once the round of observations was completed, the observers worked with the program coordinator to clarify any of their observation comments, in order to support objective feedback to the teacher concerned. An edited and agreed log of observations was prepared as a digital record completed with the photographs and short video of what occurred. The students then met with the teacher they observed and gave them a copy of the digital log to underpin a discussion that would enable the teacher to understand the students' perspective on the teaching they saw.

As the program took off, and many more students became involved, the same process applied but the random nature of visits was replaced by a more structured approach designed to ensure that, over time, all teachers were observed in a systematic way.

Having established a long tradition of classroom observation, as described in Box 4.3, the program, as the school describes, is viewed as 'just a simple extension of the culture to provide a student perspective and to add value to the program in regards to what teachers get from it and what the students can learn by participating in an authentic learning opportunity'.

Some of the flavour of the sophisticated observations that students made can be found in the following extracts from a team of three observers of a lesson aimed at teaching the writing of a procedure text. More specifically, the students observed from the lesson and their illustrative photos that the teacher:

- 'is teaching the students how to write a procedure text with the correct structure and language features'

---

[4] Further information on the Talk 4 Writing program developed in the UK can be found at https://www.talk4writing.co.uk/

- 'is taking it up to the next step to see if the students understand more procedure text'
- 'told students to go back to their tables quietly and copy the board'
- 'is helping [name deleted] to understand the steps because he wasn't here on the day when they talked about procedure text'
- decided it's time … 'to start correcting the students' work'
- 'is getting the kids to pack up so the students can play Hot Dog'
- with the students is … 'now playing a maths game called Hot Dog. It is also educational.'

The students' accompanying one minute video, in their own words, provided 'a view of what they were doing. [Teacher's name deleted] started the class by introducing the topic they are learning. They talked about procedure text'.

The value of the clarifying session with the program coordinator is then evident in this short extract from a pro forma of a lesson that focused on writing a story using capital letters and full stops.

Photo number	Observation	Clarification
Photo number 5	The students are discussing and helping each other with their buddies while doing their own work.	The students are working cooperatively so they gain more knowledge when they are writing their persuasive pieces. The students are working hard while [teacher's name deleted] is questioning all the students and giving them feedback about their work.

An evaluation of the program in its early stages, which has only been confirmed by experience since, identified that the benefits for both the students and teachers involved included:
- demonstrably improved language acquisition (vocabulary, grammar, spelling and sentence structure)
- improved participation in, and understanding of, their own teachers' lessons
- additional evidence for observed teachers to use in their performance reviews
- increased awareness of student perspectives of lesson intentions and delivery as part of the feedback to then help teachers in planning future lessons
- photographic records of teachers at their work
- conversation starters for professional discussions among observed teachers
- enhanced ICT skills for students as a result of recording their observations
- an increased focus on student agency in the school's IMOCAD (Induction, Mentoring, Observation, Coaching, Appraisal and Development) program.

CONCLUSION

We travel a lot, sometimes for holidays but primarily for work. When we do, we commonly use guide books so we learn from what others have already found and plan accordingly for the trip. It not only helps to determine the cities we want to visit, but also to prepare an outline of what we might do on different days.

It's a means of ensuring we maximise the value of our time away and see some sites we might otherwise miss. It also often reveals activities and venues that we would not have found for ourselves.

For all of that, we are well aware of Burns' 'best laid plans'[1], and the consequent recognition that things may not happen as we would want. Events will sometimes intervene, with the result we need to alter what we had planned. For example, the visit we intended to an outdoor venue will be compromised by rain, with the result we will reschedule to another day. Alternatively, someone we met on route may have raved about something we had not contemplated with the result we incorporate it into our plan replacing something else we had in mind.

Just like our travels, school improvement is a journey, and not an event. A journey that goes through the stages we have sought to identify in this book—stages that others have traversed and experienced before.

We see this book as analogous to the travel guides we use, helping schools to plan their route, and activities along the way, albeit responsive to either impediments or new opportunities that emerge.

We have sought in this context to provide some signposts towards your destination, as indicated in Table C.1, that will also help keep you on track, without constraining you to any one path along the way.

---

[1] Shortened from the (translated) reference in Robert Burns' 1786 poem, *To a mouse, on turning her up in her nest with the plough*, to 'the best laid plans of mice and men often go awry'.

TABLE C.1: SIGNPOSTS FOR YOUR JOURNEY

Chapter	Signposts and supports[2]	Destination
	The self-assessment in Chapter 4 helps you to determine where you are at, and hence where you need to head	

5	**Understanding and rating the preconditions in your school:**
	
	• Building a cohesive and effective leadership team:
	  – Evaluating and building the effectiveness of your team
	
	• Ensuring high expectations for students and staff:
	  – Evaluating expectations in the school and identifying strategies to raise them
	
	• Ensuring an orderly learning environment where students are well known by the staff:
	  – Aligning your behavioural expectations to the values of the school and developing agreed classroom rights and responsibilities
	  – Developing structures that enable students to feel well known
	  – Evaluating the orderly learning environment in your school
	
	• Ensuring a focus on what matters most:
	  – Developing your priorities and analysing the value of the strategies you adopt
	  – Abandoning strategies that no longer are required or do not work
		The four preconditions for whole-school improvement will be in place:
		• Strong and cohesive leadership
		• High expectations
		• An orderly learning environment where students are well known
		• A focus on what matters most

6	**Building teaching capacity so more teachers can work like the best:**
	
	• Characteristics of an effective teacher:
	  – Developing a shared view of effective teaching
	  – Identifying opportunities to increase engaged student learning time
	
	• Using an instructional model for consistently better teaching:
	  – Analysing how systematic teaching is in your school
	  – Developing an instructional model and supporting its adoption through the school
	
	• Ensuring structures for collaboration to underpin better lesson planning:
	  – Structuring professional learning teams (PLTs) and determining the focus of their work
	  – Developing shared norms and practices for effective PLTs
	  – Evaluating the effectiveness of PLTs
		Individual and collaborative planning of consistently good lessons guided by an instructional model developed by the school

Continued...

---

[2] It should be noted that this is a summary of some key tools, activities and pro formas included in the book, along with a number of case studies and vignettes to illustrate how you can use it to craft your own path to the destination you seek, rather than a complete list.

Table C.1 (continued)

7	**Drilling down to improve classroom practice:** Understanding evidence and theories of action for improved teaching: • Using data wisely in PLTs Using learning goals as a particularly effective means of improving teaching and learning: • Planning lessons from learning goals • Developing and writing good learning goals Adding success criteria into the mix: • Developing and writing good success criteria Ensuring constructive feedback to students: • Identifying the characteristics of effective feedback • Evaluating the effectiveness of the feedback you give Differentiating delivery to meet the full range of student learning needs: • Understanding what differentiation is and is not • Options for differentiating in class • Developing effective routines to ensure a well-run class	A shift in focus from inference to evidence in planning and delivering lessons, including the evidence of successful practice in other schools

The underpinnings for each stage

Arriving at any of the destinations crucially depends on:
- an understanding of how successful change happens in schools as outlined in Chapter 2
- leadership at every stage, as outlined in Chapter 3, since leadership is the difference between pockets of improvement that occur in any school, and improvement across the school as a whole
- the progressive introduction of classroom observation, discussed in Chapter 8, to support the consistent implementation of key strategies for improvement and the sharing of practice and feedback that supports more teachers to work like the best.

Once again, each of these chapters contains pro formas, tools and case studies to help reach the signposts that point you towards the destination you seek.

In developing the signposts and associated supports summarised in Table C.1, we have drawn heavily on work in schools that we described in the first edition of the book. As predicted at the time, this work has continued and grown as successful approaches in more and more schools have come to light, hence adding further tools, pro formas and exemplars that are now included in this second edition. This is similar to the way in which the range of travel guides available are supplemented by the features that most newspapers print or the wealth of blogs on the internet.

The other thing that sometimes happens on a trip, however, is that you meet someone who tries to steer you down an ostensibly attractive but, in reality, completely false path. For example, many visitors to the Grand Palace complex in Bangkok have been met before arrival by a tout who explains that the palace is closed today (despite the fact it is not) and they have an alternative the tourist can purchase instead. It's a path that you'd do best to avoid. Similarly, there are, as we suggested in Chapter 2, instances where people external to a school will prescribe the solution to its ills without ever having diagnosed the overall health of this school. A flexible approach to both tourism and school improvement suggests a need to carefully analyse where you are and where you are headed, examine the evidence of what is being advanced, and determine the path that best meets your needs at the time.

We hope in this book to have helped shift the focus from providing generic answers for schools to questions they may not even know they have, towards informing the solutions that schools can themselves prescribe for the specific ailments they diagnose. It's the difference between building capacity in the school and taking it away.

When gurus in the past have told us what to do, we have generally found that it fails. As the great management writer and educator, Peter Drucker, cogently observed, 'I have been saying for many years that we are using the word 'guru' only because 'charlatan' is too long to fit into a headline' (see James, 1997).

Similarly, the experience we have had of externally imposed reform is sufficient to tell us by now that we ought to beware of geeks bearing gifts; including, we hasten to add, us.

As we concluded last time around, enjoy the trip and let us know how you fare.

REFERENCES

Andersen, B., Fagerhaug, T., & Beitz, M. (2010). *Root cause analysis and improvement in the healthcare sector: A step-by-step guide.* Milwaukee, WI: ASQ Quality Press.

Archer, A. L., & Hughes, C.A. (2011). *Explicit instruction: Effective and efficient teaching.* New York: Guilford Press.

Argyris, C. (1990). *Overcoming organizational defenses: Facilitating organizational learning.* Boston: Allyn & Bacon.

Argyris, C., & Schön, D. (1974). *Theory in practice: Increasing professional effectiveness.* San Francisco, CA: Jossey-Bass Publishers.

Australian Council for Educational Research. (2019). *PISA: Key findings 2018.* Retrieved from https://www.acer.org/au/pisa/key-findings-2018

AITSL [Australian Institute for Teaching and School Leadership]. (n.d.). *Coaching toolkit for teachers overview.* Retrieved from https://www.aitsl.edu.au/docs/default-source/default-document-library/coaching-resources-complete-set.pdf?sfvrsn=8ab8ec3c_0

AITSL [Australian Institute for Teaching and School Leadership]. (2014). *'How-to' guide: Learning walks* [PDF file]. Retrieved from https://www.aitsl.edu.au/docs/default-source/default-document-library/how-to-guide---learning-walks.pdf?sfvrsn=d1acec3c_2

AITSL [Australian Institute for Teaching and School Leadership]. (2019). *Australian Professional Standards for Principals and the Leadership Profiles.* Retrieved from https://www.aitsl.edu.au/docs/default-source/national-policy-framework/australian-professional-standard-for-principals.pdf?sfvrsn=c07eff3c_4

Australian Institute of Health and Welfare. (2015). *Australia's welfare 2015: In brief.* Retrieved from https://www.aihw.gov.au/getmedia/341eec3b-3ac2-4198-966c-714ef7df9924/18940.pdf.aspx?inline=true

Australian Institute of Health and Welfare. (2017). *Australia's welfare 2017: In brief.* Retrieved from https://www.aihw.gov.au/getmedia/5c7b48ba-f5a2-46a6-96bd-2bbae02a5139/AIHW-AUS215-AW17_inbrief.pdf.aspx?inline=true

Barber, M., & Mourshed, M. (2009). *Shaping the future: How good education systems can become great in the decade ahead.* Report on the International Education Roundtable, July 7, 2009. Singapore: McKinsey & Co.

Bloom, B. S. (1956). *Taxonomy of educational objectives: The classification of educational goals. Handbook 1: Cognitive Domain.* New York: David McKay Co. Inc.

Boudett, K. P., City, E. A., & Murnane, R. J. (Eds.). (2013). *Data wise: A step-by-step guide to using assessment results to improve teaching and learning* (revised and expanded edition). Cambridge, MA: Harvard Education Press.

Brookhart, S. (2008). *How to give effective feedback to your students.* Alexandria, VA: ASCD.

Brooks, A. W. & John, L. K. (2018). Managing yourself: The surprising power of questions. *Harvard Business Review*, May–June. Retrieved from https://hbr.org/2018/05/the-surprising-power-of-questions

Brotherhood of St. Lawrence. (2016). *Australia's youth unemployment hotspots snapshot: March 2016*. Retrieved from http://library.bsl.org.au/jspui/bitstream/1/9004/1/BSL_Aust_youth_unemployment_hotspots_Mar2016.pdf

Buck, A. (n.d.). *Bringing out the best in everyone*. Retrieved from http://www.growthcoaching.com.au/articles-new/bringing-out-the-best-in-everyone

Caldwell, B. (2000). *The transformation of schools: Scenarios for leadership and 'abandonment'* (Occasional Paper No. 92). Melbourne: IARTV.

Chiu, L. H., & Tully, M. (1997). Student preferences of teacher discipline styles. *Journal of Instruction and Psychology*, 24(3), 168–175.

Clarke, S. (2003). *Enriching feedback in the primary classroom*. London: Hodder & Stoughton.

Clayton, H. (2015). Norms and protocols: The backbone of learning teams. *Making the Common Core Come Alive!* Vol. IV, Issue III. Retrieved from http://www.justaskpublications.com/just-ask-resource-center/e-newsletters/msca/norms-and-protocols-the-backboneof-learning-teams

Colaci, C., Saraikin, T., & Hilton, C. (2013). Action research for personalised learning. *Leadership in Focus: The journal for Australasian School Leaders*, Winter Issue.

Cole, P. (2004, December) *Professional development: A great way to avoid change*. (Seminar Series, No. 140) Melbourne: IARTV.

Cole, P. (2016, August). *Getting your whole-school teaching right*. PowerPoint presentation to The Education Show, Melbourne. Provided to the authors by the presenter.

Cook, H. (2015, November 23). Schools hit a wall with open-plan classrooms. *The Age.* Retrieved from http://www.theage.com.au/victoria/schools-hit-a-wall-with-openplan-classrooms-20151123-gl5vo8.html

Cotton, K. (n.d.). *Classroom questioning*. Portland, OR: North West Regional Educational Laboratory. Retrieved from https://educationnorthwest.org/sites/default/files/resources/classroom-questioning-508.pdf

Covey, S. (1990). *Seven habits of highly effective people*. New York: Simon & Schuster.

Curriculum Corporation Australia [now Education Services Australia]. (n.d.). *Learning Intentions: Background*. Professional Learning module, Assessment for Learning. Retrieved from https://www.assessmentforlearning.edu.au/professional_learning/learning_intentions/learning_intentions_landing_page.html

Dahlgren, R. (n.d.). *Remain calm and respond right when a student challenges!* Center for Teacher Effectiveness Diffusers for Teachers. Retrieved from http://www.timetoteachtrainer.com/wp-content/uploads/2010/08/Diffusers.pdf

DEECD [Department of Education and Early Childhood Development]. (2011). *Making the most of flexible learning spaces: A guide for principals and teachers*. Melbourne: Author.

Department of Education and Training. (2017). *High impact teaching strategies*. Retrieved from https://www.education.vic.gov.au/school/teachers/teachingresources/practice/improve/Pages/hits.aspx

DuFour, R. (2011). Work together: But only if you want to. *Phi Delta Kappan, 92(5)*, 57–61. Retrieved from http://journals.sagepub.com/doi/pdf/10.1177/003172171109200513

DuFour, R., DuFour, R., & Eacker, R. (n.d.). *Professional learning communities (PLC): Where do we begin?* [PowerPoint presentation]. Retrieved from http://www.powershow.com/view3/438cf3-Y2FlN/Professional_Learning_Communities_PLC_ powerpoint_ppt_presentation

Dunning, D. (2006). Strangers to ourselves. *The Psychologist, 19(10)*, 600–603. Retrieved from https://thepsychologist.bps.org.uk/volume-19/edition-10/strangers-ourselves

Edugains. (2016). *Knowing and responding to learners: A differentiated instruction educator's guide.* Retrieved from http://www.edugains.ca/resourcesDI/EducatorsPackages/DIEducatorsPackage_2016/ DI_EducatorsGuide_AODA.pdf.

Fisher, D. & Frey, N. (2013). *Better learning through structured teaching: A framework for the gradual release of responsibility* (2nd ed.) Alexandria, VA: ASCD.

Forbes, O. (2016). *Country profiles of formal and non-formal adult education opportunities in literacy, numeracy and other skills: Australia.* Retrieved from https://unesdoc.unesco.org/ark:/48223/pf0000247581

Fullan, M. (n. d). *Leading in a culture of change.* Retrieved from https://www.csus.edu/indiv/j/jelinekd/edte%20227/fullanleadinginacultureofchange.pdf

Fullan, M. (2001). *The new meaning of educational change* (3rd ed.). New York: Teachers College Press.

Fullan, M. (2002). The change leader. *Educational Leadership, 59(8)*, 16–21. Retrieved from http://www.ascd.org/publications/educational-leadership/may02/vol59/num08/The-Change-Leader.aspx

Fullan, M. (2019). *Nuance: Why some leaders succeed and others fail.* Thousand Oaks, CA: Corwin.

Garmston, R. J. & Wellman, B. M. (2016). *The adaptive school: A sourcebook for developing collaborative groups* (3rd ed.). Oberlin, OH and Concord, MA: Rowman & Littlefield.

Gladwell, M. (2000). *The tipping point: How little things can make a big difference.* Boston, MA: Little Brown and Company.

Goddard, Y. L, Goddard, R. D. & Tschannen-Moran, M. (2007). A theoretical and empirical investigation of teacher collaboration for school improvement and student achievement in public elementary schools. *Teachers College Record, 109(4)*, 877–896. Retrieved from https://education.illinoisstate.edu/downloads/casei/collaboration_studentachievement.pdf

Goodwin, B. (2018). *Student learning that works: How brain science informs a student learning model.* Denver, CO: McRel International.

Gorham, M., Finn-Stevenson, M., & Lapin, B. (2008). *Enriching school leadership development through coaching.* New Haven, CT: School of the 21st Century, Yale University.

Griffin, P. (2010, October). *Professional learning teams.* PowerPoint presentation to an AiZ Workshop, Melbourne. Provided to the authors by the presenter.

Guskey, T. R. (1983). Staff development and teacher change. *Educational Leadership, 41(3)*, 57–60.

Hattie, J. (2003, October). *Teachers make a difference: What is the research evidence?* Paper presented at the Australian Council for Educational Research Annual Research Conference on Building Teacher Quality, Melbourne.

Hattie, J. (2009). *Visible learning: A synthesis of 800 meta-analyses related to achievement.* London & New York: Routledge.

Hattie, J. (2015). *Hattie ranking: 195 Influences and effect sizes related to student achievement.* Retrieved from https://visible-learning.org/hattie-ranking-backup-195-effects/.

Hattie, J. (2019). *Hattie ranking: 252 influences and effect sizes related to student achievement, 2018 updated list.* Retrieved from https://visible-learning.org/hattie-ranking-influences-effect-sizes-learning-achievement/

Hattie, J. & Clarke. S. (2019) *Visible learning feedback.* London and New York: Routledge.

Hattie, J., & Timperley, H. (2007). The power of feedback. *Review of Educational Research, 77(1),* 81–112.

Hattie, J., & Yates, G. (2014). *Visible learning and the science of how we learn.* London & New York: Routledge.

Haynes, M. (2009, June). *NASBE Policy Update: State strategies for turning around low-performing schools and districts, 17(7).* Arlington, VA: National Association of State Boards of Education.

Herman, R., Dawson, P., Dee, T., Greene, J., Maynard, R., Redding, S., & Darwin, M. (2008). *Turning around chronically low-performing schools: A practice guide* [NCEE #2008-4020]. Washington, DC: National Center for Education Evaluation and Regional Assistance, Institute of Education Sciences, U.S. Department of Education. Retrieved from https://ies.ed.gov/ncee/wwc/Docs/PracticeGuide/Turnaround_pg_04181.pdf

Hopkins, D., & Craig, W., with Knight, O. (2015). *Curiosity and powerful learning.* Melbourne: McRel Australia.

Hopkins, D., Harris, A., Stoll, L., & Mackay, T. (2011, January). School and system improvement: State of the art review. Keynote presentation prepared for the 24th International Congress of School Effectiveness and School Improvement, Limassol, Cyprus.

Hopkins, D., Munro, J., & Craig, W. (Eds.). (2011). *Powerful learning: A strategy for systemic educational improvement.* Camberwell, Victoria: ACER Press.

Itzchakov, G. & Kluger, A. N. (2018, May 17). The power of listening in helping people change. *Harvard Business Review.* Retrieved from https://hbr.org/2018/05/the-power-of-listening-in-helping-people-change

James, D. (1997, September 15). Peter Drucker, the man who changed the world. *Business Review Weekly,* September/October issue.

Jensen, B. (2019, September 25). Improving professional development policy. *Learning First.* Retrieved from https://learningfirst.com/improving-professional-development-policy/

Jerald, C. (2007, January). *Believing and achieving.* Issue brief. Washington, DC: The Center for Comprehensive School Reform and Improvement.

Knight, J. (2009, March). What can we do about teacher resistance? *Phi Delta Kappan, 90(7),* 508–513.

Knight, J. (2018). *The impact cycle: What instructional coaches should do to foster powerful improvements in teaching.* Thousand Oaks, CA: Corwin.

Kruse, K. (2012, July 16). *Steven Covey: Ten quotes that can change your life.* Forbes online. Retrieved from https://www.forbes.com/sites/kevinkruse/2012/07/16/the-7-habits/#42bafd5139c6

Le, A., & Miller, P. (2002). *Educational attainment in Australia: a cohort analysis.* ACER Longitudinal Surveys of Australian Youth, Research Report no. 25. Camberwell, Victoria: ACER.

Leithwood, K., Seashore, K., Anderson, S., & Wahlstrom, K. (2004). *Review of research: How leadership influences student learning.* New York: The Wallace Foundation.

Lemov, D. (2010). *Teach like a champion: 49 techniques that put students on the path to college.* San Francisco, CA: Jossey-Bass.

Lemov, D. (2015). *Teach like a champion 2.0: 62 techniques that put students on the path to college.* San Francisco, CA: Jossey-Bass.

Lewis, R., Romi, S., Qui, X., & Katz, Y. J. (2005). Teachers' classroom discipline and student misbehaviour in Australia, China and Israel. *Teaching and Teacher Education, 21(6),* 729–741. Reprint available at https://www.academia.edu/21058871/ Teachers_classroom_discipline_and_student_misbehavior_in_Australia_China_and_Israel

Little, J. W. (1990). The persistence of privacy: Autonomy and initiative in teachers' professional relations. *Teachers College Record, 91(4),* 509–536.

Loughran, J. (2010). *What expert teachers do: Enhancing professional knowledge for classroom practice.* Sydney: Allen & Unwin.

Ludden, D. (2018, November 30). How to Avoid 'Death by Meeting' in the Workplace. *Psychology Today.* Retrieved from https://www.psychologytoday.com/au/blog/talking-apes/201811/how-avoid-death-meeting-in-the-workplace

MacCrindle, A. & Duginske, J. (2018, April 5). Seven qualities of an instructional coach. *ASCD.* Retrieved from https://inservice.ascd.org/seven-qualities-of-an-instructional-coach/

Marzano, R. J. (2008). *The art and science of teaching—Program 2: Effective classroom management.* Alexandria, VA: ASCD.

Marzano, R. J., Marzano, J. S., & Pickering, D. J. (2003). *Classroom management that works.* Alexandria, VA: ASCD.

Marzano, R. J., Pickering, D. J., & Pollock, J. E. (2001). *Classroom instruction that works: Research-based strategies for increasing student achievement.* Alexandria, VA: ASCD.

Maslow, A. H. (1966). *The psychology of science: A reconnaissance.* New York: Harper Collins.

Maxwell, J. (2019, February 19). *Connect with your ears.* Retrieved from https://www.johnmaxwell.com/blog/connect-with-your-ears/

McGill, R. M. (2019). *Pose, pause, pounce, bounce!* Retrieved from https://www.teachertoolkit.co.uk/2011/11/04/pose-pause-bounce-pounce/

Mealings, K. T., Buchholz, J. M., Demuth, K., & Dillon, H. (2014). *An investigation into the acoustics of an open plan compared to enclosed kindergarten classroom.* Sydney: Macquarie University and National Acoustics Laboratories.

Milne, P. W. (with update by the Federal Office of Road Safety). (1985). *Fitting and wearing of seat belts in Australia: The history of a successful countermeasure* (2nd ed.). Canberra: Australian Government Publishing Service.

Moskowitz, C. (2008, April 28). *Mind's limit found: Four things at once.* LiveScience. Retrieved from http://www.livescience.com/ 2493-mind-limit-4.html

Moss, C. M., & Brookhart, S. M. (2012). *Learning targets: Helping students aim for understanding in today's lesson.* Alexandria, VA: ASCD.

Mourshed, M., Chijioke, C., & Barber, M. (2010). *How the world's most improved school systems keep getting better.* London: McKinsey & Company.

Moyle, K. (2015, February 2), Coaching and mentoring for school improvement. *Teacher Magazine*. Retrieved from https://www.teachermagazine.com.au/articles/coaching-and-mentoring-for-school-improvement

Mroz, J. E., Allen, J. A, Verhoeven, D. C. & Shuffler, M. L. (2018). Do we really need another meeting: The science of workplace meetings. *Current Directions in Psychological Science, 27(6)*, 1–8. Retrieved from https://www.researchgate.net/publication/328399884_Do_We_Really_Need_Another_Meeting_The_Science_of_Workplace_Meetings

Munby, S. (2020). *A new paradigm for leadership development?* (Occasional Paper Number 164). Melbourne: Centre for Strategic Education.

New South Wales Department of Education and Communities. (2015). *Strong start, Great teachers—Phase 4. Differentiating content, process, product, learning environment.* Retrieved from http://ssgt.nsw.edu.au/documents/3_content_pro_etal.pdf

NHS Scotland. (2010, May). *Healthcare Strategy for NHS Scotland.* Retrieved from https://www.gov.scot/publications/healthcare-quality-strategy-nhsscotland/

Northern Illinois University Faculty Development and Instructional Design Center (n.d.), Bloom's Taxonomy [pdf]. Retrieved from http://www.niu.edu/facdev/_pdf/guide/learning/blooms_taxonomy.pdf

Northwestern University. (2018, September 17). Scientists determine four personality types based on new data: Comprehensive data analysis dispels established paradigms in psychology. *ScienceDaily*. Retrieved from www.sciencedaily.com/releases/2018/09/180917111612.htm

Oberman, M. E., & Boudett, K. P. (2015, November). Eight steps to becoming data wise. *Educational Leadership, 73(3)*. Retrieved from http://www.ascd.org/publications/educational-leadership/nov15/vol73/num03/Eight-Steps-to-Becoming-Data-Wise.aspx

OECD. (2014). *A teachers' guide to TALIS 2013: Teaching and Learning International Survey,* TALIS. Paris: OECD Publishing.

OECD. (2018). *TALIS 2018 Results (Volume 1): Teachers and school leaders as lifelong learners,* TALIS. Paris, OECD Publishing.

OFSTED with Matthews, P. (2009a). *Twenty outstanding primary schools: Excelling against the odds.* London: OFSTED

OFSTED with Matthews, P. (2009b). *Twelve outstanding secondary schools: Excelling against the odds.* London: OFSTED.

Ontario Ministry of Education. (2007). *Professional learning communities: A model for Ontario schools*. The Literacy and Numeracy Secretariat Capacity Building Series, Special Edition No. 3, 1–3. Ontario, Canada: Author.

Ontario Ministry of Education. (2010). *Learning goals and success criteria: Assessment for Learning Video Series: Viewing Guide* (1st ed.). A resource to support the implementation of Growing Success: Assessment, Evaluation and Reporting in Ontario Schools. Toronto, ON: Author. Retrieved from http://www.edugains.ca/resourcesDI/ProfLearningModules2011/DiffInst_AssessmentandEvaluation/LearningGoalsSuccessCriteriaViewingGuide2011.pdf

Platt, A. D., & Tipp, C. E. (2008). Communities that undermine learning. *Leadership*, September/October, 18–22.

Prytz, A. (2018, November 6). A big ship to turn around: The school that changed course. *The Age*. Retrieved from https://www.theage.com.au/national/victoria/a-big-ship-to-turn-around-the-school-that-changed-course-20181025-p50bt6.html

QELI. (2017). *QELI leadership framework and behaviours of effective leaders* Retrieved from https://qeli.qld.edu.au/qeli-leadership-framework-and-behaviours-of-effective-leaders/

Quaglia, R., & Corso, M. J. (2014). *Student voice: The instrument of change*. Thousand Oaks, CA: Corwin.

Robinson, V. (2018). *Reduce change to increase improvement*. Corwin Impact Leadership Series. Thousand Oaks, CA: Corwin.

Robinson, V., Le Fevre, S. M., Sinnema, C. E. L., Meyer, F. & Pope, D. (2016). *Open-to-learning leadership: How to build trust while tackling tough issues*. Moorabbin: Hawker Brownlow.

Rogers, E. M. (1962). *Diffusion of innovation*. New York: Free Press of Glencoe.

Rogers, E. M. (2003). *Diffusion of innovation* (5th ed.). New York: Simon & Shuster.

Rosenthal, R., & Jacobson, L. (1963). Teachers' expectancies: Determinants of pupils' IQ gains. *Psychological Reports*, *19*, 115–118.

Rowe, M. B. (1986). Wait time: Slowing down may be a way of speeding up. *Journal of Teacher Education, 37(1)*, 43–50.

Russell, D. (2019, 5 August). *Cognitive load theory: Teaching strategies*. ACER Teacher Bulletin. Retrieved from https://www.teachermagazine.com.au/articles/cognitive-load-theory-teaching-strategies?utm_source=CM&utm_medium=Bulletin&utm_content=August6

Sanders, W. L., & Rivers, J. C. (1996). *Cumulative and residual effects of teachers on future student academic achievement*. Knoxville: University of Tennessee Value-Added Research and Assessment Centre.

Sharratt, L. (2019). *Clarity: What matters most in learning, teaching and leading*. Thousand Oaks, CA: Corwin.

Shasta County. (2009, May). *What is explicit instruction?* Shasta County Curriculum Leads. Retrieved from https://studylib.net/doc/8923848/explicit-instruction

Sipe, A. (n.d.). *Lesson closure with examples or 40 ways to leave a lesson.* Grandview, Washington: Assembled by Ann Sipe on behalf of the Grandview School District. Retrieved from https://cpb-ap-se2.wpmucdn.com/global2.vic.edu.au/dist/c/10024/files/2011/11/40_ways_to_leave_a_lesson.pdf

Stahl, R. J. (1990). *Using 'think-time' behaviours to promote students' information processing, learning and on-task participation: An instructional module.* Tempe, AZ: Arizona State University.

Stronge, J. H., Ward, T. J., Tucker, P. D., & Hindman, J. L. (2007). What is the relationship between teacher quality and student achievement? An exploratory study. *Journal of Personal Evaluation in Education, 20(3),* 165–184.

Svenson, O. (1981). Are we all less risky and more skilful than our fellow drivers. *Acta Psychologica, 47(2),* 143–148. Retrieved from https://pdfs.semanticscholar.org/ad37/e00352406dd776bc010769489b2412951c7d.pdf

Thompson, S., De Bortoli, L., & Underwood, C. (2016). *PISA 2015: A first look at Australia's results.* Camberwell, Victoria: ACER. Retrieved from http://research.acer.edu.au/cgi/viewcontent.cgi?article=1021&context=ozpisa

Thompson, S., De Bortoli, L., & Underwood, C. (2017). *PISA 2015: Reporting Australia's results.* Camberwell, Victoria: ACER.

Tomlinson, C. A. (2000, August). *Differentiation of instruction in the elementary grades.* ERIC Digest. ERIC Clearinghouse on Elementary and Early Childhood Education.

Tomlinson, C.A. (2008, November). The goals of differentiation. *Educational Leadership, 66(3),* 26–30. Alexandria, VA: ASCD.

Tomlinson, C. A. (2014). *The differentiated classroom: Responding to the needs of all learners* (2nd ed.). Alexandria, VA: ASCD.

Top scientist Michelle Yvonne Simmons wins Australian of the Year. (2018, January 25). *Australian Financial Review.* Retrieved from https://www.afr.com/politics/top-scientist-michelle-yvonne-simmons-wins-australian-of-the-year-20180125-h0oieq

Tucson Unified School District. (2016–2017). *Professional learning communities guide.* Retrieved from http://www.tusd1.org/Portals/TUSD1/District/docs/PD/PLCGuide.pdf?ver=2018-01-28-202010-497

Victorian Department of Education and Training (DET). (2018). *Peer observation, feedback and reflection: A guide for principals and school leaders.* Melbourne: Victorian DET.

Whitmore, J. (2002). *Coaching for performance: Growing people, performance and purpose* (3rd ed.). London & Boston: Nicholas Brealey Publishing.

Wiliam, D. (2016, May). *Embedding formative assessment institute.* Paper presented at the 13th Annual Thinking & Learning Conference, Hawker Brownlow Education, Melbourne.

Wiliam, D., & Leahy, S. (2015). *Embedding formative assessment: Practical techniques for F–12 classrooms.* Moorabbin, Victoria: Hawker Brownlow Education.

Zbar, V. (2011). *Leading from the front: Turning around an under-performing school. Case studies in principal leadership.* Melbourne: Northern Metropolitan Region, Department of Education and Early Childhood Development, Victoria.

Zbar, V. (2013). *Generating whole school improvement: The stages of sustained success* (Occasional Paper No. 132). Melbourne: CSE.

Zbar, V. (2016). *We need to talk about change: No prescription without diagnosis* (Occasional Paper No. 145). Melbourne: CSE.

Zbar, V. (2017). *Effective leaders of school improvement: Development of the QELi Framework*. Melbourne: Zbar Consultancy.

Zbar, V. (2018). *Leadership to make things happen in your school* (Occasional Paper, No. 156). Melbourne: CSE.

Zbar, V., Kimber, R., & Marshall, G. (2008). *How our best performing schools come out on top: An examination of eight high performing disadvantaged schools.* Melbourne: Victorian Department of Education and Early Childhood Development.

Zbar, V., Kimber, R., & Marshall, G. (2009). *Schools that achieve extraordinary success: How some disadvantaged Victorian schools 'punch above their weight'* (Occasional Paper No. 109). Melbourne: CSE

Zbar, V., Kimber, R., & Marshall, G. (2010). *Getting the preconditions for school improvement in place: How to make it happen*. Seminar Series No. 193. Melbourne: CSE.

Zbar, V., Macklin, P., Muscat, M., Naidu, N., & Wastle, J. (2016). *How revolution happens: The full Kambrya story*. Seminar Series No. 259. Melbourne: CSE.

www.ingramcontent.com/pod-product-compliance
Lightning Source LLC
Chambersburg PA
CBHW081102070526

44584CB00021B/3173